COOKS' BOOKS

COOKS' BOOKS

AN
AFFECTIONATE
GUIDE
TO THE
LITERATURE
OF FOOD
AND
COOKING

L. Patrick Coyle, Jr.

Facts On File Publications
New York, New York ● Bicester, England

COOKS' BOOKS

An Affectionate Guide to the Literature of Food and Cooking

Library of Congress Cataloging in Publication Data

Coyle, L. Patrick.
  Cooks' books.

  Includes index.
   1. Food.   2. Cookery.   3. Food—Bibliography.
4. Cookery—Bibliography.   5. Food—Anecdotes, facetiae, satire, etc.   6. Cookery—Anecdotes, facetiae, satire, etc.   I. Title.
TX357.C65   1984   641.3   82-18193
ISBN 0-87196-683-2

ISBN 0-87196-695-6 (pbk)

Design by Jennie Nichols/Levavi & Levavi

Printed in the United States of America

10 9 8 7 6 5 4 3 2 1

Composition by Creative Graphics, Inc.
Printed by Maple-Vail

CONTENTS

Acknowledgments

The help, encouragement and expertise of a number of people contributed to the successful completion of this project. Gerry Helferich, my editor, deserves credit for his stimulating treatment of the original idea and his subsequent advice and support.

Special thanks are due to Robina Mapstone for her efforts in organizing the graphics for the book.

For assistance in researching the book, I am especially grateful to Billie Connor and members of the reference staff at the Scientific and Technical Department of the Los Angeles Public Library, main branch. Dan Strehl, also of L.A. Public, provided good advice when I needed it.

The following persons and organizations were generous with their time and/or facilites in support of the photography: Billie Connor, Dan Strehl and Sylva Manoogian of the Los Angeles Public Library; Crown Books, Venice; UCLA Research Library and the Santa Monica Public Library.

Thanks to Ann Gonzales, Dave Ott and Kathleen Coyle for their timely help with the index.

FOOD DOLLAR by Janet Spiegal. Copyright © 1981. Reprinted by permission of Chronicle Books, San Francisco, publisher.

"Potatoes and Beans" from *FUTURE FOOD* by Colin Tudge, Copyright © 1980 by Colin Tudge. Reprinted by permission of Crown Publishers.

"Noodle Doughnuts" from *THE ART OF HUNGARIAN COOKING* by Paula P. Bennett and Velma R. Clark. Copyright © 1954 by Doubleday & Company, Inc. Reprinted by permission of the publisher.

"Fresh Ham" from *COOKERY AND DINING IN IMPERIAL ROME* by Apicius, translated and edited by Joseph D. Vehling. Reprinted by permission of Dover Books, New York.

"Tartar Sauce, a Modern Recipe in the Apician Style" from *COOKERY AND DINING IN IMPERIAL ROME* by Apicius, translated and edited by Joseph Dommers Vehling. Reprinted by permission of Dover Books, New York.

"Les Oiseaux sans Têtes" from *THE JAMES BEARD COOKBOOK* by James Beard, Copyright © 1959 by James Beard. Reprinted by permission of E.P. Dutton, publisher.

"Iguana Mole" from *A GOURMET'S BOOK OF BEASTS* by Faith Medlin, copyright © 1975 by Faith Medlin. Reprinted by permission of Paul S. Eriksson, publisher.

"French Beef Casserole" from *THE I HATE TO COOK BOOK* by Peg Bracken, copyright © 1960 by Peg Bracken. Reprinted by permission of Harcourt Brace Jovanovich, Inc., publishers.

"Bourbon Corn Chowder" (page 40) from *AMERICAN FOOD AND CALIFORNIA WINE* by Barbara Kafka, copyright © 1981 by Barbara Kafka. Reprinted by permission of Harper & Row, Publishers, Inc.

"Corn Chips (page 117) from *BETTER THAN STORE BOUGHT* by Helen Witty and Elizabeth Schneider Colchie. Copyright © by Helen Witty and Elizabeth Schneider Colchie. Reprinted by permission of Harper & Row, Publisher, Inc.

"How to Cook Couscous" (page 134) from *COUSCOUS AND OTHER GOOD FOOD FROM MOROCCO* by Paula Wolfert, Copyright © 1973 by Paula Wolfert. Reprinted by permission of Harper & Row, Publishers, Inc.

"Shoulder of Pork with Sweet Wine Cakes" from *THE ROMAN COOKERY BOOK* by Apicius, translated by Barbara Flower and Elisabeth Rosenbaum. Copyright © 1958 by George G. Harrap Ltd. Reprinted by permission of the publisher.

Copyright © 1982. Reprinted by permission of Random House, publisher.

"Toulouse-Lautrec Chocolate Mayonnaise" from *CALIFORNIA ARTISTS COOKBOOK* by Chotse Blank and Ann Seymour, Copyright © 1982 by The San Francisco Museum of Modern Art. Reprinted by permission.

"Garbanzo Paste Sesame Dip" from *ASIAN FOOD FEASTS* by Sigrid M. Shepard, Copyright © 1979 by Sigrid M. Shepard. Reprinted by permission.

"Pot Roast of Veal" from *PRESSURE COOKERY PERFECTED* by Roy Andries de Groot. Copyright © 1978 by Roy Andries de Groot. Reprinted by permission of Summit Books, a division of Simon & Schuster, Inc.

"Poule au Pot d'Henri Soulé" from *THE NEW YORK TIMES 60-MINUTE GOURMET* by Pierre Franey, copyright © 1981 by Pierre Franey. Reprinted by permission of Times Books, publisher.

"Podvarak" from *THE COOKING OF VIENNA'S EMPIRE* by Joseph Wechsberg, Copyright © 1968 by Joseph Wechsberg, Reprinted by permission of Time-Life Books, Inc., publishers.

"Vegetarian Palachinki" from *A QUINTET OF CUISINES* Michael and Frances Field, Copyright © 1970 by Michael and Frances Field. Reprinted by permission of Time-Life Books, publishers.

"Marinated Snake Cooked with Rice" from *UNMENTIONABLE CUISINE* by Calvin W. Schwabe, Copyright © 1979. Reprinted by permission of the University Press of Virginia.

"Shrimp Creole" from *LITTON'S EXCITING NEW WORLD OF MICROWAVE COOKING.* Copyright © 1976 by Van Nostrand Reinhold Co., Inc. All rights reserved. Reprinted by permission.

"Tongue Creole" from Kansas State University's *PRACTICAL COOKERY*, copyright © 1976. Reprinted by permission of John Wiley & Sons, Inc., publisher.

COOKS' BOOKS

History
of
Cookbooks

HANDWRITTEN NOTES

Ancient cookbooks were written by hand, an arduous task that inspired the use of shortcuts. From the time of Imperial Rome to the Renaissance, authors tended to save space by skimping on cooking directions and often by leaving exact quantities to the discretion of the cook.

Scholars point out, moreover, that early cookbooks were manuals for professionals, people who knew their way around a kitchen and who could make do with a list of ingredients and a few hints on preparation. What's more, nobody was trying to make it easy for the beginner: Cooking was a lucrative occupation, and its secrets were not to be given away.

In their way, these early recipes were coded messages meant for the initiated. Moreover, among those who could afford fancy cooking, heaviness and disguise were in vogue. Nearly every course contained meat or other substantial protein, and Romans seemed to dislike the natural taste of things. Dishes contained a profusion of spices and often a heavy sauce. Ingredients often were molded to look like something else, usually something more expensive. Consequently, when naïve cooks many years later attempted to reproduce ancient dishes, the results often turned out to be inedible sludge.

The culinary legacy of the ancient world is embodied in the cookbook of Marcus Gavius Apicius, *De Re Coquinaria*, or *The Art of Cooking*. Dating from the first century A.D., it is the West's oldest surviving cookbook, and its influence on later cookbooks was pervasive until the invention of the printing press in the middle of the fifteenth century and the subsequent use of vernacular languages in print. As we shall see, the spirit of Apicius shines through the pages of medieval works such as *A Book of Cookery* (c. 1250), Tirel's *Le Viandier de Guillaume Taillevent* (c. 1380), the *Forme of Cury* (c. 1400), *Le Ménagier de Paris* (1420) and Platina's *De Honesta Voluptate et Valetidine* (1474).

Two modern translations of the Apicius book are in print. One is Barbara Flower and Elisabeth Rosenbaum's *The Roman Cookery-Book* (London: George G. Harrap, 1958). The other is Joseph D. Vehling's *Cooking and Dining in Imperial Rome* (New York: Dover, 1977, paperback). Vehling's translation is the older of the two, having first appeared in 1936. Its accuracy has been called into question, especially by Flower and Rosenbaum, who state in their introduction, "His text is so full of mistakes that it becomes almost useless as a translation."

APICII · LIBRI · X

QVI DICVNTVR DE OBSONIIS
ET CONDIMENTIS SIVE ARTE
COQVINARIA QVÆ EXTANT

·

NVNC PRIMVM ANGLICE REDDIDIT PROŒMIO
BIBLIOGRAPHICO ATQVE INTERPRETATIONE
DEFENSIT VARIISQVE ANNOTATIONIBVS
INSTRVXIT ITA ET ANTIQVÆ CVLINÆ
VTENSILIARVM EFFIGIIS EXORNAVIT
INDICEM DENIQVE ETYMOLOGICVM ET
TECHNICVM ARTIS MAGIRICÆ ADIECIT

·

IOSEPHVS DOMMERS VEHLING

·

INTRODVXIT FRIDERICVS STARR

Apicius was a famous Roman epicure, a symbol of fine eating. Although *De Re Coquinaria* is attributed to him, it is likely that he actually wrote only a small part of the text. It is, as it were, a celebrity cookbook, featuring the best of a centuries-old Greek cooking tradition that was inherited by the Romans along with other treasures of Greek culture.

(The history of Greek cooking is chronicled by Atheneus in *The Deipnosophists*, a work on gastronomy that dates from the same era as the Apicius book but does not mention it. The "sophists" of the title discuss 20 great cookbooks, the most famous of which was *Gastrology*, written in 350 B.C. by Archestratus. Although neither it nor the other 19 works survive, it is nevertheless clear that the Greeks had developed a high cooking style well worth inheriting and perpetuating.)

From *The Deipnosophists* and other sources we discover that Greek fine cooking first developed in the colonies of Sybaris (our word "sybaritic" derives from the lavish culinary ways of this Greek colony) in present-day Italy, as well as in Syracuse on Sicily, and grew out of contact with the richer, older cultures of Asia Minor. Another foreign influence was introduced by Alexander the Great when he campaigned in Persia during the fourth century B.C. According to Atheneus, Alexander delightedly embraced the opulent customs of the Persian kings, which he swifty adopted at his own court in Macedonia.

The Golden Age of Greece was a peak era for gastronomy as well. Athenian cuisine specialized in fish and other seafood, and wealthy Athenians feasted in a style that endured for centuries. They reclined on beds or couches, leaning on the left elbow. There were no plates for individuals, but the meal was served on a multitude of small plates, each containing a different delicacy, smorgasbord style. A diner was expected to reach into a dish with his right hand, then put the food directly into his mouth. Big eaters, to increase their share of a popular dish, resorted to such gimmicks as finger and tongue shields to protect the flesh from hot food. Or they might pass food to a personal servant (stationed behind the couch) to be taken home and eaten later, or sold. Wives were excluded from these feasts, but not courtesans.

A product of this tradition, *De Re Coquinaria* is a collection of monographs on various branches of cookery and displays a level of specialization that a highly developed civilization— such as the Greek—might produce. The work is composed of ten chapters, or books: (1) Epimeles: The Careful Housekeeper; (2) Sarcoptes: The Meat Mincer; (3) Cepuros: The Gardener; (4) Pandecter: Many Ingredients; (5) Ospreon: Pulse; (6) Aeropetes: Birds; (7) Polyteles: The Gourmet;

THE LOST MASTERPIECE

Food was apparently as fascinating a subject to the literati of Pericles' land as any other aspect of life. Athenaeus mentions the names of as many as *20* cookbook authors [none of whose work survives]; one, Archestratus, produced his masterpiece *Gastrology* in 350 B.C. Archestratus was said to have traveled widely searching for new recipes, many of which still are in use today. Not only epicurean aristocrats collected recipes; professional cooks held a respected position in Greek society. The Greek cook was an artisan, paid better than any other hired workman, often an educated man to be called in to drink with the guests when he produced a masterpiece for their enjoyment. Cooking was, in fact, a recognized art, and Greek intellectuals considered a new dish as important as a new poem.

Betty Wason, *Cooks, Gluttons and Gourmets* (Garden City, N.Y.: Doubleday & Company, 1962), pp. 18-19.

A MODERN RECIPE
IN THE APICIAN STYLE

Take liquamen [a Roman sauce similar in taste to soy sauce], pepper, cayenne, eggs, lemon, olive oil, vinegar, white wine, anchovies, onions, tarragon, pickled cucumbers, parsley, chervil, hard-boiled eggs, capers, green peppers, mustard, chop, mix well, and serve.

The result? Tartar sauce.

Apicius, *Cookery and Dining in Imperial Rome,* trans. and ed. Joseph D. Vehling, p. 27.

(8) Tetrapus: The Quadruped; (9) Thalassa: The Sea, and (10) Halieus: The Fisherman. Chapter 10 of the Vehling translation also contains the Excerpts of Vinidarius. (Vinidarius, a fifth-century A.D. Goth, was a scientist who lived in Italy and who appended certain recipes to the Apician text. Whether they were truly excerpted from earlier versions is not known.) The two books attributed to Apicius himself are Chapters 1 and 10. Incidentally, the Flower and Rosenbaum version includes the Latin text *en face.* The individual books have Greek titles, which was taken as evidence of Greek origin.

Many of the dishes will seem familiar to the modern cook—meat broth, ham with raisin sauce, duck with turnips, salads with cheese or herb dressing, jellied salads, seafood croquettes, fish balls, dumplings, stuffed vegetables, fruit compotes, custards, fruit tarts and candied dates stuffed with nuts.

Vehling, a chef himself, tested many of Apicius's recipes and found them practical, tasty, even delightful. A few, he reported, were consummate perfection in gastronomy. But others were a puzzle.

What puzzled Vehling were incorrect weights and measures, and in some cases a private code that necessitated the elimination or transposition of certain words. Perhaps his puzzlement resulted in part from his deficiencies as a translator that Flower and Rosenbaum allude to. But these aspects of the Apicius book have puzzled others as well. When a Latin edition was published in London in 1705, for instance, it inspired a number of scholars and gourmets to try some recipes, but the results were nauseating. In Victorian times, George Augustus Sala, an artist, writer and gourmet, organized a Roman feast featuring dishes from Apicius. Predictably, the food was disappointing. About these experiments Vehling remarked, "Eager gourmets, ever on the lookout for something new, and curious scholars have attempted to prepare dishes in the manner prescribed by Apicius. Most of such experimenters have executed the old precepts too literally, instead of trying to enter into their spirit."

Flower and Rosenbaum are much more sure of their ground and more helpful. They say, on page 19 of *The Roman Cookery-Book:*

Our aim in making this translation was mainly practical. We have tried out many of the recipes, and we found that many could become welcome additions to our menus. . . . The Roman cookery-book was not meant for beginners. The lack of indication of quantities in most recipes makes a basic knowledge of cookery necessary.

But we found that with common sense and a little imagination one cannot go wrong on the quantities. We have nevertheless in some cases added the quantities we think correct in a footnote.

But what of this spirit Vehling referred to? As we mentioned earlier, the Roman watchwords were "heaviness and disguise." At a Roman banquet, nearly all the courses contained meat, highly spiced and covered with a thick sauce. Moreover, many of the ingredients were dictated by fashion and ambition. The Roman gourmands were nobles who had a passion for food, and they competed for prestige and imperial favor on the basis of outrageously expensive banquets. Wealth and leisure set the scene for high gastronomic culture, but once competition set in, the flaunting of wealth occupied center stage. Good cooking took third place behind opulent display and the awe-inspiring costly ingredient (or facsimile thereof).

Two such extravagant ingredients were silphium (a flavoring agent extracted from a plant that modern scholars believe was related to asafetida) and peacock flesh. The latter was rated the top meat dish by gourmets, followed by rabbit (some translators say pheasant), spiny lobster, chicken (some translators say crane) and young pig. Emperor Heliogabalus (A.D. 204–22) carried this obsession for costly ingredients to absurd lengths, producing meals consisting of camels' heels, cocks' combs, parrot heads, mullet beards and ostrich tongues. His banquets reportedly cost from 100,000 to 3 million sesterces each, at a time when 25,000 sesterces was considered an adequate annual income for a family at the rank of knight, the lowest noble order.

Thus, *De Re Coquinaria* mixes what you might call sensible middle-class recipes with a few gourmet recipes and ingenious ruses such as extending or faking the presence of silphium, making rose wine without roses, and creating liburnium oil out of inferior ingredients. Both cooks and hosts were delighted when cheaper food could be passed off as a more expensive item, cooks on a point of cleverness, hosts on a point of economy. A second reason for disguise was to mask food spoilage. Written in an age of poor-to-nonexistent refrigeration, the book's first chapter abounds with clever ways of preserving food and restoring spoiled food to palatability.

The third Roman watchword was "overindulgence." The main meal of the upper class began between 3 p.m. and 5 p.m. and lasted up to three hours. Eating was leisurely, with long pauses between courses, and diners were soothed by readings from philosophical or literary texts. At banquets, however, the meal might last all night, or even for several

APICIAN RECIPE TRANSLATIONS COMPARED
Fresh Ham

A fresh ham is cooked with 2 pounds of barley and 25 figs. When done skin, glaze the surface with a fire shovel full of glowing coals, spread honey over it, or, what's better: put it in the oven covered with honey. When it has a nice color, put in a saucepan with raisin wine, pepper, a bunch of rue and pure wine to taste. When this [sauce] is done, pour half of it over the ham and in the other half soak specially made ginger bread in the remnant of the sauce; after most of it is thoroughly soaked into the bread, add to the ham.

Apicius, *Cookery and Dining in Imperial Rome*, trans. and ed. by Joseph D. Vehling, p. 170.

Shoulder of Pork (cured like ham) with Sweet-wine Cakes

Boil the shoulder of pork with 2 lb of barley and 25 dried figs. When it is done remove the meat from the bone, and brown its fat on a glowing hot brazier and sprinkle with honey, or—better—put it in the oven and rub with honey. When it is browned put in a sauce pan *passum*, pepper, a sprig of rue, and wine. Mix. When the pepper-sauce is mixed, pour half of it on the shoulder of pork, and the other half over pieces of sweet-wine cake. When these are saturated pour the rest of the liquid over the meat.

Apicius, *The Roman Cookery-Book*, trans. Barbara Flower and Elisabeth Rosenbaum, p. 169.

days. Many of the gourmands practiced bulimia. "Eat to vomit; vomit to eat" was the derogatory phrase coined by Roman dramatist Seneca, who was indignant that the wealthy should spend a fortune importing exotic food, then not deign to digest it. (Seneca, by the way, died a wealthy but emaciated man. In his later years, fearing poisoned food, he subsisted on a diet of wild apples and water.)

Apicius himself squandered an immense fortune on banquets. One day, according to legend, he realized that his remaining funds (10 million sesterces) could no longer support his style of living, so he gave a final banquet, then killed himself. Nevertheless, his legacy was dominant in Europe for 12 centuries. Manuscript copies of the cookbook circulated throughout the Continent, to the exclusion of others, except for certain Arabic texts, such as Ibn Gazla's *Book of Dishes and Spices*.

The next known Western cookbook is a fragmentary manuscript dating from the second half of the 13th century and entitled (in translation) *A Book of Cookery*, which was written in Latin, allegedly for a group of 12 Sienese noblemen who were known as the "Spendthrift Brigade" and who entertained accordingly. The book derives mostly from Apicius but also in small part from Ibn Gazla. *A Book of Cookery* is considered a milestone in that it is a sort of medieval equivalent of Apicius. The first known French cookbook, by the way, is an addendum at the end of a Latin manuscript copy of *A Book of Cookery*, dated about 1300.

The Middle Ages were not a period of innovation for gastronomy. The traditions of heaviness, disguise and overindulgence persisted among the landed aristocracy. Meanwhile, monks are thought to have eaten nearly as well as the gentry, and the devout alternated feasting with fasting, both of which the Church considered to be endorsed by the Bible.

The aristocratic diet was much the same throughout Europe. Meat and game predominated. Vegetables might be cooked with meat, but as a separate dish, they were despised as food for the poor. Ordinarily, a main meal would have as many as 10 courses, each consisting of 15 or more dishes. Spices were added with a heavy hand, as in Imperial Rome, to flaunt wealth, to mask spoilage and, some say, to act as a stimulant. In fact, heavy spicing didn't decline until the 16th and 17th centuries, as other stimulants such as tobacco, tea and coffee came into general use.

During the Middle Ages, soft food was the rule. Meat was chopped and pounded, since few adults had a set of teeth adequate for chewing it, especially salt meat (a staple in winter), which was especially tough.

Guillaume Tirel, Lord of Taillevent, is the first known

THE SPORT OF COOKING

Though the language seems a bit difficult at first, medieval recipes make amusing reading. To beat eggs is to "swing" them, to boil is to "seethe," to garnish is to "flourish," to cut into little pieces is to "smite to gobbets" and to bruise and press together is to "ramme hem up." The language is so much more vivid than ours it makes cooking sound like an active sport . . . . The few recipes that begin by roasting meat usually go on to smite it to gobbets or ramme hem up, or both.

Barbara Norman, *Tales of the Table* (Englewood Cliffs, N.J.: Prentice-Hall, 1972), pp. 74-75.

medieval cookbook writer. Although there is no exact date for his work *Le Viandier de Guillaume dit Taillevent*, the book is thought to have appeared in manuscript form at about 1380. Tirel lived from about 1314 to 1395 and spent his entire working life employed by the French royal house, starting as a scullion and rising to the post of head cook for Philippe VI of Valois in 1346, head cook to the Duke of Normandy in 1355, head cook to King Charles V in 1375 and finally master caterer to the king's kitchen in 1392. Tirel's book owes much of its fame to the fact that it was printed in 1492 and exerted great influence on 16th-century French cooks.

Many of Tirel's recipes bear a striking resemblance to those of Apicius. Both texts avoided tough meat from larger animals; both leaned toward purees and the parboiling of food before roasting; both showed a predilection for songbirds and finely plumed birds; both used spices and other seasonings with a lavish hand; and both favored heavy sauces. Otherwise, like *De Re Coquinaria*, Tirel's book dealt mainly with what we would consider wholesome middle-class fare rather than extravagant delicacies. He cooked poultry with fresh garden herbs; he spit-roasted hare, then cooked it in beef broth and wine with diced pork fat and croutons.

Scholars speculate, however, that the similarities between the two books resulted less from Tirel's direct borrowing from Apicius than from both works' common origin in an oral tradition dating from the Roman occupation of Gaul, as well as from a similar level of culinary technology in both cultures.

Another popular and enduring French cookbook, *Le Ménagier de Paris*, appeared in manuscript form in the 1390s. A treatise on domestic economy, the book offered, in addition to recipes, advice to young householders and hints on conjugal happiness. The work appeared anonymously, and the recipes were quite similar to Tirel's.

At the turn of the 15th century, the earliest known cookbook written in English appeared, a manuscript entitled *Forme of Cury (Art of Cooking)*. Authorship is attributed to King Richard II's master cook, and the recipes of *Forme of Cury* resemble those found in Apicius and Tirel. For an extensive discussion of this work, see Chapter Two.

The forerunner of what would become French *haute cuisine* first appeared in Renaissance Italy. The first book to give expression to this type of cooking was J.B. Platina's *De Honesta Voluptate et Valetudine (Of Honest Indulgence and Good Health)*, which was printed in Rome in 1474. The author, a Vatican librarian named Platina who expressed himself in elegant Renaissance Latin, holds forth for five chapters on

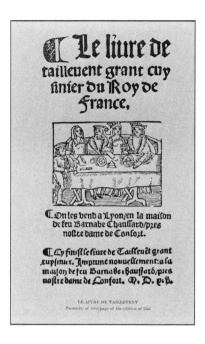

LE LIVRE DE TAILLEVENT
Facsimile of title-page of the edition of 1545

A TIREL MENU

[For a banquet served to Charles V toward the end of the 14th century.] Desserts aside, dinner . . . comprised 14 dishes (served in three courses), of which three were made up of capons in various guises (with cinnamon broth, in spiced pies, and in sour grape juice), four were of other fowl, and two were of venison. New cabbage was the only vegetable, butter bread and meat jellies were counted as dishes, and the festivities also included young hares stewed in vinegar and "a fine roast" of unspecified origin. In short, a meal as monotonously repetitive as most big medieval feeds but perhaps enlivened somewhat by Tirel's command of 20-odd sauces, including *"saulce Robert,"* his reading of the English roebuck sauce, of which a more refined version is still a mainstay of the French repertory and an excellent accompaniment to grilled meats.

Jay Jacobs, *Gastronomy* (New York: Newsweek Books, 1975), p. 85.

good food and sober living, then gives 250 contemporary recipes divided into another five chapters. Scholars had noted a discontinuity in tone between the two halves of the book, and in the 1930s they discovered that the recipes had been translated from an Italian manuscript written by Maestro Martino (fl. 1450–57), former cook to the most reverend monsignor the chamberlain and patriarch of Aguileia. The latter was almost certainly Ludovico Trevisan, who became chamberlain to the pope in 1440 and held the office until 1465, through the tenures of five popes. Martino, then, was a professional who cooked for the best circles. Detailed and precise, his recipes repudiate the old watchwords "heaviness and disguise."

Martino's cooking was characterized by a respect for the inherent flavor of the ingredients, which he emphasized by moderate cooking and judicious seasoning. He favors dishes with substantial pieces of meat in them, or whole birds in a sauce. Purees and porridges are given scant attention, and vegetables are cooked whole, or fried as fritters. He is concerned with the textures of food, and he gives a prominent place to soups. Scholars have found a marked Arabic influence in some recipes—e.g., those sprinkled with sugar and spices; sauces flavored with grapes, prunes and raisins; and telltale ingredients such as aniseed, rice, dates, pomegranates and bitter oranges.

De Honesta Voluptate et Valetudine was translated into French, German and Italian, and during the next 100 years more than 30 editions were printed. In a development all too typical in the history of cookbooks, Martino's recipes were incorporated into another contemporary book, entitled *Epulario*, by Giovanne de Rosselli. *Epulario* was being reprinted well into the 1600s and was even translated into English.

Written expression of the Renaissance cooking style culminated in 1570 with the publication of Bartolomeo Scappi's *Opera*. Containing 1,000 recipes, this book is a detailed and fully illustrated exposition, in Italian, of the state of the art. Things had progressed in the 100 years since Martino. Scappi was using some of the methods of classical cooking, such as braising and poaching. He had a penchant for marinades; he discourses confidently on the Arabic art of pastry-making (the first European cook to do so) and includes 200 pastry recipes for such things as waffles, flaky pastry and cakes called *pizze;* he acknowledges regional specialties, naming dishes for gastronomic centers such as Rome, Bologna and Milan; he includes foreign dishes such as Moorish couscous, and trout *alla tedesca* (German style). In all, the book has six chapters: meat and poultry, fish, food for meat days, food for fast days, pasta, and diets for the sick.

During the Renaissance, Italy was the center of culinary innovation, but as Scappi composed his masterwork, the ideas and techniques it contained were spreading northward to the court of France. During the next century, cooks in that country would seize the initiative and create a unified, rational *haute cuisine*, while the Italian genius would be expressed more and more in regional styles.

THE ART OF COOKING

Italian Renaissance cuisine reached its apogee in the work of Scappi. During his lifetime, an event occurred that shifted the center of cooking innovation to France, causing a revolution in taste and giving rise in 1651 to the publication of *Le Cuisinier François* by François Pierre de la Varenne. La Varenne is generally acknowledged as the founder of French classical cooking, and his book documents the strides made in French cooking under the Italian influence.

The provocative event was the marriage of Catherine de Medici to the heir of the French throne, later crowned Henry II. Catherine brought with her an army of chefs and a new fad in tableware—the fork, which northern Europeans were slow to accept, believing it profane. The cuisine she introduced to France was essentially that of the Florentine nobility; in contrast to the overindulgence of the Middle Ages, this cuisine was restrained, natural and unpretentious. The Tuscan nobleman did not confuse quality with extravagance, and emerging from medieval ways, he seemed to take the austere Roman republic as a model rather than the opulent empire.

What were some specific items of cuisine? Pasta, milk-fed veal covered with a light sauce, crisp broccoli, *piselli novelli* (later dubbed *petits pois*), truffles, juicy tournedos, quenelles, ice cream, rice pudding, kidneys, sweetbreads, cocks' combs, "royal" carp, zabaglione (called *sayabon* in France), macaroons and frangipane tarts.

Catherine herself was forceful and indulgent. She broke with custom and insisted that she and her ladies in waiting be invited to state banquets. She doted on artichokes and ate them publicly, a shocking act for the time because they were thought to be an aphrodisiac.

Catherine arrived in 1533. But by the time of La Varenne's birth in 1615, the French court had had to withstand a second invasion of Italian cooks, brought on by the marriage of Marie de Medici to Henry IV.

La Varrenne was the first French cookbook writer to assimilate the culinary revolution. He is seen as the first great

RECIPE FROM LA VARENNE— STUFFED MUSHROOMS

Choose the largest mushrooms to hold the stuffing, which you will make of several meats or good herbs, so that it is delicate, and bind it with egg yolks, then your mushrooms being stuffed and seasoned, set them on a bard [thin sheet of pork fat] or on a little butter; cook them and serve with lemon juice.

Pierre F. La Varenne, *Le Cuisinier François,* 1651.

saucier, using savory reductions of natural cooking juices bound with flour and butter mixtures. Now known as roux, these replaced highly spiced, bread-thickened broths, and they anointed a main ingredient that had not been hacked, chopped or otherwise mangled in the sport of medieval cooking. La Varrenne also developed the first *fumet*, or fish stock. He simplified menus, bringing logic and order and doing away with the plethora of ill-assorted meat dishes.

Le Cuisinier François appeared when La Varrenne was 35 years old. A master cook for the Marquis d'Uxelles, he immortalized his patron with the duxelles of mushrooms, seasoned with herbs and shallots. La Varrenne's lifetime spanned the reigns of two kings, Louis XIII and Louis XIV, the Sun King. The latter's reign was a time of gastronomic transition, as new food, brought to Europe from the New World and Asia, was being assimilated. Jerusalem artichokes, for example, were adopted more quickly than potatoes and tomatoes. We find La Varrenne suggesting that Jerusalem artichokes be braised, then sautéed with onions and a grate of nutmeg. At table, the court combined aspects of the new sensibility with the gluttony of past centuries. Louis XIV himself has been described as more glutton than gourmet. "A man who eats well, works well," was his motto. His energy and appetite were both legendary.

The royal day began with a simple breakfast of bread and wine mixed with water. The main meals, served at noon and 10 p.m., consisted of eight courses of eight dishes apiece. Louis partook of each course, but not necessarily each dish. According to contemporary accounts, the king generally ate three soups, five entrées, three fowl, two fish and vegetables, tasted various roasts, had a quick bite of shellfish, cleared his palate with the *entremens*, enjoyed some dessert and ended with a few hard-boiled eggs.

A better symbol of the increasingly serious French attitude toward food is Vatel, the master cook of the Princesse de Condé. He committed suicide in 1671 after a series of culinary mishaps during a royal visit to her residence at Chantilly. The king arrived with a horde of retainers. During the first night, there was a shortage of tables for the lesser nobles. Then the kitchen ran out of roasts. Vatel felt disgraced. The next day at dinner the fish failed to arrive on time. Agitated, Vatel tried to explain the problem to the princess, but she would not listen. He retired to his chambers and threw himself on a sword. A few minutes later, the fish arrived.

At the same time, the English were displaying a more relaxed attitude toward cooking, if not toward food in general. An authoritative cookbook of the period, Robert May's *The Accomplisht Cook* (1660), makes plain that, in contrast to the

THE WAY TO A MAN'S HEART

Louis XIV was bored by his queen but thoroughly enjoyed his many mistresses, each of whom had to be a skillful cook to qualify for his attentions. Madame de Montespan invented a sauce and a paté of lark for her king. She also once spent nine thousand livres for a wine cooler so that his wines would be of the proper temperature when they dined together. Madame de Maintenon made the most far-reaching contribution because it was she who established the famed Cordon Bleu school of cookery. Originally the school was meant only for orphaned daughters of noble army officers, but *cuisine* was one of the subjects taught the girls, and in time the school became so famous for this one subject alone that the *cordon bleu* (blue ribbon) worn by each graduate as part of her costume came to be an emblem of an excellent cook.

Betty Wason, *Cooks, Gluttons and Gourmets,* p. 180.

French, who sought perfection, the English were taking a functional approach. Three hundred years earlier, there had been little to choose between Taillevent's *Le Viandier* and its English contemporary *Forme of Cury*. Now a divergence was clear. May devotes a small section to foreign dishes such as *olla podrida*, a Spanish stew called "olio" by the English, and *quelques shoses*, fancy French dishes the English called "kickshaw." But the mainstream for May is decidedly puddings, pies and roasts. Thus English culinary tradition was already set in its ways, disdaining "roots . . . water . . . herbs, or such beggary baggage."

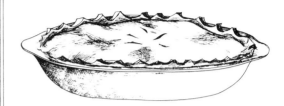

With the death of Louis XIV, gluttony suddenly became passé in the French court. Phillipe d'Orleans, regent during the minority of Louis XV, was an amateur pastrymaker who also dabbled in *haute cuisine*. He set a new style. Whereas the old king had reveled in huge public meals *(grands couverts)*, the *petits soupers* (little suppers) now captured the aristocratic fancy. It was *de rigueur* for a courtier to do some of his own cooking at these exquisite suppers, and nobles vied with one another inventing new dishes (or hiring chefs to invent dishes) that would then bear the nobles' famous names. Garnishes, *vols au vent*, cutlets and sausages bore such tags as de Berri, Villeroy, Monmorency, Mirepoix, Nesle, Richelieu and Talleyrand. Classic *haute cuisine* flowered during the Regency, and during the subsequent reign of Louis XV, it was characterized by simplicity, ingenuity, harmony and lightness. It retained some element of disguise, but this trait also disappeared from fashionable cuisine toward the end of Louis XV's reign, replaced by a passion for stressing the basic nature of the raw materials, a trait French cuisine retains to this day.

When Louis XV came to the throne, he took his cue from the Regent and adopted the *petit souper* as his style. He was a dilettante cook himself, and, besides, the intimate mode of dining suited his penchant for womanizing.

Cookbook writers followed a dual track during this period. Promoting *haute cuisine* and often working for aristocrats, they wrote with one eye on a growing audience, the upper middle class. In France the landmark cookbooks of the first half of the 18th century were Marin's *The Gifts of Comus* and Menon's *La Cuisinière Bourgeoise*. Despite his exalted status—Marin was *maître d'hôtel* for the Prince of Soubise—he addressed himself to the middle class: "I realize that the cuisine of Comus is not practical for all, but with proper pots and pans, fresh food purchased each morning and a good bouillon, even third-class persons can dine with grace." His book became a best seller, and Menon, his rival, was quick to take up a similar tone.

Menon came out ahead in this rivalry, perhaps because he

A GRAVY RECIPE FROM HANNAH GLASSE

If you live in the Country, where you can't always have Gravy Meat, when your Meat comes from the Butcher take a Piece of Beef, a Piece of Veal, and a Piece of Mutton; cut them into as small Pieces as you can, and take a large deep Sauce-pan with a Cover, lay your Beef at Bottom, then your Mutton, then a very little Piece of Bacon, a Slice or two of Carrot, some Mace, Cloves, Whole Pepper Black and White, a large Onion cut in Slices, a Bundle of Sweet Herbs, and then lay in your Veal. Cover it close over a very slow Fire for six or seven Minutes, shaking the Sauce-pan now and then; then shake some Flour in, and have ready some boiling Water, pour it in till you cover the Meat and something more: Cover it close, and let it stew till it is quite rich and good; then season it to your Taste with Salt, and strain it off. This will do for most Things.

Hannah Glasse, *The Art of Cookery Made Plain and Easy* (Hamden, Conn.: Archon Books; East Ardsley, England: S.R. Publishers, 1971). A photographic reproduction of the 1796 edition.

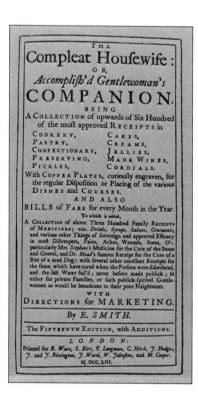

addressed himself to the female cook and openly attempted to "reduce expenses, simplify methods, and go some way towards bringing what has seemed the preserve of opulent kitchens within the range of the bourgeoisie." A favorite of a new class of entrepreneurs, the restaurateurs, the book outsold all other 18th-century cookbooks.

In England, the best-selling cookbook of the 18th century was Hannah Glasse's *The Art of Cookery Made Plain and Easy*. It was first published in 1747, and during the next 50 years it ran through 20 editions. Apart from the "plain and easy" tag, which is still effective, 20th-century critics are hard put to explain the phenomenal success of this book. It seems to differ little from half a dozen rivals; it is poorly organized, lacked (in early editions) an alphabetical index, has repetitive recipes in several sections and contains a lot of material stolen from earlier cookbooks. Yet it has certain undeniable qualities.

The author's style inspires confidence in her honesty and experience. She candidly admits "that some few of these [recipes] have been taken from other publications, the Editor does not pretend to deny. . . ." The book covers an enormous range of topics, including pickling, brewing, making vermicelli, carving, and mixing home remedies. Most charming is the insistent tone of modesty with which the author convinces the reader that the art of cooking can be mastered by all.

As the 18th century progressed, the gulf between English and French cooking widened. Crosschannel travelers began to complain of each other's cooking: the Englishman at being served "a frivolous selection of pompously titled tidbits, but no real food," and the Frenchman at the English dinner, which "generally consists of a half-boiled or half-roasted meat; a few cabbage leaves, boiled in plain water; on which they pour a sauce made of flour and butter. . . ."

Cooking in 18th-century America is mainly a footnote to English cookery. The most popular cookbook there, as in England, was Hannah Glasse's *The Art of Cookery Made Plain and Easy*. The first one printed in America, at Williamsburg, Virginia, was an English title, *The Compleat Housewife* (1742), by E. Smith, which bowed to local conditions by omitting ingredients not available in America. *American Cookery,* by Amelia Simmons and published in Hartford, Connecticut, in 1796, was the first to contain American recipes, such as roast turkey with cranberry sauce, watermelon pickles and johnnycake, and to use native foods, such as corn, pumpkins, squashes and Jerusalem artichokes. There were also "truly American" dishes such as chowder, lobster Newburg, planked shad, Boston baked beans, succotash, spoon bread,

Maryland fried chicken, hominy grits, scrapple, maple syrup and buckwheat cakes.

The only real departure from Anglo-Saxon style took place in New Orleans. Waverley Root and Richard de Rochemont explain this aberration on page 281 in their book *Eating in America* (New York: William Morrow, 1976):

> Creole cooking is that of a melting pot, but not the general American melting pot. It is a mixture of French, African, Indian and Spanish cuisines, cheerfully unconscious of the very existence of Anglo-Saxon cooking. It was put together partly in the West Indies, whose populations are also made up chiefly of the descendants of Frenchmen, Africans, Indians and Spaniards.

Examples of creole dishes are jambalaya, which is of Spanish origin and related to *paella;* and gumbo, a fish dish thickened with okra, a vegetable brought from Africa by black slaves, or with filé powder; and bouillabaisse, a fish stew of French inspiration.

French classical *haute cuisine* culminated in the works of Marie-Antonin Carême, who was born in 1784 and became the greatest chef of the early 19th century. Apprenticed at 14 to the pastry chef Bailly, Carême managed by the time of his death in 1835 to have been chef for Talleyrand (1814), Alexander I of Russia (1815–16), the prince regent of England (at Brighton, 1816–18), Prince Esterhazy and the Baron Rothschild (1829–30). A prolific writer as well, Carême's works include *Le Patissier Royal Parisien* (1827), *Le Maître d'Hôtel Français* (1821) and *L'Art de la Cuisine Française au 19ème Siècle*, in three volumes (1833).

Claiming that confectionary was a brand of architecture, Carême created masterpieces of table decoration out of marzipan, fondant and sugar. Thus he came to the attention of French statesman Charles Maurice Talleyrand, the greatest gourmet of the epoch, and of Napoleon. While still with Bailly, Carême moonlighted as an extra chef in the great houses of Paris, learning other aspects of cooking from the finest chefs of the day. A perfectionist, Carême observed critically and gave praise where due (Talleyrand) and blame where *it* was due (Cambaceres). Jean Jacques Régis de Cambacères, Prince of Parma and a minister of Napoleon, had the reputation of a gourmet, but Carême professed to be shocked at what he saw in the kitchen: "The prince occupied himself with his table every morning, expending minute care, but only to discuss and decrease expense. He

RECIPE FROM AMELIA SIMMONS— GINGERBREAD CAKE

Three pounds of flour, a grated nutmeg, two ounces ginger, one pound sugar, three small spoons pearl ash [a raising agent] dissolved in cream, one pound butter, four eggs, knead it stiff, shape it to your fancy, bake 15 minutes.

Amelia Simmons, *First American Cookbook* (Johnsburg, N.Y.: Buck Hill, 1966).

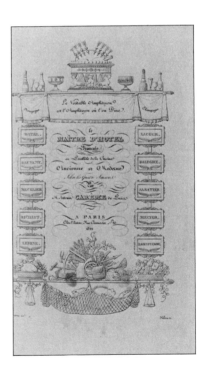

CARÊME IN ENGLAND

Carême came, and saw, but he could not conquer. The ponderous battery of Brighton shone out in its vast armament of polished copper in vain. Troops of chuckle-headed little English aides, plump and batter faced, were no aid to him, and the hecatombe of English beef, and oceans of passive and obedient fish which came to be caught within the view of the kiosks of Brighton Pavilion, involved the genius of the enlightened foreigner to no avail. To use his own expression, he was *soffoqué*. He discovered that nobody at the Pavilion could speak French, and he could speak no English, and therefore he had no way of expressing his ideas which he would have communicated. He found that he had a vocabulary to invent, a grammar to compose, and he shrank from the herculean labour imposed upon him. But above all he discovered that the women of England knew nothing at all of his art, that the presiding deity of the Pavilion scarcely rose above the cowslips appreciation of roast duck with its coarse and predominating accompaniment of sage and onion stuffing.

Lady Morgan, quoted in Edward B. Page and P.W. Kingsford, *The Master Chefs,* (New York: St. Martin's Press, 1971), p. 94.

KITCHEN CONDITIONS

Imagine yourself in a large kitchen at the moment of a great dinner, see twenty chefs, coming, going, moving with speed in this cauldron of heat, look at the great mass of charcoal, a cubic meter for the cooking of entrees, and another mass on the ovens for the cooking of soups, sauces, ragouts, for frying and the bain maries. Add to that a heap of burning wood in front of which four spits are turning, one of which bears a sirloin weighing 45 to 50 pounds, the other fowl or game. In this furnace everyone moves with speed, not a sound is heard, only the chef has a right to be heard, and at the sound of his voice everyone obeys. Finally the last straw; for about half an hour all windows are closed, so that the air does not cool the dishes as they are being served up, and in this way we spend the best years of our lives. We must obey even when physical strength fails us, but it is the burning charcoal that kills us.

Carême, quoted in Edward B. Page and P.W. Kinsford, *The Master Chefs,* (New York: St. Martin's Press, 1971), p. 79.

showed in the highest degree that worry and concern over details that mark the miser. At every service he took a note of the dishes that had not been served, or only partly eaten, and the next day he composed his meal from these vile leftovers. Heavens, what a dinner!"

Of Talleyrand, he remarked, "[He] understands the genius of a cook, he respects it, he is the most competent judge of delicate progress and his expenditures are wise and great at the same time."

Carême's watchwords were wisdom, order, efficiency, experience and excellence. After his work with ministers of state, he grew to believe that cooking could have an exalted mission: "To serve as a foil to European diplomacy . . . good cooking should strengthen the life of old societies."

With the restoration of the Bourbon monarchy in 1814, Carême worked as a free-lance chef in Paris, then accepted an invitation to head the English prince regent's kitchens at Brighton.

However, Carême gave up his past there after two years, unhappy with his work and the English weather, and returned to Paris. After a brief visit to St. Petersburg (to study the culinary system at court), he remained in Paris until his death, writing books and cooking for Esterhazy and Rothschild.

In Carême's later years he became waspish about other gastronomic writers—"unqualifed authorities" he called those who did not have his skill and experience in the culinary arts. One such was Jean Anthelme Brillat-Savarin, whom he stigmatized as a "provincial boor" and a glutton but who nevertheless achieved lasting fame, as we shall see later on.

Carême died at 51 in modest circumstances. One story has it that he was in the midst of instructing a student on how to prepare quenelles of sole. "These are good," he said, "but prepared too hastily. You must shake the saucepan lightly—see, like this . . . ," with which he collapsed and died. Another version claims the great chef died while dictating notes for a new book. Either way, Carême was advancing his profession, his obsession, as death came to him.

Carême perfected classic *haute cuisine.* He put the whole of his knowledge into *L'Art de la Cuisine Française au 19ème Siècle,* which was an exhaustive, state-of-the-art survey. He set down definitive versions of sauces that would be familiar to today's chefs. He developed a simplified menu that set the form for generations. It runs as follows: vegetable soup, roast or braised fillet of beef served with glazed vegetables or rice, and a simple *jus* as gravy, then poached or gratinéed fish, or a fish stew, then roasted fowl with vegetables, pastries, salad and dessert.

THE RISE OF THE MIDDLE CLASS

At the turn of the 19th century, the restaurant was a fairly recent phenomenon. The first one was founded in Paris in 1765, as a French adaptation of the English ale and beef-steak houses and taverns. In 1814, a restaurateur named Antoine Beauvilliers published *L'Art du Cuisinier,* a cookbook that quickly became a standard authority. Covering both *haute cuisine* and everyday cooking *(cuisine bourgeoise),* the book was considered the first worthy successor to Menon's work.

The early 19th century saw the middle class attaining new power and riches, which caused a tremendous boom in the restaurant business. But the new social leaders were uncertain about how to display their position and wealth, and to advise them a new profession was created, that of the professional gastronome, or, as we say today, the food and restaurant critic.

The most prominent of these in France was Grimod de la Reynière, who, in 1803, founded a gastronomic guide to Paris. An annual publication entitled *Almanach des Gourmands,* it soon became indispensable to fashionable people as well as to the cooks and restaurateurs of Paris. The *Almanach* was a guide to the good life and combined food and restaurant criticism with listings of shops, specialties, restaurants, the latest menus, and notes on changing customs and manners—a combined gourmet magazine and consumer report.

To put a seal of scientific objectivity on his criticism, Grimod created a jury of taste *(jury degustateur)* that functioned as a consumer panel. The jury was made up of from five to 12 distinguished gastronomes who met once a week to sample and pronounce judgment on new dishes, products and restaurants, and its verdicts were published in the *Almanach.* In the case of an unfavorable judgment, a purveyor was allowed a second chance to make up deficiencies.

In 1808, Grimod supplemented the *Almanach* with a *Manuel des Amphitryons,* a guide to the management of an affluent household. The text carefully addresses itself to the *amphitryon* (host) rather than the *seigneur* (lord) and refers to *l'homme opulent* (man of means) rather than to the nobleman.

The *Almanach* ceased publication in 1812.

In 1825, an amateur startled the gastronomic world with a small book that was to become a classic appreciation of fine dining. This was Jean Anthelme Brillat-Savarin's *The Physiol-*

APHORISMS OF GRIMOD DE LA REYNIÈRE

An overturned salt cellar is to be feared solely when it is overturned in a good dish.

Thirteen at a table is a number to be dreaded when there is only enough to go round for twelve.

There is a precise moment at which every dish should be savoured, previous to which or after which it causes only an imperfect sensation.

The etymology of the word Faisander* sufficiently proclaims that the pheasant should be waited for as long as a pension from the government by a man of letters who has never known how to flatter.

It is notorious that a dinner, however generous, has never disturbed a person who had preceded or followed it by a walk of five of six leagues; and that indigestions are virtually unknown to great pedestrians.

Life is so brief that we should not glance either too far backwards to forwards in order to be happy. Let us therefore study how to fix our happiness in our glass and on our plate.

George H. Ellwanger, *The Pleasure of the Table* (New York: Doubleday & Page, 1902), pp. 138-39.

* To keep game till it is high

Jean Anthelme Brillat-Savarin
(1755–1826)

A SELECTION OF APHORISMS

Made by the Professor for a Prologue to his work, and to be the eternal foundations of the Science when he professes.

II. Beasts feed: man eats: the man of intellect alone knows how to eat.

III. The fate of nations hangs upon their choice of food.

IV. Tell me what you eat: I will tell you what you are.

VII. The pleasures of the table are of all times and all ages, of every country and of every day; they go hand in hand with all our other pleasures, outlast them and in the end console us for their loss.

IX. The discovery of a new dish does more for the happiness of mankind than the discovery of a star.

XI. From the most substantial dish to the lightest; this is the right order of eating.

XII. From the mildest wine to the headiest and most perfumed; this is the right order of drinking.

XIV. Dessert without cheese is like a pretty woman with only one eye.

XV. A man becomes a cook; but he is born a roaster of flesh.

XVI. The most indispensable quality in a cook is punctuality: and no less is required of a guest.

XX. To entertain a guest is to be answerable for his happiness so long as he is beneath your roof.

Brillat-Savarin, Jean Anthelme, *The Physiology of Taste, or Meditations on Transcendental Gastronomy,* (New York: Dover Publications, 1960), a reprint of the 1925 Heineman edition.

ogy of Taste, or, Meditations on Transcendental Gastronomy. When the book appeared, Brillat-Savarin was a judge in the Court of Cassation (appeals). Despite the pompous title, the book is delightfully informal and witty, a charming collection of anecdotes, aphorisms and short essays ("meditations") on the pleasures of the table. Brillat-Savarin published it under a pseudonym, "the Professor."

Unlike Carême, Grimod immediately hailed the work as a masterpiece and took credit for having suggested the author's *nom de plume.* Other critics charged Brillat-Savarin with being a plagiarist of truly catholic tastes, ransacking the works of great writers from Confucius to Moncelet. This did not seem to matter to the public, The book's mixture of wisdom and erudition, leavened by a self-deprecating humor, has appealed to generation after generation, keeping the book in print to this day. It also established a genre—commentary by the gifted amateur—paving the way for such men of letters as Alexandre Dumas and Théophile Gautier.

At a less exalted level, cookbook publishing was a good business during this time. One best seller was *La Cuisinière de la Campagne et de la Ville, ou, La Nouvelle Cuisine Économique,* by Louis Eustache Audot. First published in 1818, the book remained in print (going through 80 editions) until the end of the century. The various editions of a popular cookbook by A. Viard could serve as a guide to the vagaries of French politics during the century. It started out in 1806 during the first empire as *Le Cuisinier Imperial.* When the monarchy was restored, the title was changed to *Le Cuisinier Royal.* Louis Napoleon became president of France in 1848, and the title became *Le Cuisinier National.* When a *coup d'état* transformed the president into Emperor Napoleon III, the book was reissued as *Le Cuisinier Imperial.* With the establishment of the Third Republic in 1878, A. Viard returned, permanently, to *Le Cuisinier National.*

The French Revolution and the Napoleonic wars gave the English upper classes a prolonged exposure to the best in French cooking. Chefs left France en masse and worked in English clubs or for wealthy families. Despite this, the French style did not prevail. Elmé Francatelli was Queen Victoria's chief cook in ordinary. His book, which appeared in 1845, tried to cater to all tastes—it has recipes from sheeps' jowls, ears and trotters to venison and reindeer tongues. Its stress on garnishes, however, betrayed its *haute cuisine* bias. Not so the best-selling *Modern Cookery in All Its Branches* by poet Eliza Acton, who wrote the book at the suggestion of her publisher. Well-organized, clear and particularly useful to the middle-class housewife, it stayed in print until 1905 but was overshadowed in the public fancy by Isabella Beeton's *The Book of Household Management,* which saw light in 1861 and remains in print today.

Born Isabella Mayson, the eldest of 21 children, Beeton was raised in unconventional surroundings—the racecourse at Epsom Downs, where her stepfather was clerk of the course. At 19 she married publisher Samuel Beeton and assumed editorship of his *Domestic Magazine*. Five years later, *The Book of Household Management* began to appear in installments, which were later compiled into a bound volume.

The book's strong points are a firm sense of order, a succinct, fluent style and an air of reassuring authority that left nothing to chance. Mrs. Beeton listed quantities of ingredients, cooking times and number of servings with each recipe (one of the first books to do so), and even specified that the temperature of the dining room should be "about 68 degrees."

Beeton's household tips shed light on the kind of Victorian household she was addressing: With an income of £1,000 a year, the householder was advised to employ a cook, an upper housemaid, a nursemaid, an underhousemaid and a manservant, paying a total of £65 in salaries. Critics have faulted *The Book of Household Management* because many of the recipes were of foreign origin offered under anglicized names and because many colonial recipes were also included.

Mrs. Beeton died in 1865 after giving birth to her fourth child. The rights to her book eventually passed to the publishers Ward, Lock and Tyler (now Ward Lock Ltd.), who followed a policy of frequent revision, such that the 1960 version (which is still in print) retains very little of the original. A facsimile of the first edition was published in London by Jonathan Cape in 1968, and in New York by Farrar, Straus & Giroux in 1977.

In the mid-19th century, the best-known chef in the English-speaking world was a Frenchman, Alexis Soyer. Immigrating to England in 1831, he remained there until his death in 1858. Chef at the London Reform Club for 13 years, Soyer was also a prolific author of cookbooks. An unconventional man, he shocked his Gallic colleagues by avowing that roasts, steaks and other classic English dishes could be gourmet fare. Yet when the occasion demanded it, he could turn out *haute cuisine* as elaborate as Francatelli's.

Soyer had style. A highly emotional man who often acted on impulse, he affected gaily colored clothes, with brightly polished buttons and a velvet cap set at an angle. He liked practical jokes and constantly sought public attention. He claimed, "Publicity is like the air we breathe, if we have it not, we die." His simplicity, humanitarianism and good humor won him friends by the hundreds in London. A man with a conscience, he wrote *A Shilling Cookery for the People*,

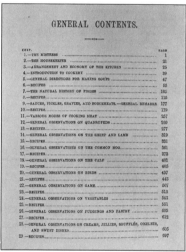

Two pages from
The Book of Household
Management *by Isabella Beeton*

IMMORAL DUCK

It is to be regretted that domestication has seriously deteriorated the moral character of the duck. In a wild state, he is a faithful husband, desiring but one wife, and devoting himself to her; but no sooner is he domesticated than he becomes polygamous, and makes nothing of owning 10 or a dozen wives at a time.

Isabella Beeton, *Mrs. Beeton's Cookery and Household Management* (Woodstock, N.Y.: Beekman, n.d.)

Soyer's stove

A HIGHER PLANE

The American housewife was given a new mantle of dignity as it became known that government bureaus were studying food and that universities were establishing departments of home economics. One cookbook editor noted that "advanced women" had been taught by higher education "to regard their domestic duties in the light of a science and an art." And Fannie Farmer, remarking the increased attention to nutrition, concluded that the study of foods and their dietetic value would soon be "an essential part of one's education."

There were those who stressed the health aspect of food almost grimly. Although American writers had rarely noticed cooking as a sensuous art, this new emphasis almost excluded the role of enjoyment. Sara Tyson Rorer, whose cookbooks were major successes, expressed the idea baldly:

. . . The teacher or cook book (an ever present teacher) that does not teach health, body building, and economy in time and money, is short-lived. There are still a few women who do elaborate cooking to please the palate and appetite, and the general habits of people. They are still in the palate stage of existence. Strive to reach a higher plane of thought—eat to live.

Richard J. Hooker, *Food and Drink in America* (Indianapolis and New York: Bobbs-Merrill, 1981)

consisting of simple and inexpensive recipes using such budget items as oxcheek and lamb's head; the book sold more than a quarter-million copies. Other popular Soyer titles were *The Modern Housewife* and *The Pantropheon*, a massive history of food and its preparation from the earliest ages. Soyer also produced innovative kitchen designs and invented culinary gadgets and devices, such as a portable stove. During the Crimean War, in cooperation with Florence Nightingale, he worked with the British Army to improve sanitary conditions, organization and equipment in the mess, and he trained cooks. He is credited with revolutionizing the English catering industry and single-handedly raising English taste from the "culinary doldrums" to an appreciation of cooking as an art. In so doing, he prepared the way for another great French chef who would practice in England, Auguste Escoffier.

By the time of the Louisiana Purchase in 1803, American cuisine was too firmly set in the Anglo-Saxon mold to be much influenced nationally by the French elements of creole cookery. More influential were the experiences of upper-class Americans who visited France as a result of the alliance during the American Revolution. Thomas Jefferson was a devotee of French cooking, laying in a collection of French wines when he moved into the White House and bringing along a French chef. The snob value of French cooking was popularly recognized. During the first third of the 19th century, the words "restaurant," "menu," and "cafe" came into use in the larger cities, along with "à la" dishes.

America soon was buffeted by successive waves of immigrants. Before the Civil War came the Germans and the Irish. While French cooking swayed the upper classes, German cooking had the most impact on the middle classes. Americans soon were using such words as sauerkraut, noodle, pretzel, pumpernickel, schnitzel, sauerbraten and zwieback. The Irish, curiously, had little influence on American cuisine, perhaps because the Irish immigrants were overwhelmingly distressed peasants whose diet had consisted mainly of potatoes supplemented by small amounts of oatmeal, buttermilk and vegetables.

In 1857, Eliza Leslie's *New Cookery Book* could boast of a variety of foreign novelties, including mutton kabob, French recipes, Irish stew, an East Indian pickle, a Turkish kabob, two recipes for curry powder and three curried dishes, pork Italian style, Scotch cake, sauerkraut and a West Indian cake.

After the Civil War there was a surge of interest in cooking. Cookbook publishing boomed, periodicals dealing with culinary matters multiplied, and cooking schools opened in the large cities. Sara Tyson Rorer, author of several popular cookbooks, founded the Philadelphia Cooking School in 1878. A short time later, the Boston Cooking School opened its doors. The first director was Mary J. Lincoln, then came Fannie Merritt Farmer.

Mrs. Lincoln and her protégée, Fannie, were preoccupied with the rationalization of measurement, timing and servings. Not for them were terms such as a pinch of salt, a "nut" of butter or a glass of wine. They wanted to know how many teaspoons, or ounces, or what size glass. Mrs. Lincoln wrote *The Boston Cook Book,* which was published in 1887. In 1896, Fannie Farmer brought out *The Boston Cooking-School Cook Book,* which, though inspired by Mrs. Lincoln's work, was mostly new material. Farmer aimed at making recipes foolproof for the novice, and overnight book sales soared. She saw the book through 21 printings before her death. The 12th edition of the *Fannie Farmer Cookbook,* as it came to be called, edited by Marion Cunningham, made the bestseller lists in 1979.

Of the several immigrant groups that arrived in America in the latter half of the 19th century—Germans, Swedes, Hungarians, Poles, Russians, Greeks, Jews—perhaps the Italians had the most impact on what Americans ate. Italians clung tenaciously to their native diet, and it was different enough to attract attention, but not so strange as to cause rejection.

This babel of ethnic cuisines was given recognition in *The Settlement Cookbook,* which was published in the early 1900s and became a culinary Bible for many immigrants, helping them translate American recipe lore into more familiar Old World measures, plus giving instructions on preparing many mid-European specialties.

Two contrasting figures highlighted French writing on food and cooking during the last quarter of the 19th century: Alexandre Dumas *(père),* the novelist and amateur gourmet, and Auguste Escoffier, the consummate professional chef.

Dumas's novels had an immense following, yet he considered his work-in-progress on cooking, which appeared posthumously in 1873, to be his masterpiece. Titled *Grand Dictionnaire de Cuisine,* the book filled more than 1,000 pages in a large folio format. It was both an encyclopedia of food and a compendium of French cooking.

The original edition contained recipes as well as facts, anecdotes and histories. Dumas's stated purpose was to take from the classic cookery books that were in the public domain all the recipes that had won a place at the best tables. To these he added "unknown dishes gathered from the ends of the earth, and the least known and liveliest anecdotes on the cooking of peoples, and on the peoples themselves." He hoped in this way to attract the practical cook while retain-

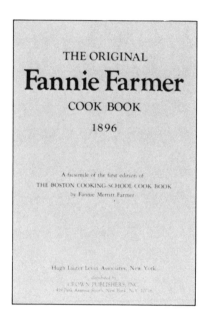

THE ORIGINAL
Fannie Farmer
COOK BOOK
1896

A facsimile of the first edition of
THE BOSTON COOKING-SCHOOL COOK BOOK
by Fannie Merritt Farmer

Hugh Lauter Levin Associates, New York

distributed by
CROWN PUBLISHERS, INC.
419 Park Avenue South, New York, N.Y. 10016

THE ABSENT POET

[Albert] de Musset's fatal passion for absinthe, which may have given some of his verses their bitter flavor, caused the dignified Academy* to descend to punning. It seems that de Musset frequently found himself in no condition to attend the academic sessions. Which prompted one of the forty Immortals to say that "he absinthes himself a bit too much."

Alexandre Dumas *(père), Dictionary of Cuisine,* p. 39.

* Académie Française

ing the readership of his fans—that is, "serious men and not-so-serious women."

Critics pounced on the book for having out-of-date recipes, but many fans found it as thrilling as *The Three Musketeers.* Nevertheless, it soon went out of print. When a new edition came out in 1882, it had been reduced to the recipes plus a few observations on dining, such as the following: "After Paris, the city with the most restaurants is San Francisco. It has restaurants from every country, even China." In France, this utilitarian edition, entitled *Petit Dictionnaire de Cuisine,* did little better than the original.

Escoffier's life spanned 89 years, from 1846 to 1935, and most of his long career was spent in England, in association with Cesar Ritz, the renowned hotelier, who considered him the best chef in the world.

Escoffier deserved this accolade for several reasons: His cooking skills were superb; he was a fertile creator of new dishes on demand; he was a brilliant designer and manager of kitchens; he created the party system of organizing the work of chefs, which cut the time needed to prepare a dish by 80 percent and made possible the "à la carte" menu; and he skillfully communicated his knowledge to both the catering trade and the general public through his articles and books.

Escoffier's masterwork, *Le Guide Culinaire,* appeared in 1902. Written in collaboration with several other well-known chefs (Phineas Gilbert, Alfred Suzanne, Émile Fétu, Apollon Caillart, Jean Baptiste Rebout and Charles Dietriche), the book demands considerable prior knowledge and skill on the part of the reader. Of the latest English translation (Mayflower Books, 1980), cooking authority Craig Claiborne wrote: "The finest and most authentic translation of the Escoffier book is that of Messrs. Cracknell and Kaufmann. They have been true in all respects to the master, who was to many generations of chefs what Hoyle was to game playing. Their translation is an outstanding, distinguished work, and indispensable to a complete library [of cookbooks]." (Craig Claiborne, *A Feast Made for Laughter* [Garden City, N.Y.: Doubleday, 1982], p. 262.)

TECHNOLOGY AND GOURMET CHIC

Escoffier had codified the rules and regulations of fine French cooking, seemingly for good. During the first half of the 20th century, his methods had the force of law among

French chefs. This rigidity was deemed a virtue: French was the finest Western cuisine, and one of its glories was that preparation of dishes from the canon did not vary, period. The same dish prepared in Tokyo, Cincinnati or Paris had to be identical, within the limits of human frailty. "Creativity" was out. The same could not be said of Italian cuisine, to cite another great Western style of cooking. Italian dishes varied from province to province, even city to city.

Still, the new French cooking introduced in the 1960s and pursued vigorously in the 1970s by such imposing figures as Paul Bocuse and the Troisgros brothers, came more as a reformation than a revolution. They billed themselves not as iconoclasts but as disciples acting in the *true* spirit of the lawgiver. They were, after all, established chefs, high priests of the old orthodoxy. Nevertheless, the changes they advocated—indeed, embodied in new dishes—revolutionized French cooking. Most subversive of all, perhaps, was the idea that it was all right to be creative. Suddenly innovation was not only "in" but even *de rigueur*. *Nouvelle cuisine* was the major ideological change in fine cooking during the 20th century. Apart from creativity, a basic premise of the new style was that the rich sauces of the 19th century were not in tune with modern needs, that, indeed, they prevented the appreciation of the essence of each ingredient, a concept harking back to Escoffier. Gone were the 10 or more heavy courses typical of Escoffier's day. Light and delicate were the new watchwords, and smaller portions. Gone were the taboos on mixing or juxtaposing various foods. Nary an eyebrow was raised at such combinations as lobster in vanilla sauce, truffles with lime ice, and ravioli stuffed with snails and peaches.

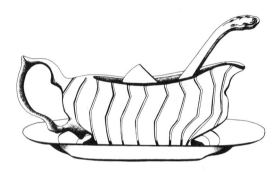

This novelty in exalted gastronomic circles was not entirely unrelated to events in the New World. In fact, the timing could not have been better. During the first half of the 20th century, Americans were paying more attention to technology than technique, and to convenience rather than high style. Cookbooks emphasized making life easier for the housewife. The big sellers of this era were *The Fannie Farmer Cookbook, Better Homes and Gardens Cook Book* (1930), Irma S. Rombauer's *The Joy of Cooking* (1931) and *Betty Crocker's Cookbook* (1950). Along with recipes, they gave instructions on how to use such technological advances as gas and electric ranges, refrigerators, freezers and such conveniences as frozen foods and cake mixes.

Pundits in the 1930s and 1940s speculated that home cooking, as the world knew it, might disappear if the trend to convenience foods continued. It was implied that that might not be a bad idea, since "American" cuisine at its best seemed to consist of watered-down and sanitized versions of

ethnic dishes, and at its worst, a form of industrial waste. Then Americans discovered eating for the pleasure of it, even the thrill of it.

Middle-class Americans achieved affluence in the 1950s, and in the 1960s they discovered European travel. Sampling various cuisines there and gaining a measure of sophistication, they began to incorporate these new tastes into their home cooking. The cookbook story of the 1960s and 1970s is one ethnic fad after another, beginning with French cooking and continuing through Italian, Chinese, Japanese and Thai, among others. As 1984 dawns, the latest far-out trend is (are you sitting down?)—American cuisine. Be it as humble as barbecued ribs or as *haute* as wild mallard glazed with molasses, American is "in."

Thus the twin American gods of convenience and technology have had to make room on the hearth for gourmet chic. These three tendencies combined perfectly, if fleetingly, in the 1970s fad of the one-dish, crockpot meal of *haute cuisine* caliber. In the 1980s, gourmet cooking has become a byword and has proved to be a natural adjunct to an affluent life-style.

Inevitably, fast, easy food and gourmet dining clashed head on with other enlightened preoccupations—the need to stay slim, and more recently, the need to be fit. *Nouvelle cuisine* to the rescue. It possessed the right combination of glamor and skimpiness, and a new name was coined for it, *cuisine minceur* (slimness cooking), which soon became interchangeable with *nouvelle cuisine*. Some landmark books about *nouvelle cuisine* are *Michel Guérard's Cuisine Minceur* (New York: Morrow, 1977), *The Nouvelle Cuisine of Jean and Pierre Troisgros* (New York: Morrow, 1978) and Roy Andries de Groot's *Revolutionizing French Cooking* (New York: McGraw-Hill, 1977).

In an interview, Jean Troisgros pooh-poohed the "revolutionary" nature of the new cuisine: "There's nothing new. They were fixing the same type of food four decades ago when I apprenticed at Lucas Carlton and La Pyramide. And what do you think Escoffier was doing?" (Jan Weimer, "Troisgros on Fish: The Secret Is in the Sauce," *Cuisine*, Vol. 10, No. 3 [April 1981], pp. 37–38.)

Preoccupation with weight loss grew steadily during the 1960s and 1970s, and by the beginning of the 1980s half of the books on the nonfiction best-seller list dealt with weight loss, exercise or both. The largest audience probably was reached by Jean Nidetch's phenomenally successful books on the Weight Watchers program. These included *The Weight Watchers Program Cookbook* (1973), *The Weight Watchers New Program Cookbook* (1978), *The Weight Watchers 365-Day Menu Cookbook* (1981) and *Weight Watchers Interna-*

tional Cookbook (New York: New American Library, 1980).

There was an earlier wave of Americans who traveled abroad before the 1960s—the GIs of World War II. Many writers trace the roots of American food sophistication in the postwar period to returned GIs. Craig Claiborne marks 1947 as a banner year for food because that's when Pan American inaugurated its first round-the-world flight.

An important voice in American food writing gained broad recognition in the postwar era: M.F.K. Fisher. Today she is considered one of the four most influential food/cookbook writers of America's Golden Age of food. (The other three are James Beard, who rose to prominence in the 1950s, and Julia Child and Craig Claiborne, both of whom became celebrities in the 1960s. In the 1980s all are deemed grand masters and retain enormous influence.) Mary Frances Kennedy Fisher is a Californian who published 13 volumes between 1937 and 1982. The best known, perhaps, is *The Art of Eating* (1954), which is a collection of five earlier volumes: *Serve It Forth* (1937), *Consider the Oyster* (1941), *How to Cook a Wolf* (1942), *The Gastronomical Me* (1943) and *An Alphabet for Gourmets* (1949). These books are a unique blend of autobiography, philosophy, recipes and storytelling. Her other works include a translation of Brillat-Savarin's *The Physiology of Taste* (New York: Knopf, 1971) and a volume of the Time-Life Foods of the World series entitled *The Cooking of Provincial France* (1968). Called the philosopher-poet of the stove, Fisher writes of an American experience of food, but with overtones drawn from familiarity with European cuisines, especially that of France, gained during residence abroad. As an indication of her standing among the arbiters of taste, consider this quotation by James Beard: "M.F.K. Fisher has been a rarity in American gastronomy. This country has produced quantities of cookbook writers—all too many who write without personality or originality—but few writers in the great European tradition of Brillat-Savarin, Maurice des Ombiaux, or George Saintsbury. . . . She writes about fleeting tastes and feasts vividly, excitingly, sensuously, exquisitely. There is almost a wicked thrill in following her uninhibited track through the glories of the good life." (From the introduction to M.F.K. Fisher's *The Art of Eating* [New York: Vintage Books, 1976], p. xviii.)

Beard himself is a native of Oregon and a man of Bunyanesque size and energy. He learned cooking at home from his mother, who operated a hotel in Portland. Beard trained as an actor, and cooking remained a sideline until the mid-1950s, when he became one of television's first performer-chefs. A prolific writer, he broke into print in 1942 with a book on hors d'oeuvres; the book is still available to-

day. It was based on his experience as the proprietor of a New York catering service. His important books began to appear after he achieved fame. They include *The James Beard Cookbook* (1958) and its sequel, *The New James Beard* (1981); *Delights and Prejudices* (1964), which is an autobiography recounted meal by meal; *James Beard's American Cookery* (1972) and *Theory and Practice of Good Cooking* (1977). Beard has exercised much of his influence through the medium of television and through the operation of his cooking school in New York City. His works present an exhaustive knowledge of techniques and recipes, combined with an upbeat philosophy, expressed most succinctly in his *Theory and Practice of Good Cooking:* "In my 25 years of teaching I have tried to make people realize that cooking is primarily fun and that the more they know about what they are doing, the more fun it is."

Craig Claiborne, a native of Mississippi, first made his mark as food editor of *The New York Times,* a post he occupied from 1959 to 1972. It is generally conceded that he ushered in a new era of American restaurant criticism. Until then, restaurant reviews mostly served as a device to stimulate advertisements and could hardly be considered objective criticism. It was precisely this impartiality he strove for in his reviews, and he used food quality as his sole criterion.

Claiborne brought unusual qualifications to his task, including 18 months' study in a respected Swiss hotel school and experience working in a hotel and a restaurant. He introduced measures to ensure his credibility: Rather than accept free meals from restaurateurs, he got *The Times* to pay for them. He also attempted to maintain (but did not always achieve) anonymity in restaurants. Before rating a new restaurant, he waited several months to allow the staff to settle in. He ate several meals in a place before reaching a conclusion, and he made follow-up visits. Most important for his credibility, he had the courage to do negative reviews.

An excellent and exacting cook himself, Claiborne compiled in 1961 *The New York Times Cook Book,* a selection of 1,500 recipes from the pages of *The Times* from the previous decade. It quickly became a best seller, and played a commanding role in the growing sophistication of American cooks. Other influential publications followed, including *The New York Times International Cook Book* (1971); *The New New York Times Cook Book* (1981) with Pierre Franey, a compilation of *Times* recipes from the 1970s; and a *A Feast Made for Laughter* (1982), an autobiographical essay with two appendices: a recommended cookbook library and Claiborne's 100 favorite recipes.

Julia Child became a cooking guru to millions during the 1960s through her PBS television program *The French Chef.*

Her style combined a sound knowledge of the subject and a down-to-earth attitude ("I tried to take a lot of the la-dee-dah out of French cooking. . . .") with the quick wit and aplomb of a stand-up comedienne. The television program was founded on the runaway success of her book *Mastering the Art of French Cooking*, Vol. 1 (with Simone Beck and Louisette Bertholle), which was published in 1961. The book stresses good technique (which happen to be French) applied to fresh ingredients. She playfully suggests that a good subtitle might have been *French Cooking from the American Supermarket*. Volume II (with Simone Beck) followed in 1970. Then came *From Julia Child's Kitchen* (1975), a sort of synthesis of the two earlier volumes, derived from her colorful television series. As time passed Child put less emphasis on things French, underlining her contention that there's nothing ethnic about good technique. *Julia Child and Company*, a menu cookbook much more American than its predecessors, appeared in 1978, then *Julia Child & More Company* in 1980. These last two are based on television programs, which continue in 1984 with an innovative series entitled *Dinner with Julia*.

The early trend in convenience continued in the postwar era with the proliferation of franchise restaurants and junk food. Although some commentators were alarmed by these developments, others took comfort in the fact that the number of cookbooks published and their total sales soared all the while. Between 1965 and 1975, some 3,168 new cookbook titles were published in the United States alone. And despite the dwindling necessity for cooking, more people today buy cookbooks and flock to gourmet cooking schools than ever before, while the print media devote more space to recipes and food news.

The growing trend in *reading* about food can be explained in another way, as a kind of fascination with a forbidden subject—that is, dieters often take an engrossing interest in food. Rationing in England had a similar effect, according to Elizabeth David, who has been that country's most influential writer on food in the postwar era. In her *French Country Cooking* (1951), David writes: "Rationing, the disappearance of servants, and the bad and expensive meals served in restaurants, have led Englishwomen to take a far greater interest in food than was formerly considered polite." A similar upswing in cookbook sales was noted during the 1871 siege of Paris, which created drastic food shortages.

Since World War II David has written about French, Italian, Mediterranean and British food. Some of her best-known titles are *Mediterranean Food* (1950), *Italian Food* (1954), *Summer Cooking* (1955), *Spices, Salt and Arummer Cooking* English Kitchen (1970) and *Bread and Yeast Cookery*

BEST-SELLING COOKBOOKS

Better Homes and Gardens Cook Book (1930)	18,684,976
Betty Crocker's Cookbook (1950)	13,000,000
The Joy of Cooking, by Irma S. Rombauer and Marion Rombauer Becker (1931)	8,992,700
The Good Housekeeping Cookbook, ed. by Zoe Coulson (1942)	5,250,000
The Pocket Cook Book, by Elizabeth Woody (1942)	4,900,000
The Boston Cooking-School Cook Book, by Fannie Farmer (1896)	4,100,000
Better Homes and Gardens Meat Cook Book (1959)	3,609,105
The American Woman's Cook Book, ed. by Ruth Berolzheimer (1939)	3,549,276
The I Hate to Cook Book, by Peg Bracken (1960)	2,929,782
Better Homes and Gardens Casserole Cook Book (1961)	2,613,948
The Weight Watchers Program Cookbook, by Jean Nidetch (1973)	2,575,000
Better Homes and Gardens Barbecue Book (1956)	2,439,001
Betty Crocker's Good and Easy Cookbook (1954)	2,400,000
Better Homes and Gardens Salad Book (1958)	2,341,060
Let's Cook it Right, by Adelle Davis (1947)	2,151,439
Better Homes and Gardens Fondue and Tabletop Cooking (1970)	2,022,529

Alice Payne Hackett and James Henry Burke, *80 Years of Best Sellers: 1895-1975* (New York: Bowker, 1977), pp. 47-49.

Update

Cookbooks That Have Sold at Least 100,000 Copies Since 1975

Better Homes and Garden Crepes Cookbook (1976)

Better Homes and Gardens Crockery Cookbook (1976)

Better Homes and Gardens Microwave Cookbook (1976)

Better Homes and Gardens All-Time Favorite Salad Recipes (1978)

Better Homes and Gardens Meals for One or Two (1978)

Pure and Simple, by Marian Burros (1978)

Weight Watchers New Program Cookbook, by Jean Nidetch (1978)

The Fannie Farmer Cookbook, ed. by Marion Cunningham (1979)

Fix It Fast Cookbook (1979)

Food Processor Cookbook (1979)

Betty Crocker's International Cookbook (1980)

Better Homes and Gardens New Cookbook (1981)

Weight Watchers 365-Day Menu Cookbook (1981)

Compiled from *Publishers Weekly.*

in the English Kitchen (1976). She is treasured for a fine writing style as well as expertise in the kitchen. Her popularity in England has never been matched in America, perhaps because of her very Englishness—she does not give recipes in the concise, detailed style Americans are used to, and she employs imperial measures exclusively. Yet, according to James Beard,

> She is to me probably the greatest food writer we have, a purist and perfectionist, intolerant of mediocrity and totally honest, yet not above breaking with tradition to get at what she feels is the essential nature of a dish. (From his introduction to *Elizabeth David Classics* [New York: Knopf, 1980], p. vi.)

America's discovery of the outside world gastronomically has been reciprocal. Ordinary people worldwide have welcomed such manifestations of American gastronomy (if such it be) as hot dogs, corn flakes, and hamburgers, either as pale imitations (Blimpie Base sandwich shops in England) or as the real thing (McDonald's golden arches in Tokyo).

For the future, commentators half seriously expect to see a world divided between the few *cognoscenti* and the many victims of mass marketing. Middle- and upper-class epicures would shuttle among the gourmet store, the spice parlor and the trusted market, while ordinary people would live (blissfully perhaps) under the sway of fast-food manipulators and food packagers.

Some see the new trend in American "cuisine" as a significant reexamination of our culinary roots, while others take a darker view, noting that restaurants are beginning to characterize themselves as "classic American" and "*nouvelle* American." "Nouvelling" *American* food is just too trendy for James Beard, who in January 1984 told *The Wall Street Journal:*

> There has been so much delving into nouvelle American cuisine—a term I loathe, by the way—that it's become almost a contest as to who can do the most imaginative thing. It often has tragic consequences. (*The Wall Street Journal*, Vol. CX, No. 6 [Jan. 10, 1984] p. 14.)

CHAPTER TWO

Classic
Books
by
Great
Chefs

The chef's image is one of unusual contrasts. On the one hand, he exudes authority. In fact, David Ogilvy, writing in *Confessions of an Advertising Man*, says the chefs he trained under as a youth in Swiss hotels exercised more power than any business executive he met during his advertising career. They demanded and got instant and unquestioning obedience from their staffs, due partly to their special training and personal authority, and partly to the state of emergency that prevailed in the kitchen at mealtimes.

At the same time, chefs are figures of fun. They are popularly depicted as foreign, flamboyant, overweight, excitable, voluable, by turns charming and threatening, ulcer-ridden, alcoholic and, if provoked, murderous. Doubtless the ridicule reflects our fear of authority, as was the case with that other stock tyrant of yore, the German professor, who was lampooned unmercifully in vaudeville and is still occasionally to be seen in comic turns on television.

Both the tyrant and the showman are to be found among chefs who wrote classic books. Carême was arrogant and bitingly scornful of rival and patron alike; Charles Ranhofer became a gastronomic dictator over New York's social elite; Escoffier was a genius of austere habits who wielded crushing authority; and Soyer played the French chef with outrageous gestures and motley garb. Luckily, neither extreme did their cooking, or writing, any harm.

FORME OF CURY

Forme of cury is an old English expression for the art of cooking. As noted in Chapter One, it is also the title of the first known cookbook written in the English language—it first appeared in manuscript form at about the beginning of the 15th century. The author, or compiler, of the manuscript is reputed to have been the master cook of King Richard II, but his name is not known. The *Forme of Cury*'s introduction notes that King Richard is "the best and royallest viander of all Christian Kings," meaning in our terms that he was an advanced gourmet and spent lavishly on feasting. Accordingly he employed more than 300 cooks, so perhaps this first cookbook was a cooperative effort.

Perhaps only a king would need a cookbook, given the low rate of literacy in that era and the primitive cooking arrangements of most households. King Richard's cooks faced an extraordinary task even in royal terms, that of feeding as many as 10,000 of the king's retainers and guests on a daily basis. As a way of spending public money, it seems less

TO THE KING'S TASTE Richard II's book of feasts and recipes *adapted for modern cooking by* LORNA J. SASS

The Metropolitan Museum of Art

wasteful than the foreign wars that preoccupied earlier kings.

The *Forme of Cury* contains 196 recipes, many of the ordinary sort but others grand and exotic, requiring the services of artist-chefs who specialized in pastry architecture and *sotelties,* sweet dishes made of jelly or marzipan, which would be molded or sculpted into a splendid image of a lion, eagle or crown, or even as the depiction of an honored guest. These cooks had much need of variety, and the manuscript seems to bring together all manner of dishes served during the 350 years since the Norman conquest. The nomenclature is mostly Norman French, with a sprinkling of Saxon names.

Forme of Cury was not printed as a book until 1780, when Dr. Samuel Pegge, a noted antiquarian, presented it with his comments, an index, a glossary and an appendix consisting of a manuscript of the Rolls of Provision of Henry VIII. The most recent edition appeared in 1975, edited and modernized by Lorna J. Sass and entitled *To the King's Taste: Richard II's Book of Feasts and Recipes* (New York: Metropolitan Museum of Art, 1975). This is a handsome little volume, embellished by medieval woodcuts, with a selection of recipes adapted for modern cooks and an introduction that illuminates 15th-century attitudes toward food and practices in the kitchen.

One thing that might strike the reader as quite modern is the author's assurance that *Forme of Cury* was compiled with "the Assent and avyssement of Maisters of phisik and philosophie who dwelt in Richard's court." Thus it lays claim to being scientific and healthful. Perhaps the author had in mind the fate of King Henry I (1068–1135), who is said to have hastened his own demise by indulging a gluttonous appetite for lamprey flesh even after his physicians had warned him it was "feble," that is, indigestible "mete."

A list of provisions for a feast given September 23, 1387 by King Richard and the Duke of Lancaster gives a good idea of the sort of meat and fowl considered fit for the royal table. It includes 14 salted and two fresh oxen, 120 live sheep and 120 sheep carcasses, 12 boars, 14 calves, 140 pigs, three tons of salt venison, three fresh does, 50 swans, 210 geese, 50 larded capons, 60 dozen hens, 400 large rabbits, four pheasants, five herons and bitterns, six kids, 12 dozen roasting pullets, 100 dozen pigeons, 12 dozen partridges, 12 dozen curlews, 12 cranes and assorted wild fowl. Practically no meat or fowl emerged onto the table in recognizable form. It was "hewed in gobbets," pounded in a mortar, and if necessary to achieve the desired smoothness, put through a sieve. Exceptions were swans and peacocks, which were often skinned, stuffed, roasted, slipped back

RABBITS IN SYRUP

The cony, a variety of mature rabbit, is not mentioned in English literature before the Norman period and certainly was not native to England. But by the late Middle Ages it was a popular meat, and there are many recipes for cooking it. *Conying* was served at Henry IV's coronation feast.

This dish, with its sweet, highly spiced syrup, might be served over rice.

2½-pound rabbit (or chicken), cut into pieces

⅓ cup flour seasoned with salt and pepper

3 tablespoons oil

3 cups Muscatel, Vernaccia, or any sweet, heavy wine

4 tablespoons cider vinegar

¼ cup raisins

½ cup currants

¼ teaspoon cinnamon

2 teaspoons freshly minced ginger

20 cubebs, finely ground

10 cloves, finely ground (scant ¼ teaspoon)

---

1. Dredge rabbit in seasoned flour and brown in oil in a heavy skillet.
2. In the top of a double boiler, combine remaining ingredients. Heat and stir until blended. Check seasoning.
3. Pour syrup over the rabbit, stirring to combine the dregs. Cover and cook over a gentle flame for about 40 minutes, or until rabbit is tender.
SERVES 4

Lorna J. Sass, *To the King's Taste* (New York: Metropolitan Museum of Art, 1975), p. 53.

MENU FOR A MEDIEVAL FEAST

THE FIRST COURSE

Venison with frumenty (sliced venison in a sauce of boiled, hulled wheat)

A potage called Viaundbruse (a broth made of choice meats)

Hedes of Bores

Grete Flessh (roasted haunches of meat)

Swannes rosted

Pigges rosted

Crustade Lumbard in paste (custard with dried fruit, parsley, and bone marrow baked in a crust)

And a Soltelte

THE SECOND COURSE

A potage called Gele (jellied soup)

A potage de Blandesore (capon or hen cooked in a broth of almond milk, spiced with ginger, mace, and cubebs, and thickened with rice flour)

Pigges rosted

Cranes rosted

Fesauntes rosted

Herons rosted

Chekons endored

Breme (bream)

Tartes

Broke braune (carved flesh)

Conyngges rosted (roasted rabbits)

And a Sotelte

THE THIRD COURSE

Potage. Bruete of Almonds (almond soup)

Stwde Lumbarde (a stew prepared in the style of Lombardy)

Venyson rosted

Chekenes rosted

Rabettes rosted

Quailes rosted

Larkes rosted

Payne puff (egg yolks, bone marrow, dates, raisins, and ginger baked in a pie crust)

A dissh of gely

Longe Frutours (curds, eggs, and flour fried and cut into small pieces with sugar sprinkled on top just before serving)

And a Sotelte.

Lorna J. Sass, *To the King's Taste* (New York: Metropolitan Museum of Art, 1975), pp. 31-32.

into their skin and, in the case of peacocks, triumphantly served with gilded comb and spread tail feathers.

Medical opinion declared raw fruit difficult to digest, although it was occasionally served at the end of a meal with sweetened spices, nuts or hard cheese, which were considered aids to digestion. Usually fruits were cooked in sugary syrups, fermented into ciders or made into pies. Those most frequently mentioned in *Forme of Cury* are Warden pears, bullace and damson plums, medlars, quinces, apples, grapes, cherries, mulberries, strawberries, pomegranates, peaches and, imported from the Levant, oranges and lemons.

Hot spices were considered an essential luxury, most probably because of the medieval faith in their digestive qualities, but also because they masked unpleasant odors and tastes due to food spoilage. Pepper was the most highly prized, followed by ginger and a related root called galingale, then cubeb, a berry whose taste suggests allspice and peppercorn, and clove, cinnamon, cardamom, cumin and coriander. It is the assertive presence of all these spices that makes many recipes in the in original form uninviting to the modern palate.

Here is a sample of typical 14th-century dishes. *Mortrewes* contained the meat or poultry that had been mortared, then mixed with such things as bread crumbs, egg yolks and *poudre fort* (a spice mixture), and boiled with ginger, saffron, salt and honey until it was stiff. *Blank-manger* consisted of shredded or mortared chicken flesh boiled with rice and the milk of almonds until thick. It was sweetened with honey and sugar, and sometimes seasoned with salt. *Frumenty*, the standard accompaniment of venison, was a thick pudding made of whole wheat, almond milk and often egg yolks, and colored with saffron. *Mawmony* was a porridge made of ground capon flesh boiled with wine, sugar, oil, spices, ginger, cinnamon and galingale. *Bucknade* mixed meat "gobbets" with mortared almonds, raisins, sugar, cinnamon, cloves, ginger, onions, salt and herbs. The result was thickened with rice flour and colored with saffron.

LE CUISINIER FRANÇOIS

It would be hard to underestimate the importance of *Le Cuisinier François* in the development of French cooking, which is to say Western cooking in its highest form. The book records the pivotal change in court cooking that took place under the influence of Renaissance Italians who flooded aristocratic purlieus after the royal marriages of Catherine and Marie de Medici. Until *Le Cuisinier François* came along in 1651, cooks had only one printed book in French to refer to, *Le Viandier de Guillaume Tirel dit Taillevent*, which had appeared originally 300 years earlier in manuscript form. Like *Forme of Cury*, *Le Viandier* was medieval in spirit. True, Bartolomeo Scappi's *Opera*, which featured Renaissance Italian cooking, had been printed in 1570. But it had not been translated into French and was, in any case, out of print by 1650. So *Le Cuisinier François* filled a void, and it was immediately recognized as a classic. Amid acclaim and denunciation, it went through 30 editions during the next 75 years.

Not much is known about the author. François Pierre de la Varenne was born in 1615 and died in 1678. At the time the book was published, he was a master cook for the Marquis d'Uxelles. Apparently the name La Varenne was a pseudonym, and an oft-told anecdote about La Varenne is now believed to relate the adventures of an earlier cook. The story goes that La Varenne started his career as a scullion in the kitchen of the Duchess of Bar, sister of Henry IV (1553–1610), and, proving useful to the king as a bearer of love notes to various courtesans, was swiftly promoted. In later years the duchess told him, "You earned more by acting as a porter for my brother's *poulets* [double meaning—"chicken" or "love letter"] than you did for turning mine on a spit."

Le Cuisinier François, while laying the groundwork for *haute cuisine*, retained many elements of medieval cooking. The recipes were divided into two sections—*grasses* and *maigres* (meat days and fast days). Familiar and favorite recipes were retained, such as venison pie, blancmange and larded roast loin of veal. On the other hand, gone were the huge displays of meat and fowl overloaded with spices that had characterized the exaggerated medieval banquets.

A manual for the working cook or *maître d'*, *Le Cuisiner* begins with a recipe for bouillon, just as Escoffier's *Guide Culinaire* would 250 years later. Escoffier used his basic stocks *(fonds de cuisine)* as elements in a modular system that becomes increasingly more elaborate as one progresses in

POTAGE DE PROFITEOLLES

It is made thus: you take four or six rolls, you take out all the crumb from them through a little opening made in the top. You take off the lid and you dry it out with the rolls; you cook them in lard or bacon fat, and then you put your rolls in your *potage* to garnish it, and fill them with cockscombs, sweetbreads, forcemeat balls, truffles, and mushrooms. Add broth just until the rolls are soaked; before serving pour the *jus* and what you have over them, then serve.

François Pierre de la Varenne, *Le Cuisinier François*, p. 8.

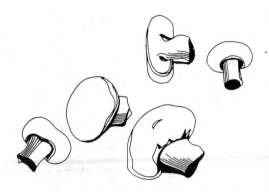

CHAMPIGNONS À L'OLIVIER

[It is said that the following recipe is for the mushroom dish that has come to be known as *duxelles*. La Varenne worked for the Marquis d'Uxelles, but nowhere does he name the dish for his patron.]

Clean them [the mushrooms] well, cut them in quarters, and wash them in several changes of water to take off the earth. Put them between two dishes with an onion and some salt, then on the chafing dish so they will give off their liquid. When they have been pressed between two plates, take some good fresh butter, with some parsley and scallions, and fricassée them; after that put them to simmer and when they are well cooked you may add some cream or some blancmange, and serve.

François Pierre de la Varenne, *Le Cuisinier François*, p. 121.

his book. Here, in La Varenne, we see the beginning of that modular system, although he used only two basic stocks, one for meat days and the other for fast (fish) days. Other elements of the system were liaisons, stuffings *(farcés)* and herb and spice mixtures. Among his liaisons was roux, made with pork fat rather than butter, but appearing here in print for the first time. Many of these elements could be prepared ahead of time and form part of the cook's basic equipment for coping with what food might be on a particular day. Once he'd learned this system, an illiterate cook could get by without refering to recipes. Seventy-five years later the system had been elaborated into full-blown *haute cuisine*.

The book was meant for professionals, so La Varenne skimps on details, giving few quantities and leaving much to the judgment of the cook. Indeed, his instructions are less detailed than Scappi's. Nevertheless, many innovations are recorded here for the first time. La Varenne noted the importance of reducing cooking juices to intensify the flavor. He also blended roux with bouillon to make velouté sauce. Breaking with medieval tradition, he emphasized vegetables as separate dishes, especially such novelties as asparagus, cauliflower, cucumbers, artichokes and the green pea, which was a recent import from Italy. He flavored stocks and sauces with bouquet garni. He featured many new recipes for variety meats, in the Italian style, and introduced many dishes that have a modern look to them, such as omelets, beignets, pumpkin pie and such standards as *boeuf à la mode* and *oeufs à la neige*.

If one wished, one could re-create from *Le Cuisinier Fran-çois* some of the older tastes and textures, such as spiced sweet and sour combinations. But old standbys, such as blancmange, were given a modern twist: Its base of sweetened meat broth, made from veal, chicken and milk, flavored with lemon rind and almonds, survived, but as a smoothly textured jelly. La Varenne also pioneered the use of egg whites to clarify a jelly.

Important though it was, *Le Cuisinier François* was not the peak of *haute cuisine*. Cooking became increasingly refined and sophisticated, and as the 18th century dawned, fine cooking came into fashion among court nobles. However, La Varenne's masterpiece bumped down a notch or two on the social scale every 10 years, exercising an ever broadening field of influence.

L'ART DE LA CUISINE FRANÇAISE AU 19ÈME SIÈCLE

L'Art de la Cuisine was the masterwork of Marie-Antonin Carême, who died the year it was published, 1833. In final form it consisted of five volumes. Carême planned the book and completed the first three volumes before his death. The final two volumes were completed by M. Plumeret, a friend of Carême's and head cook at the Russian Embassy. An exhaustive survey of *haute cuisine*, which Carême himself had done much to perfect, *L'Art de la Cuisine* stood as holy writ for the professional chef until the appearance in 1902 of Escoffier's *Le Guide Culinaire*. Not only does *L'Art de la Cuisine* cover *haute cuisine* in its entirety, but it does so with force and wit. The supreme self-confidence that characterized Carême as *chef de cuisine* spilled over into his writing. It led him to denounce rivals as imposters but kept his books from being dull.

Carême was the *premier chef* during the period of the Bourbon Restoration, from about 1815 until his death. His only rival for the title was Antoine Beauvilliers, a chef and restaurateur, who had had great success with his book *L'Art du Cuisinier* (1814), and when Beauvilliers died in 1820, Carême was left without peers. The details of Carême's career are given in Chapter One. Suffice it to say here that he rose from very humble circumstances, apprenticing himself to a pastry cook at age 14. Legend has it that talented cooks figured among his ancestors and that the family name, Carême (which means Lent), was acquired by a cook who created an excellent Lenten soup for Pope Leo X.

Lady Sydney Morgan, an Irish novelist, left this description of a dinner prepared in the summer of 1828 by Carême at the home of the Baron de Rothschild: "To do justice to the science and research of this dinner would require a knowledge of the art equal to that which produced it." As to its character, she wrote: "It was in season, it was up to its time, it was in the spirit of the age, there was no *perruque* in its composition, no trace of the wisdom of our ancestors in a single dish; no high-spiced sauces, no tincture of catsup and walnut pickle." On the cooking, she commented, "Every meat presented in its own natural aroma; every vegetable is own shade of verdure. The *mayonase* was fried in ice (like Ninon's description of Sevigné's heart) and the tempered chill of the *plombière* (a fruit ice of nectarines), which held the place of the eternal fondu and soufflets of our English tables, anticipated the stronger shock which, with the hue

CARÊME'S APHORISMS ON THE COOK'S LIFE

The Charcoal kills us, but what does it matter? The shorter our lives, the greater our glory.

SERVICE
The man who knows how to appreciate a good servant is always well served, his house is a happy one.

ON ARCHITECTURE
Of the five fine arts, the fifth is architecture, whose main branch is confectionary.

ROUTINE COOKS
The routine cook is without courage, his life passes away in mediocrity.

THE COOK'S POSITION
The cook is always envied his position by the servants of the household who do not understand it at all.

GLUTTON VS. GOURMAND
The man who calls himself a gourmand but who eats gluttonously is a glutton and not a gourmand.

Edward Page and P. W. Kingsford, *The Master Chefs: A History of Haute Cuisine* (New York: St. Martin's Press, 1971).

and odour of fresh gathered nectarines, satisifed every sense, and dissipated every coarser flavor." She likened Carême to Titian hired "at a salary well beyond what any sovereign in Europe might be able to pay, even though assisted by M. Rothschild; without whose aid so many sovereigns would scarcely have been able to keep cooks at all." She asked to meet Carême and found him "a well bred gentleman . . . and when we had mutually complimented each other on our respective works, he bowed himself out, and got into his carriage, which was waiting to take him to Paris."

A culinary issue of the day was *service à la Française* vs. *service à la Russe*. French service, which was traditional for high-style dinners, involved putting most of the food on the table at the same time, including hot and cold dishes, roasts, starches, vegetables and soups. The rich spectacle was meant to amaze and delight the guests as they entered the dining room. The drawbacks were serious: The food often was cold by the time guests were seated, and it was not customary to pass dishes around, so where one sat determined which dishes one could partake of.

Russian-style service, on the other hand, began with a table bare except for flowers and assorted sweetmeats. Meat was cut from roasts at a sideboard, and all other dishes were rushed in hot from the kitchen. Guests got hot food and could sample all dishes. This was the style preferred by the many Russian noblemen who sojourned in Paris. Carême first witnessed it during a visit to St. Petersburg and liked it.

It met stiff resistance, though, in France and England. The French loved the spectacle and claimed they couldn't pace themselves without knowing what was to follow. The English rejected it as an instance of Russian barbarism. Carême finally came out against it, preferring the dazzling show of *service à la Française*. He also suspected Russian service was a way of cutting costs, a sure way of arousing his hostility. But in this one area he did not make a precedent. During the Second Empire, *service à la Russe* triumphed at the best tables. Indeed, it was the Russian style of service that enabled Escoffier to make many of the refinements he later codified in *Le Guide Culinaire*.

Despite Carême's statement in *L'Art de la Cuisine*, "My book is not written solely for the great ones; on the contrary, I want it to be of service to all," it was evident that French cooking had split into two traditions: *haute cuisine* and *bourgeoise cuisine*. Beauvilliers's book was the established authority on the latter, while Carême went on to say, "It is an error for those of lesser station to try to pattern their tables after the rich . . . better to serve a simple meal, well prepared." A good sentiment, but he managed to make the simplest preparation an onerous chore. That, and his inalterable aversion to leftovers, put him in the camp of *les grands*.

THE GASTRONOMIC REGENERATOR

The French issue of the two cuisines—*haute* and *bourgeoise*—was brought to the attention of the English public in 1846 by *The Gastronomic Regenerator*. Though the book was written in English, the author was French. His name was Alexis Soyer, and he was destined to become the public symbol of what Englishmen thought a French chef should be. *The Gastronomic Regenerator* was divided into two sections, one entitled "Kitchen of the Wealthy" and the other "Kitchen at Home." The latter was the smaller of the two, as perhaps befitted the modest needs of the middle-class family, but it does contain plenty of sound, simple and inexpensive recipes clearly set out with none of the distractions, such as puns and purple patches, that characterized Soyer's later style. The "Kitchen of the Wealthy" section is far more expansive and, armed with the instructions and recipes it contains, a cook could cater to the most refined and expensive tastes. This is as it should be, because since 1836 M. Soyer had been *chef de cuisine* at the exclusive Reform Club in London, where he had built a reputation as a superlative chef in the grand manner. Yet it also displayed one of his enduring and most attractive traits, a concern for the gastronomic well-being of the less fortunate social classes.

Details of M. Soyer's career were given in Chapter One, but it should be noted here that he was born in 1809 at Meaux-en-Brie, a small town on the Marne, some 25 miles north of Paris. Blessed with talent, intelligence and an amiable disposition, he rose quickly in the cooking profession, becoming a head cook at age 17. He left for England in 1831, both to escape the political upheavals in France and to cash in on the fad among English lords and ladies of hiring French chefs. He had been preceded by grander names—for example, Marie-Antonin Carême in 1816. Soyer worked for a series of aristocrats, then settled at the Reform Club, where he remained until 1850. Famous for his flamboyant dress and personality, he was lampooned in William M. Thackeray's *The History of Pendennis* (1849) as M. Mirobolant, "in his usual favorite costume, namely, his light green frock, his crimson velvet waistcoat, with blue glass buttons, his pantalon Écossais, of a very large and decided check pattern, his orange satin neckcloth, and his jean-boots, with tips of shiny leather—these, with gold embroidered cap, and a richly gilt cane . . . formed his usual holiday costume." Soyer died in 1858 after helping to reform the cooking arrangements for the British forces in the Crimea.

The Gastronomic Regenerator was well received by the critics, but more than one wondered what the title meant—

Portrait of Alexis Soyer, by his wife

POMMES DE TERRE À LA MAÎTRE D'HÔTEL

There is no potato to equal the French red kidney potato, which will keep as it is cut, while a round mealy potato would crumble to pieces.

Being rather difficult to procure, obtain some waxy kidney potatoes, which boil and stand by to get cold. Peel and cut them into slices, which put in a stewpan, with a little pepper, salt, and about half a pint of stock. Set them upon a fire, and let them boil two or three minutes; then add three quarters of a pound of fresh butter. Keep shaking the stewpan around over the fire until the butter is melted, it will thus form its own sauce. Finish with a tablespoon of chopped parsley and the juice of a lemon.

Turn out upon your dish and serve.

Alexis Soyer, *The Gastronomic Regenerator.*

apparently, nothing less than the regeneration of British gastronomy. Soyer declares in the introduction that to be worthy of the title he "closely studied to introduce the greatest novelty in every department." The book went through five printings in two years and remained in print until 1870. It contained 2,000 recipes, and although Soyer makes a bow toward *bourgeoise cuisine,* there is no doubt where his real sympathies lie, with the emphases on the finest ingredients, time-consuming preparations of *fonds de cuisine,* and the problems of large establishments. His culinary asides are addressed to "the real gourmet" and "the real epicure." The chapters deal will all branches of cookery: sauces, soups, fish, *hors d'oeuvres,* removes for the first course, flancs, entrées, savories, vegetables, entremets, removes for the second course, soufflés and preserves. One novelty for cookbooks of that period was a section on kitchens, which included plans for kitchens appropriate to various income levels and disquisitions on vaious labor-saving devices, plus illustrated lists of utensils.

As for the reviews, Helen Morris, Soyer's biographer, writes:

> All seemed to agree with the reviewer who thought Soyer "a wit and a wag of the first water," and so most of the reviews were only half serious. But even the writer in *Blackwood's,* after pages of laughing with—and at—the author, becomes serious for long enough to insist that the work is "strictly and most intelligibly practical," and "as full of matter as an egg is full of meat." (Helen Morris, *Portrait of a Chef* [New York: The Macmillan Company; Cambridge, Eng.: At the University Press, 1938].)

It is said that *The Gastronomic Regenerator* had a profound effect on the cooking and eating habits of several generations of Britons, although it is hard to see how many housewives could afford to get the full benefit from a recipe for a "simple foundation sauce" that required three days of constant boiling, skimming and straining to achieve the desired clarity. Perhaps the book's greatest contribution was to bring Soyer to public attention and create a favorable climate of opinion for his later works—*The Modern Housewife* (1846) and *Soyer's Shilling Cookery* (1854)—which influenced the middle and working classes directly.

YOUNG CARROTS IN THEIR GLAZE

Scrape forty young carrots, which put into a stewpan with a teaspoon of sugar, four young onions, a bunch of parsley, and a bay-leaf.

Just cover them with a good white stock and stew till the carrots are tender. Carefully take them out and dress in the form of a dome by sticking them into a bed of well-mashed potatoes. Strain the stock they were stewed in through a napkin into a stewpan; add to it half a pint of Brown Sauce, and reduce it till it adheres to the back of a spoon.

Add two pats of butter, sauce all over and serve.

Alexis Soyer, *The Gastronomic Regenerator.*

THE EPICUREAN

There's a side to American gastronomy that was ignored by popular and earnest cookbook writers of the 19th century, such as Catherine Beecher, Mrs. D.A. Lincoln and Fannie Farmer. It might be called the dionysian side. It flowered in the great restaurants whose fortunes rose with those of East Coast "society" in the post-Civil War era. The number of millionaires in America grew from about 20 in 1830 to more than 40,000 in 1916. Ostentatious eating was one form in which this new wealth chose to display itself, especially in fine restaurants or at affairs catered by those restaurants. New York became a center of fine dining second only to Paris. At the foundation of its reputation was a restaurant called Delmonico's, which opened its doors in the 1840s and outshone all rivals until well into the 20th century. The chef at Delmonico's in its heyday was Charles Ranhofer, whose eminence was such toward the end of his career that he was termed a "culinary dictator."

In 1893, Ranhofer published a huge cookbook entitled *The Epicurean*, which is now available in facsimile reprint (New York: Dover, 1971). Ranhofer's book runs to 1,200 pages and contains more than 3,500 recipes. Unlike Escoffier's cookbook, which would appear within 10 years, *The Epicurean* condescended to small matters, giving detailed instructions of shopping, elementary cooking methods and techniques, profuse illustrations of utensils, exhaustive restaurant bills of fare and perhaps most fascinating, menus from historic banquets.

Despite the Germanic surname, Ranhofer was French, born in Alsace. He was a precocious lad who, by the time he came to Delmonico's in 1861 at the age of 20, had already served an apprenticeship in one of the princely houses of Europe, moved to the United States to cook at the Russian Consulate and worked as chef for the Maison Dorée, a competitor of Delmonico's. He presided over the kitchens at Delmonico's for 34 years, growing very imperious as time wore on, to the point where he would flatly refuse to prepare requested dishes if the season wasn't right for them to "cook well." Wealthy and powerful clients meekly accepted his edicts.

During its lifetime, Delmonico's had eight different locations in New York City, four of which were operated simultaneously. The most imposing branches were at Fifth Avenue and 14th Street and at Broadway and Pine. An influential customer was Ward McAlister, a social arbiter who had dreamed up the designation "The Four Hundred" to indicate the *crème de la crème* of society, this being the number

that fit comfortably into Mrs. William Astor's ballroom. In the late 1860s McAlister played host to a series of dinner dances, called cotillions, at Delmonico's. He was so pleased with the results that he began to recommend Delmonico's to his wealthy friends with the airy advice, "Tell Ranhofer the number of your guests and nothing more, and you will have perfection."

A decade or so later, Diamond Jim Brady began to frequent Delmonico's, heralding an era when opulent dining would give way to grotesque excesses. James Buchanan Brady (1856–1917) sold railroad equipment for a living, but his true vocation was eating. He turned a talent for splashy extravagance into a sales tool, and he pioneered expense-account entertaining with spectacular results. Brady was a standout in an era of big spenders. He acquired his nickname, "Diamond Jim," with a collection of diamonds valued at more than $2 million, a figure to be multiplied by 20 to approximate their value in 1984 dollars.

Brady's style made him the darling of the tabloids and a treasured customer at fancy restaurants such as Delmonico's, the acknowledged pinnacle of fashionable dining. Often, however, Brady favored Rector's, an up-and-coming, less formal rival. George Rector, son of the founder, Charles, reckoned that "Jim Brady is the best 25 customers we have."

According to contemporary accounts, Brady's appetite defied belief. At breakfast he usually had hominy, eggs, corn bread, muffins, flapjacks, chops, fried potatoes and beefsteak, all washed down with a gallon of orange juice (he never drank anything stronger).

He followed this at 11:30 a.m. with a snack of two or three dozen clams and oysters. An hour later he lunched on two or three deviled crabs, a couple of boiled lobsters, more oysters and clams, a roast of beef, salad and several kinds of pie. This was accompanied by orange juice or lemon soda.

He staved off hunger pangs at teatime with a huge platter of mixed seafood and more of his usual libations. But the foregoing was a mere prelude to the big meal of the day.

According to Charles Rector, a typical dinner for Brady began with two or three dozen Lynnhaven oysters (each six inches long and chosen especially for Brady by Maryland dealers), six crabs (claws and all), green turtle soup (two bowls), half a dozen lobsters, two whole canvasback ducks, two portions of terrapin, a sirloin steak, vegetables and dessert, usually a platter of pastries and two pounds of chocolate.

At the peak of his fame, Brady frequently squired Lillian Russell to dinner. She was the reigning American beauty and the most popular music hall performer of the 1880–1910 era. In point of gastronomy, it was a match made in heaven, because, if she wanted to, Lillian Russell could rival Brady bite for bite. She weighed 200 pounds, but her bounteous hourglass figure captivated American men for 35 years. Of the example she set, A.J. Liebling wrote: "In building up to a similar opulence, I suppose, a younger woman developed eating habits that were hard to curb after she reached the target figure. . . . A popular dessert named for the star, the Lillian Russell, was a half-cantaloupe holding about a pint and ¾ of ice cream. If an actress had a dish named after her now, the recipe would be four phenobarbital tablets and a jigger of Metrecal." (A.J. Liebling, *Between Meals* [New York: Simon & Schuster, 1962], pp. 48–49.)

Brady was felled by stomach trouble at age 56 and died five years later. An autopsy showed his stomach to be six times normal size.

One reason Brady favored Rector's was that prices were lower there. Yet Ranhofer maintained that Delmonico's was not outrageously expensive, and to back it up produced a sample menu for three of first-rate Delmonico's dishes that cost a total of $12 with wine. He also proclaimed that the most expensive dishes were not always the most palatable. Indeed, Delmonico's pioneered the balanced diet for the elegant diner, emphasizing vegetable dishes and salads, some of whose ingredients were so rare in mid-19th century New York that they had to be grown on a restaurant-owned garden plot in Brooklyn.

Still, Ranhofer's book *is* entitled *The Epicurean*, and both he and Delmonico's will best be remembered for the sort of affair typified by the Swan Banquet of 1873. Hosted by Edward Luckmeyer, an importer and shipowner who had received a windfall tax refund of $10,000, the feast was attended by 73 guests, who sat at a "table 18 feet wide and as long as the hall." The centerpiece was an oval pond graced by swans rented from Prospect Park. Unfortunately, it was mating season, and in midbanquet the male swans staged a riot of sexual dueling. The evening was a resounding success anyway—or perhaps the swans contributed to the success by relieving the torpor that such a lavish eight-course meal normally will produce. See the menu in the accompanying illustration.

ESCOFFIER COOK BOOK

This is the classic of classics for modern French cuisine. Its author, Auguste Escoffier, was a chef who flourished between 1870 and 1914, spending much of his distinguished career in England, in association with illustrious hotelier Cesar Ritz. Escoffier compiled the approximately 5,000 rec-

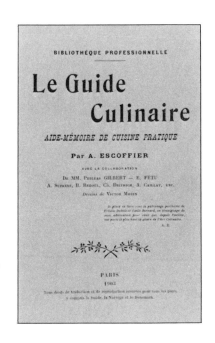

ipes in the book in collaboration with other chefs, most notably Philias Gilbert and Émile Fétu, and it first appeared in French in 1902, under tht title *Le Guide Culinaire,* and in English in 1907, under the title *A Guide to Modern Cookery.* A current American translation in print is *Escoffier Cook Book* (New York: Crown, 1941).

Escoffier, the son of a blacksmith, was born in 1846 in the Alpes-Maritimes Department of France. At 13 he began his career as an apprentice in his uncle's restaurant in Nice, and at 19 he went to Paris to work in the fashionable restaurant Le Petit Moulin. After serving in the Franco-Prussian War (as chef at an army headquarters), he returned to Le Petit Moulin as head of kitchen, then held similar posts at several of the best restaurants. His big break came in 1880 when he was appointed chef at Cesar Ritz's Grand Hotel in Monte Carlo, beginning a fruitful association that brought both men to the pinnacle of fame during the next 30 years. Cesar Ritz took over the management of the Savoy Hotel in London in 1889, bringing Escoffier with him. The restaurant quickly became the rage among the upper crust. In 1896 they moved their talents to the Ritz Hotel on the Place Vendôme, Paris, where they met with similar success in smaller quarters. In 1899 Escoffier returned to London to become chef at the new Ritz-Carlton Hotel. By this time the name Ritz was such a byword for snobbish luxury that it had entered the language as an adjective (ritzy) and a verb ("Don't try to ritz me!"). Escoffier had become known as the greatest chef in the world.

He'd earned this title in part because of his fertile imagination in creating new dishes. He complains of the demands made on him, "Novelty! It is the prevailing cry; it is imperiously demanded by everyone. . . . What feats of ingenuity have we not been forced to perform, at times, in order to meet our customers' wishes?. . . Personally, I have ceased counting the nights spent in the attempt to discover new combinations, when, completely broken with the fatigue of a heavy day, my body ought to have been at rest." He met the demands with such original delicacies as *pêches Melba* (named for diva Nellie Melba), *poularde Adelina Patti* (another diva), *consommé favori de Sarah Bernhardt* (the actress) and *salade Tosca.*

When he began assembling his notes in 1898, he saw himself as working very much in the grand tradition, harking back to Carême, and even to Taillevent's *Le Viandier.* Escoffier was a master of French cuisine, adapting it, modernizing it to meet the needs of a changed society. What was society demanding, apart from novelty? *Lightness.* That today they are demanding still more lightness probably would elicit no more than a Gallic shrug from the master; nor would he be

surprised that French chefs are providing it while invoking the spirit of Escoffier. He observed that the venue of *haute cuisine* had shifted from manor house to chic restaurant. The splendor, heaviness and complication of bygone dinners did not fit into the light and frivolous atmosphere of restaurants nor suit the new class of moneyed customers "who only had eyes for one another."

He codified the new rules, setting the policy with this *obiter dictum:* "The number of dishes set before the diners being considerably reduced, and the dishes themselves having been deprived of all the advantages which their sumptuous decorations formerly lent them, they must recover, by means of perfection and delicacy, sufficient in the way of quality to compensate for their diminished bulk and reduced splendor. They must be faultless in regard to quality; they must be savory and light."

The casual reader should be warned that Escoffier's book is not a lighthearted romp through the basics of French cuisine. It is a manual for chefs, for experts who need a reference book to use around the kitchen. Escoffier's style is a model of Cartesian logic and Gallic clarity. He deals with the basics first—*his* idea of basics, that is—foundation sauces and stocks. The first recipe makes ordinary or white consommé. On first reading it does not seem to require a high level of skill, but it would take all day. There are vague references to "moderate fire," "cook for 4 or 5 hours" and "add a little cold water occasionally." Also, the beef shins must be from an animal at least eight years old; three or four years old won't do. As one proceeds through the chapter, the recipes become increasingly shorter, as in No. 16, Poultry Glaze: "Reduce the poultry base indicated in Formula 10, and proceed in exactly the same way as for meat glaze (Formula 15)." Even experienced cooks have found this need to refer back and forth annoying.

These foundation sauces and stocks are the first building blocks. He then works through warm sauces, compound sauces, cold sauces, aspics, court-bouillons and elementary preparations to soups. Chapters 11 through 20 are the complicated pieces, and many incorporate the building blocks from the early chapters. For example, Langue de Beouf Choucroûte says to "braise the tongue as described under No. 247, and glaze it at the last moment. Dish it, and send to the table separately (1) a timbale of Well-braised sauerkraut; (2) a timable of potato purée; (3) a Madeira sauce, combined with the braising-liquor of the tongue, cleared of all grease, and reduced."

This book was the definitive word until the late 1960s. In addition, Escoffier advanced kitchen management by his introduction of the *parti* system. Traditionally, different

SOUPS

I shall not make any lengthy attempts here to refute the arguments of certain autocrats of the dinner-table who, not so many years ago, urged the total abolition of soups. I shall only submit to their notice the following quotation from Grimod de la Reynière, one of our most illustrious gastronomists: "Soup is to a dinner what the porch or gateway is to a building," that is to say, it must not only form the first portion thereof, but it must be so devised as to convey some idea of the whole to which it belongs; or, after the manner of an overture in a light opera, it should divulge what is to be the dominant phrase of the melody throughout.

I am at one with Grimod in this, and believe that soups have come to stay. Of all the items on a menu, soup is that which exacts the most delicate perfection and the strictest attention, for upon the first impression it gives to the diner the success of the latter part of the meal largely depends.

Auguste Escoffier, *Guide to Modern Cookery,* p. 92.

sections of the kitchen produced all their own specialties—sauces, pastry goods—independently of other sections. Escoffier organized the kitchen into five interdependent sections, or *partis*, which produced certain specialties, or performed needed services for the others. They were the pastry cook; the pantryman, who kept supplies and supervised cold dishes; the *entremettier*, who did soups, vegetables and desserts; the roaster, in charge of roasts and broiled or fried dishes; and the saucemaker. The system, with minor changes, endures to this day.

THE PREFERRED MINCEUR SALAD DRESSING

To serve four:

5 tablespoons of fromage blanc
2 tablespoons of wine vinegar
1 tablespoon of soy sauce
1 tablespoon of Dijon mustard
1 teaspoon of minced fresh herbs (chervil, tarragon, parsley, chives)
Salt sparingly to taste
Pepper

Mix all the ingredients together in a bowl with a whisk, or in an electric blender.

Michel Guérard's Cuisine Minceur, Morrow edition, p. 94.

MICHEL GUÉRARD'S CUISINE MINCEUR

Cuisine minceur means "slimness cooking," but of course this is far more than a diet cookbook. Michel Guérard works within the new mode of French cooking *(nouvelle cuisine)* and takes the style to its natural limits. Nevertheless, the result is recognizably *grande cuisine*. How is this miracle achieved?

Not easily. High French cooking is noted for the richness of its sauces, based upon much-reduced stocks and bound with high-calorie butter, flour and cream. It is noted for its use of absolutely fresh and often expensive ingredients. It is noted for its complex, time-consuming procedures and the fanatical attention the chef devotes to the appearance of the final product in all its detail.

Conceptually, Guérard's approach was simple: He retained the virtues of the high style while removing a lot of the calories. He did not come to this new style easily, but at the cost of much personal travail. As he notes in the introduction to *Michel Guérard's Cuisine Minceur*, when he and his wife were courting, she hinted he would be a lot more attractive if he lost a few pounds. After some soul-searching (after all, he was not only a three-star chef but also an enthusiastic eater), he went the broiled-meat-and-grated-carrot route. Soon he was feeling "isolated, quarantined" and overwhelmed by "claustrophobic frustration." Then he did what came naturally and began to create new recipes that would shed the pounds but satisfy not only his aesthetics but also his craving for the "unctuous and voluptuous" sauces.

He called this *cuisine gourmande*. At the time he was the owner of a small bistro named Pot-au-Feu, in the obscure Paris suburb of Asnières; this bistro quickly became a famous magnet for gourmets. After their marriage, he and his wife moved to Eugénie-les-Bains, a town near the Basque coast of France, where they opened a restaurant and spa called Les Près d'Eugénie. Together they perfected his *cuisine minceur,* and together they wrote the book. In the first four years of the restaurant's existence, it was rated two-star by *Michelin* and four-star by the *Guide Gault-Millau.*

In his new approach, Guérard tackled the *grande cuisine* at its cornerstone, the sauces. He kept the traditional *fonds*—veal, chicken and fish—intact, but for the usual liaisons composed of butter, flour and cream, he substituted vegetable purées, mushroom purée or *fromage blanc,* a fresh cheese traditionally made in Luxembourg and very popular in France but having very few calories. The resulting sauces are somewhat thinner but manage to salvage the unctuousness and *volupté* of the old. They also enhance the flavor of food without masking it, which is a prime tenet of *nouvelle cuisine.*

Michel Guérard's Cuisine Minceur (New York: Morrow, 1976; London: Macmillan, 1977) is divided into two principal parts. Part One is a review of the traditional methods of cooking and of preparing stocks, liaisons and sauces. After each is explained, he adds a *cuisine minceur* twist. After "Sautéing," for example, he notes:

> After the food has been sautéed, put it on absorbent paper to rid it of every trace of fat. Degrease the pan completely so that only the juices are left in the bottom.
>
> In deglazing, reduce the wine or brandy until it has almost completely evaporated; this will eliminate the alcohol content and leave only the aroma.
>
> Obviously you will have to find some thickening agent for the *liaison* other than butter and cream! Use only those suggested later on in our *minceur* recipes. . . . (Morrow edition, p. 42)

The recipes, mostly Guérard originals, are contained in Part Two, which makes up three fourths of the book. They are arranged under such topics as soups, sauces, first courses, salads, shellfish and fish, meats, poultry and game, vegetables and desserts. Recipes are clearly laid out, have copious notes and even specify the utensils used, which are identified in an illustrated appendix.

Guérard has a poetic touch, and the recipes make interesting reading, but a sampling of the titles will give you an idea of the difficulties to be encountered: Vineyard Thrush Soup, Truffle Soup, Oysters Baked in Champagne. Without, for example, *grive de vigne,* a thrush that feeds on grapes, one can't achieve exactly the right effect, and, ounce for ounce, truffles are one of the most expensive substances on earth. Many of the preparations are time-consuming. Under desserts, Orange Custard calls for orange peels to be cut "into *julienne* sticks as fine as pine needles, then cut cross-

APPLE AND APRICOT COMPOTE

To serve two:

---

4 small apples (see Note), peeled, quartered, and cored

---

4 fresh apricots, rinsed, halved, and pitted, or 8 canned unsweetened apricot halves

---

Artificial sweetener equivalent to 2 tablespoons of granulated sugar, or to taste

---

UTENSILS

Heavy-bottomed saucepan, with a lid

Electric blender

To serve: Small serving bowl and 2 chilled dessert bowls

Note: The apples called for are *pomme reinettes,* russet apples, which you will not find unless they are grown locally. Use crisp apples with a good, winy flavor. Greenings and Golden Delicious are possible choices. Ed.

In the saucepan cook together, covered, the apples, 4 of the apricot halves, and the artificial sweetener, plus a spoonful of water, for 15 minutes. Meanwhile, cut the remaining 4 apricot halves into ¼-inch dice. Purée the cooked fruit in the electric blender, add the diced apricots, and pour the compote into the serving bowl. Chill before serving.

Michel Guérard's Cuisine Minceur, Morrow edition, p. 270.

wise into tiny dice." A dish such as Stuffed Chicken Drumsticks Steamed over Vapor of Marjoram would take a full day of preparation.

Guérard gets around a major objection—that of the day-long cooking time of his stocks and purées—by suggesting you celebrate a *minceur* week two or three times a year. That way you spend a day getting your stocks and purées together in advance, thus cutting preparation time for each meal drastically.

Most of his recipes treat foods very simply, and the effects depend on flavor and texture contrasts. Guérard's dishes look completely natural when served, yet stunning.

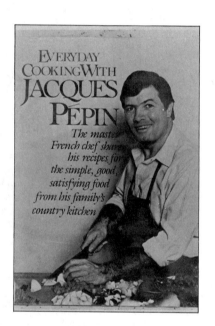

EVERYDAY COOKING WITH JACQUES PÉPIN

Jacques Pépin is a French chef who has become familiar to many Americans through his cooking show on the PBS television network. As an author, he has established himself in two particular areas: techniques and home cooking. Pépin's first book in English appeared in 1975 under the title *A French Chef Cooks at Home*. He followed this in 1976 with *La Technique: The Fundamental Techniques of Cooking—An Illustrated Guide*. His *La Méthode*, which appeared in 1979, was acclaimed best cookbook of the year. Most recently he has written *Everyday Cooking with Jacques Pépin* (New York: Harper & Row, 1982). It was meant to accompany a new television series in which he re-creates a number of the recipes, but the book functions very well as a separate entity.

Jacques Pépin's parents were restaurateurs. He was born in 1935 in Bourg-en-Bresse (near Lyon), France, and he served a traditional apprenticeship beginning at age 13. He rose to the rank of chef at the prestigious Plaza Athénée in Paris. From there he moved into high political circles, becoming personal chef to the president of France, a post he retained through the terms in office of three incumbents, including Charles de Gaulle. Moving to the United States in 1959, Pépin became chef at the renowned Le Pavillon Restaurant in New York City. In his off-hours he obtained two college degrees at Columbia University (in philosophy and French literature). Since the middle 1970s, he has made his living as an author, lecturer and teacher.

In his writing, Pépin shows a talent for convincing the reader that the dishes under discussion can be prepared by the merest novice, provided he or she can read and look at photographs. The trick is accomplished partly through excellent step-by-step photographs and partly through the author's knack of incorporating simple explanations of techniques right into the recipes' notes. If the reader needs more coaching, he or she can refer to an appendix containing tips on techniques.

In *Everyday Cooking,* Pépin has concentrated on ease of preparation and economical ingredients. Efficiency is something of an obsession with Pépin, as he illustrates with this example: "You'll never see a professional chef start to make a simple mushroom omelet by breaking the eggs and then slicing the mushrooms. He'll first put a pat of butter in a skillet, set it on the heat, and by the time the skillet is ready, the one or two mushrooms will have been sliced and the one or two eggs broken. No time is lost sitting around waiting for the butter to melt." Accordingly, each recipe bears timing indications, one for cooking and one for preparation. Rarely does preparation time exceed 20 minutes, or cooking time an hour. These seem quite realistic, provided the reader develops some efficient moves.

A second kind of efficiency is promoted, too, that of avoiding waste. If the reader catches Pépin's spirit, saving food will become second nature. He shows how to put trimmings to good use in making stocks for sauces. Leftovers are transformed into cold salads or casseroles.

Pépin shows his partiality for southern-European cooking in his selection of recipes. Many were plucked from memory—the very dishes his mother and grandmother put on the table—and refurbished for this book. He has frequent recourse to garlic, onions and tomatoes, and one recipe— vegetable soup with corn dumplings—calls for a basil-and-cheese sauce called *pistou,* the southern French version of *pesto.*

Many dishes are stylish as well as inexpensive. Pépin has demonstrated his dazzling showmanship on television, yet he makes it seem likely that the ordinary cook could reproduce the simple, elegant decoration he creates on his chicken liver pâté out of scallion stems and tomato skins. Equally attractive is his mayonnaise of fish (preparation time, 30 minutes), which is molded on the platter in the shape of a fish, replete with mouth and gills of carrot peelings and gills of thin-sliced cucumbers.

The book contains 53 recipes grouped into chapters as follows: "The Menus," "First Courses and Accompaniments," "The Main Dishes" and "Desserts." Some of the memorable main dishes include chicken cassoulet with beans and sausages; roast lamb breast Provençal; potato ragout with bacon, onions, garlic and thyme; and gratin of pasta with vegetables. Salads include a highly flavored coleslaw with white and red cabbage and either iceberg lettuce

or curly endive. For desserts he favors fresh fruits, or such elaborations as peach gratiné baked with brown sugar, and almonds with heavy cream.

In sum, *Everyday Cooking with Jacques Pépin* is a book of savory French country recipes that are easy to prepare and often beautiful to behold. The author, meanwhile, has managed to incorporate—painlessly, in most cases—a surprising amount of technique and kitchen savvy.

CHAPTER THREE

Famous
Cookbooks
by
Food
and
Cookery
Experts

The great Alexis Soyer once remarked that it was up to women to preserve our culinary heritage, because men chefs were apt to neglect it in their relentless drive to be creative. This was a typical bit of exaggeration, perhaps, but Soyer had doubtlessly noticed that women—in England and America, at least—tended to dominate the writing of popular cookbooks in the 18th and 19th centuries.

The role of chef in the public image remained firmly masculine, but that of the humbler cook was feminine. Popular cookbooks addressed not sophisticates at the sharp edge of culinary invention, but housewives concerned with putting three meals a day on the table for their families.

They were also concerned with the issues that continue to preoccupy women today, status and power. Earnestly and often piously, these books never ceased to point out that knowledge was power, that competence in cooking and household management enhanced the status of a woman. This applied equally to the domestic servant, to the housewife who did her own cooking and to the upper-class lady saddled with managing a staff.

By the third quarter of the 20th century, this issue seemed less pressing. Women had begun to seek other paths to status and power. Perhaps because of this, female predominance in home cooking is not quite so marked, at least in point of popularity, if not in numbers. The flood of cookbooks is so overwhelming that one is left to judge by the few names that break the surface into the sunlight of celebrity.

Certain well-known food writers, such as Julia Child, Craig Claiborne, and Pierre Franey, are not discussed here because their work is covered elsewhere in the book.

THE ART OF COOKERY MADE PLAIN AND EASY

The Art of Cookery was first published in London in 1747 and rapidly became a best seller. It retained its hold on public attention for the next 100 years, before it was finally eclipsed by *Mrs. Beeton's Book of Household Management*, which appeared in 1859. Authorship of the first two editions of *The Art of Cookery* was ascribed to "A Lady," but the third edition was signed, "H. Glasse."

This did little but deepen the mystery of authorship, since no one knew who H. Glasse was. It was widely believed in literary circles that a literary hack who styled himself Sir John Hill was the author. This idea was debunked by Dr. Samuel Johnson, who claimed that the book displayed an ignorance of elementary chemical compounds of the sort used around the house that Hill (who had trained as an apothecary) could never be guilty of.

The fourth edition returned to the anonymity of "A Lady," but subsequent editions on into the 19th century were signed by "Mrs. Glasse." Who was Mrs. Glasse? A definitive answer to this question was not obtained until 1938, when Madeleine Hope Dodds, of Newcastle upon Tyne, published the facts in a local history journal. Hannah Glasse was the half sister of Sir Lancelot Allgood, head of an old Northumberland family. Hannah was born in 1708, and at the age of 16 she eloped with John Glasse, an impecunious young man. For the next two decades they lived part of the time in Broomfield, Essex, and part in London. Hannah bore eight children. In the 1740s she began to show entrepreneurial spirit, first in marketing a patent medicine, then in writing her cookbook. John Glasse died in 1747, the year *The Art of Cookery* was published, and shortly thereafter, strapped financially, Hannah set up in business with her daughter Margaret as a dressmaker. Business flourished, and a 1754 edition of Hannah's cookbook has a frontispiece bearing an advertisement for "Hannah Glasse, Habit-Maker to her Royal Highness the Princess of Wales, in Tavistock Street, Covent Garden." Despite this impressive client, Hannah Glasse went bankrupt that very year, to the tune of £10,000, an enormous sum in that era. Astutely, she had registered as a trader, thus avoiding personal liability and the consequent debtor's prison. There are scant details of her life after this disaster, because it distanced her from the family. She wrote other cookery books, including *The Complete Confectioner*, and something called *The Servant's Directory*. She died in obscurity in 1770.

What made *The Art of Cookery* such a solid favorite with the British and later with the Americans? Perhaps it was lack of pretension. A facsimile edition of the 1796 edition is still in print, (*The Art of Cookery Made Plain and Easy* (Hamden, Conn.: Archon Books; Wakefield, Yorkshire: S.R. Publishers, 1971). In an introductory note entitled "To The Reader," Hannah declares, "If I have not wrote in the high polite style, I hope I shall be forgiven; for my intention is to instruct the lower sort, and therefore must treat them in their own way." She ends this section with the hope that "my Book will answer the ends I intend it for; which is to improve the servants, and save the ladies a great deal of trouble."

Fanny Cradock, in a modern introduction, finds the

TO FRY EGGS AS ROUND AS BALLS

Having a deep frying-pan, and three pints of clarified butter, heat it as hot as for fritters, and stir it with a stick, till it runs like a whirlpool. Then break an egg into the middle, and turn it round with your stick, till it be as hard as a poached egg. The whirling round of the butter will make it as round as a ball. Then take it up with a slice and put it in a dish before the fire. They will keep hot half an hour, and yet be soft, so you may do as many as you please. You may serve them with what you please, nothing better than stewed spinage, and garnish with orange.

Hannah Glasse, *The Art of Cookery Made Plain and Easy*, p. 236.

TO MAKE AN ENGLISH RABBIT

Toast a slice of bread brown on both sides, then lay it in a plate before the fire, pour a glass of red wine over it, and let it soak the wine up; then cut some cheese very thin, and lay it very thick over the bread, and put it in a tin oven before the fire, and it will be toasted and browned presently. Serve it away hot.

Hannah Glasse, *The Art of Cookery Made Plain and Easy*, p. 230.

book's virtues to be several: The "plain and easy" line was a significant inducement that was borne out honestly by the text; that Hannah Glasse was that rare bird, a truthful cookbook writer, in that she owns up to having borrowed 150 new recipes from other published cookbooks; that her style convincingly portrays a person who has performed all that she recommends, thus persuading the reader that an ordinary person can do likewise.

Cradock cites a case in point to illustrate how Hannah's trial-and-error experience shines through her style. The recipe for lemon cream on page 322 directs, "When it [the lemon cream] is as hot as you can bear your fingers in, pour it into glasses." This, says Cradock, bespeaks experience. Yet a check of Eliza Smith's *The Compleat Housewife* finds identical wording in *her* recipe for lemon cream (page 185)—and the first edition was published 20 years before *The Art of Cookery*. Looking for truth in style is a tricky business. The facsimile edition of *The Compleat Housewife* (London: Literary Services and Production Ltd., 1968) was taken from a 1753 edition (the 18th), so one could suppose that the publishers actually stole the lemon cream recipe from Hannah Glasse. Another critic points out, however, that Glasse lifted the entire cream section word for word from Smith's 1727 edition. However, Smith (or the publisher of her book) evened the score by borrowing wholesale from Glasse, and as time wore on both books got increasingly fatter on gleanings from contemporary rivals. This was ordinary publishing practice of the times for cookbooks, and the larceny should not necessarily be attributed to the authors.

Despite the lack of originality, the lack of an index (a fault later corrected), and repetitive recipes, *The Art of Cookery* did have much to recommend it to the beginner. The recipes were clear and precise. Instructions to the experienced were lucid and easy to follow. The book contained many excellent recipes for English fare. Its scope was broad, covering topics such as baking, preserving and carving ("To unlace a Coney," "To allay a Pheasant or Teal," "To thigh a Woodcock"). Under "Miscellaneous," she offers cures for the bite of a mad dog, the plague and heartburn, plus tips on "How to keep clear from Bugs."

Glasse's most enduring claim to fame, perhaps has been that of having added a phrase to the language, "First catch your Hare," a bit of basic advice to the naïve reader. However, scholars have searched in vain for this line in *The Art of Cookery* and have discovered that what the author actually said was to "case" the hare, a culinary term meaning to dress it—i.e., clean, trim and truss it.

AMERICAN COOKERY

American Cookery, the first American-written cookbook, was published in Hartford, Connecticut, in 1796. All we know about the author, Amelia Simmons, is what she volunteered about herself, that she was an "American orphan." The book, a slender volume of about 130 recipes, was not a literary masterpiece. The author admitted to "being without sufficient education to prepare this work," and indeed the original edition contained many errors of grammar, typography and usage. Nevertheless, the first edition sold briskly at a price of two shillings, three pence a copy. In the preface to a later, revised edition, Simmons complained that many of the imperfections of the first edition "were occasioned either by the ignorance, or evil intention of the transcriber for the press."

The object of the book, according to the author, was to further "the improvement of the rising generation of *Females* in America." She was especially concerned with the development of character, by which she meant "having an opinion and determination." This was not mere obstinacy, she hastened to add, but a holding fast to maxims that had stood the test of the ages in the matter of perfecting good wives and useful members of society. Character was above all essential for those who shared her sad estate of being an orphan and who had no family to defend their "indiscretions." After sounding this note of high moral purpose in the preface, the author confines herself in the next to the pragmatics of shopping, cooking, preserving and baking.

A version of the book is in print in the United States, *First American Cookbook* (Johnsburg, N.Y.: Buck Hill, 1966). This is not a facsimile reprint but an imaginative re-creation of the original with some of the rough edges taken off and enriched by lovely 18th-century engravings.

The book makes clear that American cooking, though firmly based on English methods, was developing distinctive qualities of its own. Some of the differences were due to American use of maize, or corn. For example, we find recipes for johnny or hoe cake, a type of cornbread, Indian "slapjack," made with cornmeal, and Indian pudding also based on cornmeal, as well as the use of corncobs to smoke bacon. Simmons also suggests "cranberry" sauce as an accompaniment to that American game bird, the turkey. None of the contemporary English cookbooks had these recipes, although, following the publishing practice of the day, they soon would have. Susannah Carter's *The Frugal Housewife*, an English cookbook, appeared in an American edition in 1803

AMERICAN COOKERY

or the art of Dressing

VIANDS, FISH, POULTRY & VEGETABLES

and the best Modes of Making

PASTES, PUFFS, PIES, TARTS, PUDDINGS
CUSTARDS & PRESERVES

and All Kinds of

CAKES

from the

IMPERIAL PLUMB TO PLAIN CAKE
adapted to This Country & All Grades of Life

BY AMELIA SIMMONS
an American Orphan

1796

TO MAKE A FINE SYLLABUB FROM THE COW

Sweeten a quart of cyder with double refined sugar, grate nutmeg into it, then milk your cow into your liquor, when you have thus added what quantity of milk you think proper, pour half a pint or more, in proportion to the quantity of syllabub you make, of the sweetest cream you can get all over it.

Amelia Simmons, *American Cookery*, p. 54.

APPLES

Apples are still more various, but rigidly retain their own species, and are highly useful in families, and ought to be more universally cultivated, excepting in the compactest cities. There is not a single family but might set a tree in some otherwise useless spot, which might serve the two fold use of shade and fruit; on which 12 or 14 kinds of fruit trees might easily be engrafted and essentially preserve the orchard from the intrusions of boys, etc. which is too common in America. If the boy who thus planted a tree, and guarded and protected it in a useless corner, and carefully engrafted different fruits, was to be indulged free acess into orchards, whilst the neglectful boy was prohibited—how many millions of fruit trees would spring into growth—and what a saving to the union. The net saving would in time extinguish the public debt, and enrich our cookery.

Amelia Simmons, *American Cookery,* p. 29.

with an appendix containing 30 American recipes, many of which coincided with those in *American Cookery*. A subsequent edition of Hannah Glasse's *The Art of Cookery*, published for American readers, included that appendix word for word. On the other hand, it is quite likely that Amelia Simmons based some of her more English recipes on Susannah Carter's book.

Other novelties include a recipe for "pumpkin pie" and another for pickled watermelon rinds (called "American citron"). Several recipes called for the use of a leavening agent called pearlash, an American contribution to the culinary world. Consisting of potassium carbonate produced through a wood-burning process, when mixed with dough and baked, it produced carbon dioxide, which caused the dough to rise. Pearlash was a big American export in the 1790s (8,000 tons to Europe in 1792), and whole forests were leveled to produce it.

Some of Amelia Simmons's terminology must have struck the English as strange. She called scones "biscuits," and biscuits "cookies," distinctions in usage that continue to this day, while fat used in pastry-making she called "shortening."

Amelia attacked the problem of cooking in what is now thought to be the European manner—i.e., a good deal of knowledge of everyday technique was taken for granted. The author did not waste words on the simpler dishes but did pay quite a bit of attention to party dishes, such as dressing and cooking a turtle, or a calf's head turtle fashion. The recipes were clear sailing for an experienced cook, but a novice would need guidance on many.

Simmons offers many household hints, especially in shopping. She warns, "veal bro't to market in panniers, or in carriages, is to be preferred to that bro't in bags, and flouncing on a sweaty horse." On fish: "Deceits are used to give them freshness of appearance, such as peppering the gills . . . and even painting the gills, or wetting with animal blood." As to poultry, she wrote, "All birds are known, whether fresh killed or stale, but tight vent in the former, and a loose open vent if old or stale."

American Cookery offers some insights into the daily life of postrevolutionary America. The recipes, if nothing else, can provide an amusing jolt to modern readers to whom food processors, cake mixes and frozen foods have become second nature.

GRAND DICTIONNAIRE DE CUISINE

Alexandre Dumas *(père)*, a pillar of the Romantic movement in French literature and author of some 500 books, died in 1870, three years before the publication of his final work, *Grand Dictionnaire de Cuisine*. It was a whale of a book, the original edition running to about 600,000 words. The text, arranged alphabetically, was an assortment of anecdotes, tall tales and "facts" (often incorrect) about food and cooking, interspersed with recipes, many of which were outdated or impractical.

In his introduction, Dumas expressed the hope that this work would be his crowning literary achievement and that he wanted it "to be read by the sophisticated and used by the practitioners of the art." It is safe to say he achieved the first aim, but about 80 or 90 years later than he might have expected. He failed in the second aim, most probably because it is not a practical book.

Apparently Dumas thought about writing a definitive book on food for years but put it off repeatedly. The time arrived when it could no longer be put off. It was near the end of his life, and he was, unfortunately, feeling old and ill. He retired to Roscoff on Cape Finisterre in 1869 to do the writing, and he delivered the manuscript in March of 1870. What emerged from the publishing house of Alphonse Lemerre three years later was described as follows by translator Alan Davidson:

> The text was often repetitive, the balance between subjects inexplicable, the punctuation and paragraphing erratic, the incubus of perfunctorily drafted recipes borrowed from other authors almost intolerable, and yet . . . it was an engaging and impressive jumble. (Alan and Jane Davidson, *Dumas on Food* [London: Michael Joseph, 1978] p. 7).

It might have been a better, more consistent book had the author lived to shape it at the proofs stage. As it was, the publisher hired two well-known authors, Leconte de Lisle and Anatole France, to polish the manuscript. The result, however, is unmistakably a Dumas production.

The original edition did not sell out; indeed, according to the Davidsons, unsold copies were found in the cellar of the publishing house when it went out of business in the 1950s. An abridged edition entitled *Petit Dictionnaire de Cuisine* was published in 1882, leaving out many of the recipes and most

Alexandre Dumas (père)

EGGS

To some people an egg is an egg. This is an error. Two eggs laid at the same moment, one by a hen that runs loose in a garden, the other by one that feeds in the henyard, can be utterly different in flavor.

I am one of those who insist that my egg be put in cold water and slowly brought to a boil. In this manner, the whole egg is uniformly cooked. Otherwise, if an egg is dropped into boiling water it is likely to break, and the white might be hard and yolk uncooked.

Poached Eggs. Here is the recipe from the *Cuisinier Imperial de 1808*, repeated in the *Cuisinier Royal de 1839*. You are free to adopt for your own:

Have 15 poached eggs drained and placed on a platter. At the same time have 12 ducks, almost done, roasted on the spit. Take the ducks off the spit, cut them to the bone, drain off their juices, season juice with salt and coarse pepper. Reheat but do not boil and pour over the poached eggs.

Louis Colman (ed., tr., abr.), *Alexandre Dumas' Dictionary of Cuisine* (London: Spring Books, 1958), pp. 108-9.

of the anecdotes. The press run was small and the sales disappointing, apparently, because the *petit* edition was not reprinted. And there the matter rested. The book had received mixed reviews 10 years earlier, but it seemed to fall between two stools. Literary critics ignored it; it was not a book for food professionals, and what might appeal to amateurs was buried in the jumble.

Interest suddenly revived in the 1950s with the discovery at Lemerre of the original copies (which were destroyed) and the publication of a new Dumas biography by André Maurois. Several modern editions appeared in rapid succession, one introduced by André Maurois, with a foreword by Raymond Oliver, an important French gastronomic writer. The first version in English appeared in 1958, translated, edited and abridged by Louis Colman and entitled *Alexandre Dumas' Dictionary of Cuisine* (London: Spring Books, 1958). A second was published in 1978, translated by Alan and Jane Davidson and entitled *Dumas on Food: Selections from Le Grand Dictionnaire de Cuisine by Alexandre Dumas* (London: Michael Joseph, 1978). Both versions pare down the text to what might interest the sophisticated amateur—i.e., the anecdotes and the reliable (or interestingly unreliable) facts and recipes. The Davidson version runs about 50 pages longer (327 pages) and in its scholarly apparatus contains a wealth of fascinating detail about the author, the history of the book's publication, subsequent bibliography of writings about it, and French cooking practices and utensils of the period.

The book was "discovered" by working foodwriters, particularly the late Waverley Root, who specialized in the history of food and cuisines, with all its social and literary ramifications. Root wrote for the *International Herald Tribune* (in Paris) a weekly column that was syndicated worldwide, and Dumas dictionary entry frequently served Root as a starting point for a witty and erudite discussion of a food item. Root also drew on much of this material for his *Food: An Authoritative and Visual History and Dictionary of the Foods of the World* (New York: Simon & Schuster, 1980).

Perhaps he fell under the spell of Dumas's peculiar charm, as did the Davidsons, who remarked in their introduction that working on their translation "gave us an admiration and affection for Dumas which was quite absent when we began. His genius was a warm one, which kindles a reciprocal warmth."

Dumas borrowed material from the best sources, sometimes with attribution, sometimes without. The original edition printed a letter from the publisher to chef Denis-Joseph Vuillemot, a longtime friend of Dumas, thanking him for his

CURLEW

Called the sea crow because of its resemblance to the common crow. About three feet long, it is dark, almost black, with green and purple lights. It lives along the shores of lakes and feeds entirely on fish.

The curlew is a sad and sombre bird, said to bring misfortune. Its flesh has a bitter, swampy odor, which makes it very disagreeable to the taste. Be that as it may, the Mexicans who sometimes eat it find it pretty good.

Louis Colman (ed., tr., abr.), *Alexandre Dumas' Dictionary of Cuisine* (London: Spring Books, 1978) p. 100.

contribution of advice and recipes. Dumas quoted liberally from Brillat-Savarin's *Physiologie du Gout* and adopts many of the latter's philosopical musings without acknowledgment. Dumas has high praise for and frequently refers to Grimod de la Reynière's *Almanach des Gourmands*, a work discussed elsewhere in this volume. Lesser-known but important sources of recipes were Urbain Dubois's *La Cuisine Classique* (1868) and M. le Comte de Courchamps' *Néo-Physiologie du Goût* (1839) and *Mémoires de la Marquise de Créquy* (1853). Dumas in his introduction testifies to his indebtedness to the great Carême and to Beauvillier's *Art du Cuisinier*.

Dumas was much criticized by his contemporaries for his habit of quoting and paraphrasing all and sundry, but with the perspective afforded by history, it is now clear that Dumas has himself been quoted and paraphrased enough to more than even the score.

THE ORIGINAL BOSTON COOKING-SCHOOL COOK BOOK 1896

The Boston Cooking-School Cook Book was first published in 1896. Its author was Fannie Merritt Farmer. Succeding editions of this book—and there were many—came to be known simply as "Fannie Farmer." Miss Farmer, who became a nationwide celebrity both as a writer and a lecturer, earned the sobriquet "Mother of Level-Measurement" due to her insistence on precision in the measurement of ingredients and in the way she went about achieving it.

Fannie Farmer inherited a tradition of precision from a predecessor at the Boston Cooking School, Mrs. D.A. Lincoln. Mrs. Lincoln was a formidable lady—in print, at least—who believed there was a right way to do each recipe. She had no patience with the then-current language of recipes, which called for "pinches" of this or that, and pieces of "butter the size of an egg." This could lead to confusion, and the wrong way. In her formulations, such vague phrases became two ounces, or one-fourth cup. Fannie Farmer perfected this concept, stating, "Correct measurements are absolutely necessary to insure the best results. Good judgment, with experience, has taught some to measure by sight; but the majority need definite guides." She decreed the use of volume measurement for dry ingredients (rather than by weight, as was customary in Europe) and specified that teaspoons and cups be *measured level*.

THE
ORIGINAL
BOSTON
COOKING-SCHOOL
COOK BOOK
1896
BY
Fannie Merritt Farmer

A facsimile of the first edition of
THE BOSTON COOKING-SCHOOL COOK BOOK
by Fannie Merritt Farmer

Hugh Lauter Levin Associates, New York
distributed by
CROWN PUBLISHERS, INC.
419 Park Avenue South, New York, N.Y. 10016

In 1887 Mrs. Lincoln published *The Boston Cookbook*. The same year she wrote a textbook for use in the Boston public schools. One of her practices was to tabulate the ingredients at the head of each recipe. Elsewhere she offered a detailed table of weights and measures. Mrs. Lincoln's format and Miss Farmer's volume measurements have since become trademarks of America-style recipe writing.

Fannie Farmer was one of four daughters of a respectable middle-class Boston family. In early childhood she suffered a stroke that crippled her for life. Despite the handicap, she developed into a person of redoubtable character and energy. At the age of 30 she enrolled in the Boston Cooking School for a two-year course. On graduation she was appointed assistant to the director, and upon the latter's death, director.

Although Mrs. Lincoln's book served as a starting point, Miss Farmer found it wanting in many respects. Mainly there were not enough recipes and not enough detailed instructions for the book to serve as a general cooking reference book. Thus her 1896 publication was a completely new book, written much in the spirit of Mrs. Lincoln's philosophy, but larger in scope and much more detailed.

A facsimile reprint of this work is *The Original Boston Cooking-School Cook Book 1896* by Fannie Merritt Farmer (New York: Hugh Lauter Levin Assoc., dist. by Crown, 1973; paperback, New York: New American Library, 1973). Miss Farmer published the original edition at her own expense. The publisher who printed and distributed it, Little, Brown, had doubts about its commercial possibilities and refused to underwrite it, a decision that redounded greatly to the benefit of Fannie Farmer.

The book was quickly and lastingly successful. It has sold more than 3 million copies since 1896, going through 12 editions. The latest appeared in 1979 under the title *The Fannie Farmer Cookbook* (New York: Alfred A. Knopf), edited by Marion Cunningham.

The original is no celebration of food or hymn to the pleasures of eating. Its objectives and tone are as earnest as those of the cooking school. Household management and cooking were taught as disciplines to enhance the skills, but also the status, of homemakers. In the early days of Miss Farmer's tenure the school mainly taught teachers of cooking, but as the new century dawned, she broke out of this mold and attracted a large clientele of middle- and upper-class girls who would apply the skills directly and assume the housewife-as-domestic-scientist role. The book begins with a lecture on food and nutrition, then moves to general conceptions of cookery, starting with how to build a fire. It moves systematically through beverages, baking (very ex-

HOW TO BUILD A FIRE

Before starting to build a fire, free the grate from ashes. To do this, put on covers, close front and back dampers, and open oven-damper; turn grate, and ashes will fall into the ash receiver. If these rules are not followed, ashes will fly over the room. Turn grate back into place, remove the covers over fire-box, and cover grate with pieces of paper (twisted in centre and left loose at the ends). Cover paper with small sticks, or pieces of pine wood, being sure that the wood reaches the ends of the fire-box, and so arranged that it will admit air. Over pine wood arrange hard wood; then sprinkle with two shovelfuls of coal. Put on covers, open closed damper, strike a match,—sufficient friction is formed to burn the phosphorus, this in turn lights the sulphur, and the sulphur the wood,—then apply the lighted match under the grate, and you have a fire.

Fannie Merritt Farmer, *The Original Boston Cooking-School Cook Book 1896*, pp. 19-20.

tensive), cereals, eggs, soups, and so on through 34 chapters. Its strong points are its comprehensive approach, instructions that are clear enough for any beginner to follow and, above all, its precision. Fannie Farmer is not discursive or chatty in the manner of Mrs. Beeton, whose *Book of Household Management* so dominated the English cookbook market.

The recipe selection of the original edition was biased toward the New England region and French cuisine. Subsequent editions brought the reader up to date on technical advances and corrected the biases. The second edition, for example, instructs the reader on gas-fueled stoves (the first had discussed only wood- and coal-burning). Fannie Farmer No. 12, according to Marion Cunningham, favors the heartland, "our bounty flowing from sea to shining sea." The original offered 1,500 recipes, while the latest edition contains close to 3,000.

Given the American preoccupation with food, it is safe to say in retrospect that Fannie Farmer's wish, as stated in her introduction, has been realized:

It is my wish that the book may not only be looked upon as a compilation of tried and tested recipes, but that it may awaken an interest through its condensed scientific knowledge which will lead to deeper thought and broader study of what we eat. [p. vii]

THE ART OF EATING

M.F.K. Fisher, author of *The Art of Eating* (New York: Macmillan, 1954), is sometimes referred to as the greatest American foodwriter. Few would dispute that she is one of the four most influential American foodwriters of the past 50 years (the others being James Beard, Julia Child and Craig Claiborne). Granted that this is so, wherein does her greatness lie? The names of others are household names, while hers is not. Others attract large television audiences, while she does not. Others write vastly more popular cookbooks. The answer seems to lie in her ability to charm a relatively small elite who appreciate both good writing and good food. What they admire in the writing of M.F.K. Fisher is its passion, its honesty and its wit.

In the world of gastronomic writing, Fisher is most often compared to Jean Anthelme Brillat-Savarin, a Frenchman who died in 1826, leaving behind a single, slender volume of essays, or "meditations," on what he called "transcendental gastronomy." It was entitled *The Physiology of Taste*. The im-

BOSTON BAKED BEANS

Pick over one quart pea beans, cover with cold water, and soak over night. In morning, drain, cover with fresh water, heat slowly (keeping water below boiling point), and cook until skins will burst,—which is best determined by taking a few beans on the tip of a spoon and blowing on them, when skins will burst if sufficiently cooked. Beans thus tested must, of course, be thrown away. Drain beans, throwing bean-water out of doors, not in sink. Scald rind of one-half pound fat salt pork, scrape, remove one-fourth slice and put in bottom of bean pot. Cut through rind of remaining pork every one-half inch, making cuts one inch deep. Put beans in pot and bury pork in beans, leaving rinds exposed. Mix one tablespoon salt, one tablespoon molasses, and three tablespoons sugar; add one cup boiling water, and pour over beans; then add enough more boiling water to cover beans. Cover bean-pot, put in oven, and bake slowly six or eight hours, uncovering the last hour of cooking, that rind may become brown and crisp. Add water as needed. Many feel sure that by adding with seasonings one-half tablespoon mustard, the beans are more easily digested. If pork mixed with lean is preferred, use less salt.

The fine reputation which Boston Baked Beans have gained, has been attributed to the earthen bean-pot with small top and bulging sides in which they are supposed to be cooked. Equally good beans have often been eaten where a five-pound lard pail was substituted for the broken bean-pot.

Yellow-eyed beans are very good when baked.

Fannie Merritt Farmer, *The Original Boston Cooking-School Cook Book 1896*, pp. 211-12.

posing title concealed a delightful collection of philosophical musings on the subject of food and dining that have made the book a classic. It is no coincidence that M.F.K. Fisher admires *The Physiology of Taste*. Indeed, she has produced one of the finest English translations of it, and she considers this to be her best work. On the similarity between the two writers, Clifton Fadiman writes:

> Of all writers on food now using our English tongue she seems to me to approach most nearly, in range, depth, and perception, the altitude of Brillat-Savarin himself. And, with that said the treasure of praise is exhausted. (Quoted from the introduction to M.F.K. Fisher's *The Art of Eating* [New York: Macmillan, 1954], p. xv.)

The Art of Eating is a collection of five books, all written before 1950. The first is *Serve It Forth* (1937), a series of essays on the history of cookbooks and gastronomy, interlarded with anecdotes based on the author's experiences in Europe, mainly in France and Switzerland. She first charts the changes in an individual's appetites as he moves from childhood to old age, then moves through the history of mankind, considering such topics as "Greek Honey and the Hon-zo," "Dark Ages and the Men of God" and "A Pigges Pettie Toes" (Elizabethan England). She consciously emulates Brillat-Savarin, boldly stating, "There are two kinds of books about eating: those that try to imitate Brillat-Savarin's, and those that try not to." Despite her best efforts, she admits he "haunts" her work.

The second book, which is the shortest, is entitled *Consider the Oyster* (1941). It considers not only oysters in their many varieties but also oyster restaurants and oyster-eaters. These last, with her passion for classification, she divides into three groups: "those loose-minded sports who will eat anything, hot, cold, thin, thick, dead or alive, as long as it is an *oyster;* those who will eat them raw and only raw; and those who with equal severity will eat them cooked and no other way." She offers some 30 recipes, including one to make a pearl, which winds up, "Supervise things closely for seven years, with the help of your diving girl. Any time after that you may open your oyster. . . ."

The third volume, *How to Cook a Wolf* (1942), strikes most commentators as the most useful of the five. It was written as America went to war and was meant to help the housewife cope with food shortages—i.e., the wolf sniffing at the door. Fisher offers consoling words on "How to Be Cheerful Though Starving" and definitive instructions on "How to Boil Water." In a 1951 update, she amended many recipes, adding touches of extravagance—e.g., 16 eggs in one recipe. Still, the book stands up as a lighthearted manual for anyone having to cope with lean times.

The Gastronomical Me (1943), the fourth book, is a series of autobiographical sketches noted usually for its eloquent apologia for foodwriting: "There is a communion of more than our bodies when bread is broken and wine drunk. And that is my answer, when people ask me: Why do you write about hunger, and not wars or love?"

The final book, *Alphabet for Gourmets* (1949), celebrates the presence of food in all parts of the fabric of life. These essays frequently dwell on the sensual implications of dining: "B Is for Bachelors" (their approach to gastronomy is basically sexual), "R Is for Romantic" (gastronomy is and always has been connected with its sister art of love) and "W Is for Wanton" (a wanton woman is one who with cunning and deliberation prepares a meal that will draw another person to her). She writes with discernment about the joys of dining alone but insists that the perfect dinner be shared with five friends.

Mary Frances Kennedy Fisher was born in Wisconsin in 1909, was raised in Whittier, California, and now makes her home in Sonoma County, amid the vineyards of northern California. She has written 14 books, and innumerable short stories and essays for *The New Yorker* magazine. Much of her writing is not gastronomical—hence her reputation as a fine writer who happens to write about food. A good deal of her work is found in libraries under the name of Parrish (Mary Frances Kennedy), the surname of her second husband.

A IS FOR DINING ALONE

. . . And so am I, if a choice must be made between most people I know and myself. This misanthropic attitude is one I am not proud of, but it is firmly there, based on my increasing conviction that sharing food with another human being is an intimate act that should not be indulged in lightly.

There are few people alive with whom I care to pray, sleep, dance, sing or share my bread and wine. Of course there are times when this latter cannot be avoided if we are to exist socially, but it is endurable only because it need not be the only fashion of self-nourishment.

There is always the cheering prospect of a quiet or giddy or warmly somber or lightly notable meal with "One," as Elizabeth Robins Pennell refers to him or her in *The Feasts of Autolycus.* "One sits at your side feasting in silent sympathy," this lady wrote at the end of the last century in her mannered and delightful book. She was, at this point, thinking of eating an orange in southern Europe, but any kind of food will do, in any clime, so long as *One* is there.

I myself have been blessed among women in this respect—which is of course the main reason that, if *One* is not there, dining alone is generally preferable to any other way for me.

M.F.K. Fisher, *The Art of Eating*, p. 557.

ELIZABETH DAVID CLASSICS

Elizabeth David is for reading. All who know her work agree upon that. Of course, her books are collections of recipes and are meant to be cooked from. Yet the casual American reader might be a little put off by her way of formulating a recipe. Her recipes are not cast in the mold Americans have become used to, a style described by one writer as "owner's manual instructions," but in a simple conversational style that leaves some details to the imagination and judgment of the reader. Inescapably, one is led to the conclusion that she believes her readers to be endowed with imagination, judgment and intelligence, a flattering impression encountered all too infrequently in the pages of recent cookbooks.

Another attractive trait is David's custom of plucking a recipe intact from a quaint, often obscure source—a literary or travel memoir, perhaps—and presenting it to the reader with the comment that she can think of no better way of pre-

POACHED EGGS

My own method for poaching eggs I learnt from a cookery book published by the Buckinghamshire Women's Institute, and it has proved infallible.

First boil a saucepan of water, and into this dip each egg whole, in its shell, while you count about 30, then take it out. When it comes to actually poaching the eggs, have a pan of fresh water boiling, add a dessertspoon of vinegar, stir the water fast until a whirlpool has formed, and into this break the eggs, one at a time. 1-1½ minutes cooks them. Take them very carefully out with a draining spoon. They will be rounded and the yolks covered with a "transparent Veil" instead of the ragged-looking affair which a poached egg too often turns out to be, and the alternative of the egg-poached pan, which produces an over-cooked sort of egg-bun, is equally avoided.

It is interesting to note that Dr. Kitchiner [author of the *Cook's Oracle* (1829)] instructs his readers to place poached eggs on bread "toasted on one side only." How right he is; I have never been able to understand the point of that sodden toast. . . .

Try serving poached eggs on a piece of fresh, buttered bread; alternatively on a purée of some kind—split peas, sweet corn, or mushrooms, with pieces of fried bread around, but not under, the eggs.

Elizabeth David, *French Country Cooking*, pp. 73-74.

paring that particular dish. It adds a kind of historical continuity to the subject—say, Mediterranean food—and she frequently clarifies or updates the text by means of footnotes. She carries this habit to its extreme by leaving one recipe in *Mediterranean Food* in its original French with the observation, "this dish [Gigot à la Provençale] is supportable only to those who are accustomed to the cooking of the *Midi*" (this owing to the quantity of garlic called for).

Another quirk is her insistence upon British (imperial) measures. In his introduction, James Beard remarks, "She is adamant about refusing to alter British weights and measures, which is one reason her books have never been as popular here as in Britian." This limitation, of course, requires more from the reader, but the present edition is amply supplied with conversion tables, both in the endpapers and by the index, and a glossary to translate British usage into American as in, for example, aubergine to eggplant.

Elizabeth David Classics (New York: Alfred A. Knopf, 1980) contains three works: *Mediterranean Food* (1950), *French Country Cooking* (1951) and *Summer Cooking* (1955). They make up a fat, hardbound volume of 672 pages, including a consolidated index.

Elizabeth David is well qualified to speak of Mediterranean food, having lived in various Mediterranean countries, including southern France, Italy, Greece and Egypt. She has broadened the base of her recipes to include all lands from Spain to the Middle East. If these 300 recipes could be said to have a common motif, it would be garlic. Other recurring elements are olive oil, saffron and pungent local wines, but "peace and happiness begin, geographically," she quotes, "where garlic is used in cooking." The book was written for austerity-ridden Britons, so most dishes do not require exotic ingredients, although the way relatively simple ingredients are treated may seem unusual. The recipes may strike the reader as a bit too picturesque for every day, she says, but "who wants to eat the same food every day?"

French Country Cooking sketches in the characteristics of the major French provincial areas, though the arrangement is by course rather than by area. These 225 recipes aim for what is honest, simple and sincere in French cooking. She sets aside such distinctions as *haute cuisine* and *cuisine bourgeoise*, opting for "cookery which uses raw materials to the greatest advantage" without the absurd complication of what passed for the height of refinement in the 19th and early 20th centuries. Customs and flavors vary with region, and the author stresses the seasonal and regional availability of products. Useful chapters are included on how to outfit a kitchen *("Batterie de Cuisine")*, how to use wine in the kitchen and menu planning.

Summer Cooking is somewhat longer than the other two works, offering approximately 1,000 recipes. The emphasis here is on cold dishes, although many hot ones are included, but all are light, easy to prepare and employ ingredients available in the summer. Separate chapters consider such topics as fresh herbs, hors d'oeuvres and salads, soups, eggs, fish, meat, poultry and game, vegetables, sauces, sweets, jams, jellies and other preserves, buffet food and picnics. The chapter on summer soups contains 26 recipes, ranging from potage printanière (purée of potato soup with green peas and diced carrots) to gazpacho. The section on picnics intersperses recipes with recollections of picnics past from such diarists as T. Earle Welby, Col. Kenney Herbert, Ford Madox Ford, William Hickey and Logan Pearsall Smith.

THE NEW JAMES BEARD

James Beard was once described as a nonchef, meaning he has had no formal culinary training and held no important head-of-kitchen posts. The point the author wished to make was that professionals with the training who *do* run top-ranked kitchens frequently turn to Beard for well-paid advice. Why is that?

Part of the answer might be found by examining *The New James Beard* (New York: Alfred A. Knopf, 1981). To begin with, it was his 19th book. His book-writing career started back in 1940 with something on hors d'oeuvres and has included dissertations on barbecuing, bread, casseroles, all courses of the meal, American cooking and even a volume of autobiography entitled *Delights and Prejudices* (New York: Atheneum, 1964; paperback, 1981). This last contains some of his best writing. Here, for example, is the first paragraph:

When Proust recollected the precise taste sensation of the little scalloped *madeleine* cakes served at tea by his aunt, it led him into his monumental remembrance of things past. When I recollect the taste sensations of my childhood, they lead me to more cakes, more tastes: the great razor clams, the succulent dungeness crab, the salmon, crawfish, mussels and trout of the Oregon coast; the black bottom pie served in a famous Portland restaurant; the Welsh rabbit of our Chinese cook, the white asparagus my mother canned, and the array of good dishes prepared by the two of them in that most memorable of kitchens. [p. 3]

EGYPTIAN PICNIC

In Egypt the picnic season starts sometimes in March, with *Shem el Nessim,* the "smelling of the Zephyrs," a day which is kept as a public holiday, when the whole population goes out to eat in the open air and greet the first day of Spring.

An agreeable form of picnic in Cairo was the felucca party; on board a hired Nile sailing boat Arab servants would carry the food; there were copper trays of pimentos, small marrows and vine leaves stuffed with rice, large, round shallow metal dishes filled with meat and spiced pilaff, bowls of grapes and peaches and figs and melons cooled with lumps of ice, mounds of flat Arab loaves stuffed with a salad of tomatoes, onions and mint; there would be music and the wailing of Arab songs as the boat swung rather wildly about, the crew made Turkish coffee, and we drank the odd, slightly salty red Egyptian wine from the Mariut, one of the oldest wine producing regions in the world.

Elizabeth David, *Summer Cooking,* pp. 241-42.

This is a book to be read with delight but not on an empty stomach. Before 1981, his two most solid and wide-ranging books had been *The James Beard Cookbook* (1959) and *James Beard's Theory and Practice of Good Cooking* (1977). As late as 1983, the former was picked by Craig Claiborne as part of his recommended cookbook library with the justification that it was one of the first and best basic cookbooks and that, while somewhat dated, it contained excellent recipes for beginning cooks. The latter is integrally related to *The New James Beard* which makes frequent reference to *Theory and Practice* on points of technique.

The New James Beard, however, is not just a revision of the original. Beard remarks in the introduction that he started to write a "Revised Standard Beard," but something happened along the way. He discovered that the inner man had changed too radically and that the new could not be a mere extension of the old. Here is one reason why Beard is valuable to his consultees: He moves with the times.

In a 1981 interview, he articulated the change as follows: "Well, thinking that it's healthy once in a while to hang yourself on a hook like a piece of meat and analyze yourself, I did so about two years ago. I decided to do and write what I pleased about food. I had never done that before . . . we've been stuffing ourselves, and that's not necessary. I now find great big meals oppressive." As part of his reassessment, Beard, who stands six feet, four inches and suffers from heart trouble, lost 50 pounds, going down to 250 pounds. To do this he emphasized such things as fresh fish and vegetables in his diet and avoided butter almost completely.

How has this change surfaced in *The New James Beard?* As he put it, "a shift straight across the whole spectrum of my cookery." Specifically, this means less salt, more vegetables, less red meat, fewer sweets and lighter food. The book calls for fewer sauces than the original; heavy cream is rarely called for, and butter, his old standby, is used sparingly. He praises yogurt and has eliminated the day-old sponge cake he described so lovingly in the 1959 book. Not a vegetarian by any means, Beard nevertheless features vegetable dishes, nudging meat to the margin: "We are not thinking in the same stiff categories that we used to. Meat can be a seasoning, not a prime ingredient." Having done time on a salt-free diet, he achieved a new reverence for the plain baked potato, recommending to the reader "the nutty, delicate earthiness of a perfect baked potato."

The approximately 1,000 recipes range from very basic things such as boiled cauliflower and veal scallops with lemon to exotic creations that mix textures, flavors and ingredients in exciting ways, such as marrow soufflé and roast quail on scrapple.

The book has 12 chapters arranged by type of food (salads, vegetables, meats, etc.) plus a concordance, in which he discusses ingredients from apples to yeast, giving shopping advice and tips on technique, with copious reference to *Theory and Practice*.

How did Beard rate this book? "For me," he wrote in the introduction, "the two books [*The New James Beard* and *Theory and Practice*] would add up to a fairly complete kitchen guide; for me, they would be the culmination of my long cooking career."

Craig Claiborne thought the new book difficult to categorize but excellent nonetheless. In selecting it for his recommended cookbook library, he wrote that although it was not terribly innovative, it made a nice reference book for home entertaining. Jane Salzfass Freiman, writing in *Cuisine* magazine, thought it a fitting addition to the Beard canon, likely to enhance his reputation as the dean of American gastronomic writers. Especially gratifying to her was the additional space devoted to appetizers, soups, salads, vegetables, fish, eggs and cheese, pasta, rice and grains. Evan Jones, writing in *Quest* magazine, hailed it as the new Gospel according to Beard for the 1980s.

With its encyclopedic range, sound technique, good writing and response to change, the book does seem to epitomize Beard, the invaluable nonchef. Meanwhile, Beard, now over 80, has moved on. He continues to teach cooking at his school in New York, plus a summer session in his native Oregon. He has written yet another cookbook, entitled *James Beard on Pasta* (New York: Alfred A. Knopf, 1983). Fashion has again swung around to one of his great specialties, American cuisine, and he is much in demand as a commentator. He lives his philosophy: "Feel free and take a fresh look. My emphasis is on options. My motto: 'Why not?'"

General
Cookbooks

These general cookbooks usually share three characteristics: they are big, they are international in scope and they leave nothing to chance.

It is very comforting to have a whopper cookbook on the shelf. One is defended against any eventuality. With a good reference book in hand—and this is what they are, really—the cook can't be daunted by unfamiliar food, the need of a new technique, or the looming special event. How should it be handled? Check James Beard, Craig Claiborne, *Gourmet*, *Good Housekeeping* or Irma Rombauer.

General cookbooks are melting-pot cookbooks. Indeed, this vaunted aspect of the American experience, the intermingling of ethnic identities, may really exist only in such abstract settings as phonebooks and cookbooks. Ethnic groups tend to stick together. Even in this country, ethnic communities can exist for decades, keeping to the old ways. Yet we have learned since 1960 that their cuisines are quite likely to be taken up as fads. After the rage has died down, a few dishes find their way into general cookbooks, toned down a bit, with some ingredients substituted but retaining the old name and the charm of novelty.

Last, these books are kind to the beginner. They have exact measurements, technical explanations, conversion charts and substitution lists, anything to guarantee the success of a meal, short of a free consultation with the author.

JEAN ANDERSON COOKS

Though not a basic cookbook of the all-encompassing sort, *Jean Anderson Cooks* (New York: William Morrow, 1982) is mostly preoccupied with fundamentals. It should prove attractive to experienced cooks was well as novices because of the appealing way it balances basic information with a collection of international recipes.

Jean Anderson is a food editor of 25 years' experience and the author of nine cookbooks, including *The Grass Roots Cookbook*, the *Doubleday Cookbook* and *Jean Anderson's Processor Cooking*. In this book she presents a lot of material usually left out of cookbooks, such as an examination of why things happen in cooking—why a cake humps and cracks in the middle, or why green vegetables turn brown.

The core of the book is Part One, "Kitchen Reference," which takes up two thirds of the work and gives detailed, specific information about buying, storing and preparing all the common foods found in the supermarket, ticking off (in boldface) such important points as season, hallmarks of quality, how much or how many per serving, best way to store, basic preparations and best ways to cook. A recipe or two is given for each type of food, but the implication is that having read the material, a cook would be able to do a decent job without needing a specific recipe. This section is packed with interesting charts and tables that provide quick reference for a cook who wants, for example, to check the description, market weights and number of servings for the popular tender roasts, or discover what went wrong in baking a cake or bread.

Part Two offers more than 300 recipes from around the world, arranged by course. The following is taken from "Appetizers & Hors d'Oeuvres":

FRESH BASIL SORBET
(serves 6 to 8)

This is not a dessert but a between-the-courses, palate-clearing ice. It is very tart and best when served after the fish and before the meat course.

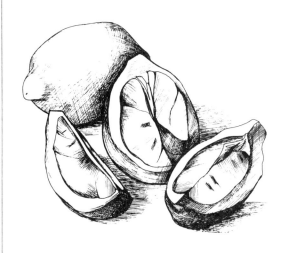

3 medium-sized bunches of fresh basil (you will need about 4 cups or 1 liter lightly packed leaves)
5 cups (1¼ liter) boiling water
½ cup (about) or 120 ml sugar
1 envelope plain gelatin
2 medium-size lemons, juiced

Carefully separate the basil leaves from the stems; discard the stems and any seriously blemished leaves. Wash the reserved basil leaves carefully in cool water, then pile them in a medium-size heatproof bowl. Pour the boiling water over the basil, then let cool to room temperature.

In a medium-size heavy saucepan, combine the sugar and gelatin. Add 4 cups (1 liter) of the basil infusion, set over moderate heat and heat, stirring frequently, about 5 minutes or until sugar and gelatin both dissolve. Set aside.

In a food processor fitted with the metal chopping blade (or in an electric blender), purée the basil leaves in the 1 cup (240 ml) remaining infusion. NOTE: *The leaves should be as uniformly fine as possible, so you may need to give the processor or blender four to five 15-second churnings.* Combine the basil purée with the gelatin mixture, then stir in the lemon juice. Taste and if too tart to suit you, add another tablespoon or two of sugar.

Pour the mixture into two refrigerator trays or into one large shallow aluminum pan and freeze until firm. Break into small chunks and beat very hard, a few at a time, until fluffy in an electric mixer set at high speed or in a food processor equipped with the metal chopping blade. Pack the sorbet into freezer containers and store in the freezer.

JAMES BEARD COOKBOOK

James Beard, author of many cookbooks, here offers one for beginners. The *James Beard Cookbook* is available in two formats, a paperback (New York: Dell, 1959) and a revised edition in hardcover (New York: Dutton, 1983). Beard opines that the book might also be of use to an experienced cook who needs encouragement to try something new. In any case, the 1,000 recipes are meant to be practicable for the rank beginner.

So as not to be misunderstood, Beard begins at the beginning with instructions on how to boil water. There's no catch to it; he simply wants to make it clear that this is a book for someone who can't even boil water.

Once that hurdle has been cleared, he moves quickly into such areas as fundamental do's and don'ts, a list of basic cooking equipment and a glossary of cooking terms. Recipes are divided up by courses of the meal and important cooking ingredients, but the chapters are arranged alphabetically—appetizers, bread, on through to vegetables. Technical instruction is placed right in the recipe that uses the particular technique.

The *James Beard Cookbook* has been enormously popular and is generally considered by critics as one of the best basic cookbooks to have appeared since World War II. It provides a well-rounded selection of American recipes spiced with a few from international traditions, some of which, such as the following, have an exotic touch to them:

LES OISEAUX SANS TÊTES
(serves 6)

Translated literally, "Birds without Heads," this is a good party dish, attractive, tasty and actually not difficult to do. For 6 persons order 12 pieces of round steak cut thin.

12 pieces of round steak ⅜ inch thick and 5-6 inches square.
1 large onion, chopped
Butter
6 mushrooms, finely chopped
½ teaspoon of thyme

1 teaspoon of salt
1 teaspoon of pepper
1 clove of garlic, chopped
3 tablespoons of chopped parsley
1½ cups of bread crumbs
1 egg, beaten
¼ cup of melted butter
12 thin slices of ham
4 to 6 tablespoons of fat
Flour
1½ cups of broth or wine

Make a stuffing first: Brown the onion in 4 tablespoons of butter. Add the chopped mushrooms, thyme, salt, freshly ground black pepper, chopped parsley, chopped clove of garlic and fine bread crumbs. Beat the egg and add to the mixture with enough melted butter to moisten the stuffing (about ¼ cup). Spread out the pieces of steak and place on each one a thin slice of ham. Then add a little stuffing, roll up, jelly-roll fashion, and tie securely with string.

In a large skillet melt 4–6 tablespoons of butter or beef fat. Roll each "bird" in flour and then brown in the hot fat, turning to sear all sides. When all the "birds" are brown, add 1½ cups of broth or red wine, cover tightly, lower the flame and simmer slowly for 1½ to 2 hours. Turn the "birds" often during the simmering to be sure they cook evenly and stay moist. Add more liquid if necessary. Serve with pan juices. Suggested accompaniments: sautéed potatoes and string beans with bacon. [pp. 236–37]

THE NEW YORK TIMES COOKBOOK

One of the cornerstones of the American gastronomic revolution, Craig Claiborne's *The New York Times Cookbook* (New York: Harper & Row, 1961) is also a good, general all-purpose cookbook. Its 1,500 recipes were drawn from the pages of *The New York Times*, where they appeared between 1950 and 1960. The selection is varied, including recipes from many European cuisines and a good many American favorites as well.

At the time this book appeared, Claiborne was food editor

of *The New York Times*, a post he occupied for many years afterward. His brilliant career as a restaurant critic and his authorship of some 15 cookbooks have raised him to the level of a gastronomic oracle. His books generally are simply written, sparkling with interesting anecdotes and are models of clarity when it comes to intricate explanations of technique. *The New York Times Cook Book* is also available in a boxed set (New York: Harper & Row, 1965) along with *The New York Times Menu Cookbook*.

In his 1961 preface, Claiborne observed that despite the proliferation of new "instant" food products, it seemed to him that there was a growing interest in fine cuisine. Accordingly, he provided not only a well-rounded assortment of recipes but also sound instruction in technique. Indeed, assiduous use of this book might be all the beginner would need as a teacher. In addition, there are chapters on wine, other beverages, herbs and spices and sources for ingredients (which, being 23 years old, probably are in serious need of updating).

The volume is well served by fine color photographs of finished dishes, and black-and-white series of how-to's on techniques.

Recipes are arranged by course, with substantial chapters on such main-dish foods as meats, poultry, fish and shellfish.

THE NEW NEW YORK TIMES COOKBOOK

The full title is *Craig Claiborne's The New New York Times Cookbook* (New York: Times Books, 1979), by Craig Claiborne with Pierre Franey. This is a companion volume to Craig Claiborne's 1961 bestseller, *The New York Times Cookbook*. Like its forerunner, it draws upon material previously published in the *Times*, including items from his "De Gustibus," in which he discusses matters of taste, gastronomy and food awareness, and from his "Q&A" column.

This new effort is Claiborne's way of dealing with the gastronomic revolution that has rocked America during the past 20 years. Since 1961 America has discovered fine food, foreign cuisines and gourmet cooking. This is why the new volume supplements the old, rather than updating it. The latter is seen as a period piece—a masterpiece, too—but an artifact from an earlier era.

Claiborne attributes the food revolution to several factors: affluence, foreign travel, growth of cooking schools, and a flood of excellent cookbooks that has swept away all the old assumptions. Also, television demonstrations, such as those offered by Julia Child on *The French Chef*, greatly modified the public's attitude toward fine cooking.

In *The New New York Times Cookbook*, Claiborne presents us with an encyclopedic study of the changes in the American kitchen. It includes 1,000 recipes that embrace regional and ethnic cooking as well as *haute cuisine*, many of them contributed by amateur or professional chefs. Among the more than 100 names he acknowledges figure such luminaries as Paul Bocuse, Jean Troisgros, Paula Wolfert and Marcella Hazan. The recipes are clearly laid out (ingredients on the margin in boldface, directions in a parallel column) and are written in a leisurely, conversational style, replete with cultural asides, and anecdotes about well-known cooks.

He takes advantage of the "Q&A" section to clarify points rarely raised in cookbooks. For example:

NOMENCLATURE
Whenever I read French menus I become confused by some of the nomenclature. In my French class I was taught that adjectives should have the same gender as the nouns they modify. And yet this doesn't happen on French menus. Take beef in burgundy wine sauce. Beef is masculine, yet the dish is listed a boeuf bourguignonne; snails is masculine, but are listed as escargot bourguignonne. Why do they not have the masculine ending, bourguignon?

Because there is an elision involved in most French menu terminology. Spelled out in toto these dishes would be listed as boeuf à la mode bourguignonne and escargots à la mode bourguignonne and so on. The à la mode is dropped for the simple reasons that it would be unnecessary clutter and boringly repetitive if spelled out for each dish. [p. 695]

THE COOK BOOK

Terence and Caroline Conran's *The Cook Book* (New York: Crown, 1980; London: Mitchell Beazley, 1980) is an all-in-one reference book for the home cook. It is billed as the complete guide to selecting, preparing, cooking and presenting good food, and its bias is away from *haute cuisine*, emphasizing simple food, cooked without pretension but served attractively.

Terence Conran is a restaurateur who also has a furniture and design business and a chain of shops specializing in kitchen equipment and utensils. Caroline Conran is a cookbook author, former cookery editor of several prominent English periodicals and translator of the English edition of *Michel Guérard's Cuisine Minceur*, which is discussed in Chapter Two of this book.

The Cook Book is divided into four parts: "The Purchase and Preparation of Food," "Recipes," "Presentation" and "Equipment." The first part, which takes up about half the book, is an encyclopedia of raw materials with bilingual titles (French and English); a text that includes description, buying guide and best cooking method; and excellent color illustrations (drawings and photographs). An attractive feature of this section is a bottom-of-the-page cross-reference grouping that guides the reader to specific recipes that incorporate the fish, meat or vegetable discussed on the page.

Part Two contains 500 recipes, ranging from stocks and soups through main dishes to desserts, preserves and drinks. Recipes emphasize simplicity; thus a beginner should have no problem with most of them. They are clearly written and include both American and metric measures. Again, cross references at the bottom of the page take the reader to the material on how to identify, purchase and prepare the raw ingredients.

The last two sections make up the final 20 percent of the book, dealing with table settings, menus (for example, "Farmhouse Supper," "Summer Tea," "Romantic Supper"), and equipment. Equipment appears in keyed photographs along the bottom of the pages, and the accompanying text explains how to use it. It is all very clear and untaxing. Menus and equipment are neatly tied into the previous text by references to both raw ingredients and recipes.

Though the format is unusual, this book can be used as a first-rate introduction for the beginner, or as a reference book for the experienced cook.

THE GOOD HOUSEKEEPING ILLUSTRATED COOKBOOK

"What you see is what you get," the phrase goes. This was never more true than for the recipes in Zoe Coulson's *The Good Housekeeping Illustrated Cookbook* (New York: Hearst Books, 1980). Part I of his lavishly illustrated volume consists of 916 color photographs of finished dishes, each with a caption bearing the name of the dish, its ingredients, preparation time, number of servings and the page number of the recipe. Part I is, in effect, an illustrated catalog for Part II, which contains the recipes. Menu planning is facilitated by the arrangement, which begins with appetizers and works its way through main dishes, cakes, breads and desserts.

A preliminary chapter entitled "Before You Cook" gives basic information on measuring ingredients and on saucepans, skillets, bakeware, cutting tools, equivalent amounts, mixing tools and other useful equipment. However, an amazing amount of data on ingredients, cooking techniques and reference charts is integrated into the recipes, which are lucidly written and easily understood, thanks in great part to the 5,000 two-color, how-to drawings.

A final section, "Useful Information," discusses menu planning and entertaining, table settings, napkin folding and outdoor eating. It also offers a herb-and-spice chart, a storage guide (for both cupboard and refrigerator), a calorie chart and a glossary of food and cooking terms.

Designed for the busy person, each of the 1,300 recipes has been pared to essentials, with attention given to such things as identifying crucial steps, eliminating steps that take extra time or unnecessarily dirtying another bowl, specifying exact pan sizes and setting up the recipe so you measure the dry ingredients before the wet (so you don't continually have to wash and dry the measuring cups).

This is a bulky book, but the size ensures that the print and drawings are large enough for easy reading.

The treatment of the recipes eases their use by beginners, but the selection is large and varied enough to interest the experienced cook, too.

EGGS MORNAY
(Begin 40 mins. ahead)

2 tablespoons butter or margarine
2 tablespoons all-purpose flour
1 tablespoon salt
½ teaspoon dry mustard
⅛ teaspoon pepper
dash hot pepper sauce
2 cups milk
¼ cup grated Parmesan cheese
8 eggs

1. In 2-quart saucepan over medium heat, into hot butter or margarine, stir flour, salt, mustard, pepper and hot pepper sauce. Gradually stir in milk; cook, stirring constantly, until mixture is thickened. Stir in cheese until melted. Preheat oven to 400 degrees F.
2. Pour half of sauce into 4 buttered 10-ounce custard cups or individual baking dishes. Break 2 eggs into each dish over sauce; spoon remaining sauce over eggs leaving yolks partially uncovered. Bake eggs 15 minutes, or until of desired doneness. [p. 143] 4 servings.

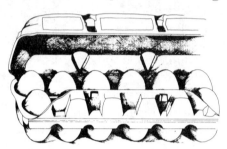

COOKING TECHNIQUES

This is a chink-filling book that would be of general use to any cook, novice or expert. If your regular cookbook takes knowledge of a technique for granted, and you don't have it, *Cooking Techniques* (Boston: Little, Brown, 1981), by Beverly Cox with Joan Whitman, can bridge the gap. It is subtitled *How to Do Anything a Recipe Tells You to Do,* and it presents 400 techniques, illustrated step by step with more than 2,000 black-and-white photographs. Another 50 color plates are reserved for the food presentation section, which pictures dishes of eye-popping allure or complexity. Fortunately, footnotes refer the reader to pages where the intricacies of forming a "lamb duck," or cutting a "watermelon whale" are gone through by the numbers.

Techniques are divided into 15 chapters: vegetables and herbs, meat, poultry, fish and shellfish, stock, pâtés, pasta and rice, the techniques of presentation, eggs, butter, pancakes and crêpes, breads, pastry cakes and cookies, and fruits.

The book deals with such seemingly trivial things as seeding a tomato or lining a mold, to such complexities as the 42-step technique for boning and stuffing a duck for a galantine (a very elegant pâté).

Chapters generally proceed from the general (techniques that apply to most foods in the class, such as fruit) to the particular (techniques that apply to specific items, which are then taken in alphabetical order—apple, banana, etc.).

THE NEW YORK TIMES 60-MINUTE GOURMET

The recipes collected here have not been tampered with to make them "quick and easy." Pierre Franey, author of *The New York Times 60-Minute Gourmet* (New York: Fawcett, 1981, paperback), says they were selected from thousands of dishes in his repertoire that simply require 60 minutes or less to bring to perfection.

Although Franey is a former chef of impeccable credentials, the "gourmet" tag here is not a code word for fancy food—most of the dishes would be considered bourgeois fare by the French—but more the author's hope that the reader will take seriously his high standards of freshness and technique that can raise any dish, however simple, to the gourmet level. Also, there is a class of dishes that don't fit into the 60-minute category, desserts, and he has omitted them, saying, "The preparation time for a first-rate dessert is simply too elaborate. In the long run, fruit with cheese is the best way to end a meal."

In his introduction he divulges some "secrets" for quick preparations without frustration: Get the best equipment you can afford and organize, organize, organize. There are some 300 recipes included here, all of them selected from his successful column of the same title in the *Times*. They are arranged in menus, and each menu consists of a main dish and, more often than not, a sauce and/or side dish, self-contained on a double-page spread. Franey introduces each menu with serving suggestions, preferred accompaniments, helpful procedural hints, and an occasional amusing anecdote from the history of cooking. The menus are grouped into categories by main dish: poultry, eggs, fish, shellfish, lamb, veal and calves' liver, beef, port and ham, pasta and cold dishes. Some examples are Chicken Breasts Veronique with curried rice, Filet Mignon Sauce Madère with sauté of vegetables Fermière and Parsleyed Rack of Lamb with Grilled Tomatoes Provençale. Following is an all-in-one dish named after Franey's former boss at Le Pavillion, Henri Soulé:

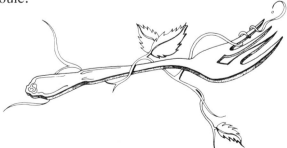

POULE AU POT d'HENRI SOULÉ
(Henri Soulé's chicken in the pot)

1 3-pound chicken
3 carrots, scraped, quartered lengthwise and cut into 1½ inch lengths
3 ribs celery, trimmed, split lengthwise and cut into 1½ inch lengths
2 or 3 turnips, about ½ pound, trimmed and cut into pieces about the same shape as the celery and carrots
1 cup leeks, quartered lengthwise and cut into 1½-inch lengths
1 zucchini, trimmed, quartered and cut into 1½ lengths
6 cups fresh or canned chicken broth
¼ cup rice
Salt and freshly ground pepper to taste

1. Truss the chicken and place it in a kettle. It should fit snugly or else too much water must be added and the subsequent soup will be weak and watery. Cover with water and add the carrots, celery, turnips, leeks and zucchini. Bring to a full boil and drain well.
2. Return the chicken to the kettle and add the chicken broth. Add all the vegetables except the zucchini. Simmer 20 minutes. Add the zucchini and simmer 5 minutes longer.
3. Add the rice and salt and pepper to taste, and cook until it is tender, about 10 minutes.
4. Untruss the chicken. Cut it into serving pieces and serve in four hot soup bowls with equal amounts of vegetables and rice in each bowl.

Yield: four servings. [p. 49]

THE GOURMET COOKBOOK

The Gourmet Cookbook, Vol. 1 (New York: Gourmet Books, 1965), was first published in 1950, which makes it something of an early classic of the fine-cooking genre. The 1965 book, which is the second revised edition, is essentially a selection of some 2,500 recipes that appeared in *Gourmet* magazine and are biased mainly toward French and American cuisines but represent many others as well.

The attitude of self-conscious gastronomy expressed in

the book's introduction foreshadowed the American gastronomic revolution of the 1960s and 1970s. What distinguishes this book from many others, and what probably keeps it in print, is the comprehensive nature of the recipe selection and the quantity of information conveyed. For that reason it makes a good reference book, and, as noted earlier in the introduction, it makes good reading even for the gourmet who never goes near a stove.

A second similarly sized and similarly priced volume was first published in 1957 and also was issued in a second revised edition in 1965. While Volume One covers all aspects of food and its presentation, Volume Two enters into more detail on such things as French pastry, outdoor cookery, the buffet and its garnishes, pâtés and wine. As in Volume One, recipes in the second book range in difficulty from the relatively simple to culinary masterpieces requiring considerable prior knowledge and skill.

The volumes are well illustrated with color photographs and charming, informal line drawings. Each volume is provided with an adequately detailed index, but there is no consolidated index for both volumes.

Recipe titles are set in the margin in eye-catching red ink. Recipes are cast in a narrative style, with no separate listing, or boldface type, for ingredients, a style that may take some getting used to.

PRACTICAL COOKERY

Kansas State University's *Practical Cookery: A Compilation of Principles of Cookery and Recipes*, 24th ed. (New York: John Wiley & Sons, 1976), has a plodding, take-nothing-for-granted approach to the subject. Compiled by the school's Department of Foods and Nutrition, it is widely used as a home economics textbook.

This approach has certain advantages. All the basics are here, and they are expressed with admirable succinctness. That this is a sound approach is evident from the longevity of this book, which has been in print since 1912 and has gone through 23 revisions. On the other hand, it leads to such statements as, "Hot food should be hot, cold foods cold, and neither type should stand long enough to lose quality."

The 700 recipes are divided among 28 chapters that cover all phases of the meal (appetizer to dessert), and principal foods (meat, vegetables, etc.), including baking, preserving and the etiquette and service of the table. A general-information chapter discusses nutrition, food groups, basic processes in food preparation, techniques, temperatures, measurements and equivalents, and presents an extensive table giving the number of servings per pound of common foods as purchased.

The few illustrations in this book are reserved for the etiquette and service chapter. Black-and-white photographs depict proper ways of holding utensils, while table settings are illustrated with diagrams.

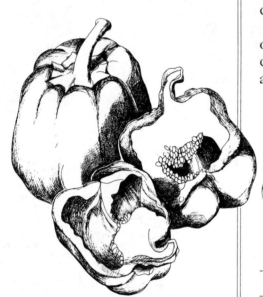

TONGUE CREOLE

| 1 tablespoon fat |
| 1 slice onion, finely chopped |
| 1 shallot, if desired, chopped |
| 1 clove garlic, if desired |
| 1 tablespoon green pepper, chopped |
| 1 tablespoon red pepper, chopped |
| 1 teaspoon paprika |
| ½ tablespoon flour |
| 2 cups tomatoes |
| 1 teaspoon salt |
| 1 teaspoon sugar |
| 1 boiled tongue, fresh small |

Cook onion, garlic, shallot, peppers, and flour in fat 3 to 5 minutes. Add tomatoes, sugar, and seasonings. Mix well. Place tongue in casserole. Add sauce. Bake ½ hour in moderate oven (375 degrees F.). One and one-half pound tongue, six servings.

THE COMPLETE GALLOPING GOURMET

A TV chef of the 1969–71 seasons, Graham Kerr here collects the more than 600 recipes presented on his show for CBS. *The Complete Galloping Gourmet* (New York: Grosset & Dunlap, 1972; London: W.H. Allen, 1973) is also notable for its excellent lessons in basic techniques.

Kerr trained in a hotel school and managed restaurants in his native England before becoming a food consultant to the New Zealand armed forces. He produced his first cooking show in Auckland, then had a four-year run on Australian television before coming to the United States.

His approach to technique is basically French, with, as he puts it, "the hard edges somewhat softened." He agrees with Escoffier that stocks are the foundations of cuisine. After bowing to the master, he suggests alternatives called "short stocks" that take 1½ to two hours to make rather than the 12 the classic stocks require.

However, this is not, generally speaking, a shortcut book. There is a well-rounded selection of recipes covering all courses. Each is labeled with a series of symbols that tell the reader at a glance whether it is an inexpensive or luxury dish, time-consuming or quick, for hot or cold weather, and an original or borrowed recipe.

There are excellent step-by-step color photographs illustrating the preparation of many dishes, plus many more of finished dishes.

SECRETS OF BETTER COOKING

Behind the piquant title lurks a good, basic cookbook. Reader's Digest's *Secrets of Better Cooking* (Pleasantville, N.Y.: Reader's Digest Association, 1973) seems principally aimed at the beginner, although many of the 600 recipes will also appeal to the experienced cook.

The title does promise secrets, though, and the publisher delivers. The text is studded with little symbols marking the "simple secrets expert cooks use to produce gourmet dishes quickly and easily." For example, "To a French chef, nutmeg is a must with fresh spinach," and "When cooking tomatoes, always add 1 teaspoon sugar for each four tomatoes. It does not make them sweet, but brings out their flavor and color."

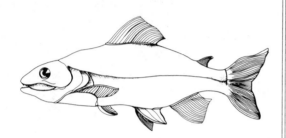

The author's approach is comprehensive. There are preliminary chapters on nutrition, shopping, equipping the kitchen, the mechanics and chemistry of cooking, and herbs and spices. Principal recipe chapters start off with stocks (as do many great chefs) and sauces, then work through main courses, vegetables, baking, cold cookery, freezing, cheese and nuts, wines and spirits, and entertaining.

The text is replete with handy reference charts ("Weekly Food Plans for Low-Cost Budgets" and "Maximum Storage Times at 0 Degress F. for Meats") and useful color drawings ("Retail Cuts of Pork and Where They Come From" and "Correct Glasses" for various wines and spirits).

The writing style is businesslike, uncluttered and easy to follow, even where the going gets a little complicated, as in the following recipe:

MONSIEUR MANIÈRE FISH SOUP

Fish soups and chowders are also made by poaching. For this you can use any white-fleshed fresh or frozen fish.

3 tablespoons olive oil
1 garlic clove, minced
1 onion, chopped
½ teaspoon dried thyme
Pinch of ground saffron
1½ pounds fish fillets
½ teaspoon salt
¼ teaspoon pepper
1 cup dry white wine
2 cups water
⅓ cup tomato paste
½ teaspoon crushed fennel seeds
3 tablespoons brandy
2 cups heavy cream

Heat olive oil. Add garlic and onion. Brown lightly, then add thyme and a pinch of saffron. Stir until blended. Add fish fillets, salt and pepper. Stir lightly over medium heat, to heat and break up the fish while mixing with the onion. Add wine, water, tomato paste and fennel seeds. Bring to a boil, cover, then simmer over low heat for 15 minutes. Add brandy and heavy cream. Stir until hot. Serve with hot toast. Makes 6 to 8 servings.

Leftover poached fish can be used in countless ways—for salads, sandwich spread, soufflés and to fill omelets. [p. 390]

THE JOY OF COOKING

An American classic, Irma Rombauer and Marion R. Becker's *The Joy of Cooking,* rev. ed. (Indianapolis, Bobbs-Merrill, 1975; New York: New American Library, 1983 paperback) has been in print since 1931 and has sold about 15 million copies. In that time it has been through five major revisions and several minor ones, growing from a privately printed collection of recipes to an all-embracing kitchen bible for millions of Americans. Its more than 900 pages contain 4,500 recipes, basic cooking instructions, notes on special appliances, definitions of terms in common use, nutritional facts, tips on entertaining and menu suggestions. About the only global criticism of it is that the print is small.

An easy, conversational style and charming sense of humor have been the hallmarks of all editions. On learning to cook, the authors note, "We are told that a hard-boiled professional cook, when asked what she regarded as primary briefing for a beginner, tersely replied, 'Stand facing the stove.'" On ham, they quip, "Someone defined eternity as a ham and two people." In the midst of a recipe for cassoulet, they insert, "For this recipe you almost need a routing sheet. If, however, you follow directions, you may proceed with the self-confidence of the bullfighter who put mustard on his sword." On judging the heat of a brazier fire, they advise, "Hold your hands above the grill at about the same distance from the coals that the food will be while cooking, and think of the name of a four-syllable state—"Massachusetts" or "Mississippi" will do nicely. If you can pronounce it once before snatching your hand away, your coals are delivering high heat; twice, medium heat; if three times, low heat."

The Joy of Cooking is a treasure trove of charts and tables. They are placed strategically in the text, and there is, unfortunately, no master list of them; access is by subject through the index. One of the more useful and unusual occurs in the chapter "Know Your Ingredients" and is entitled, "Equivalents and Substitutions for Common Ingredients." For example, if you want to know what can be substituted for one ounce of chocolate, the chart tells you 3 tablespoons cocoa plus 1 tablespoon butter or fat, or 3 tablespoons carob powder plus 2 tablespoons water.

Early on, Irma Rombauer developed a recipe style all her own, a format that works the ingredient listings into the directions, setting them apart in boldface columns.

THE COMPLETE ASIAN COOKBOOK

Charmaine Solomon's *The Complete Asian Cookbook* (New York: McGraw-Hill, 1976) is an all-inclusive survey of the major cooking styles of a large triangular area bounded by Karachi to the west, Tokyo to the east and Jakarta to the south. This is a considerable achievement, considering the diversity of the area and the intricacies of the cuisines. On the other hand, as the author points out, food crosses geographic and political boundries, so that many similarities are found in the styles of Malaysia and Indonesia, and likewise for those of India, Pakistan, Bangladesh and Kashmir.

With this in mind, she groups the recipes into 13 chapters, covering countries as follows: India and Pakistan, Sri Lanka, Indonesia, Malaysia, Singapore, Burma, Thailand, Cambodia and Laos, Vietnam, the Philippines, China, Korea and Japan. Accompanying these chapters are four others presenting an introduction to Asian ingredients and special techniques, a guide to weights and measures, a useful guide to where to buy Asian ingredients, and two glossaries. The main glossary attacks the vexing problem of identifying ingredients common to several cuisines and that (such as chili) may have as many as nine different names (in Hindi, *lal mirich;* in Thai, *prik chee pha;* in Indonesian, *lombok,* etc.). The second glossary (under "Equivalents or Substitutes") addresses another language problem caused by the book's Australian origin, that of translating their kitchen lingo into ours—e.g., their cornflour is our corn starch, their bream is our sole, and their skirt steak is our flank steak.

Apart from that possible source of confusion, the recipes are clearly detailed (weights in both metric and avoirdupois) and give good results. They total approximately 750. The book is particularly well served by excellent color photographs that depict not only finished dishes but also groups of ingredients. The latter are an invaluable aid in familiarizing oneself with exotic items.

Charmaine Solomon is a native of Sri Lanka. The following dish is a staple of the Sri Lankan diet:

LUNU MIRIS SAMBOLA
Ground Onion and Chilli Sambol

(This simple sambol is as basic to the food of Sri Lanka as salt and pepper are to Western food. Very hot, very acid and distinctly salty, it is often the only accompaniment to serve with rice, boiled yams, manioc or sweet potato, or any of the starches that are the staple of the native diet.)

10 dried chillies
1 tablespoon pounded Maldive fish* or dried prawns
1 small onion, chopped
lemon juice and salt to taste

Remove stalks from chillies and, if a less hot result is preferred, shake out the seeds. Pound all together in a mortar and pestle. In Sri Lanka this would be either pounded or ground on the grinding stone. It can be done in a blender, but a wet result is not desirable. It should be a paste. Serve with rice or pittu**. [p. 155]

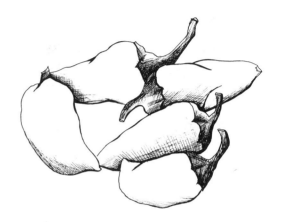

THE CHEZ PANISSE MENU COOKBOOK

Alice L. Waters's *The Chez Panisse Menu Cookbook* (New York: Random House, 1982) bears careful reading and rereading. The author's passion for fresh food and fine cooking is inspiring. At the same time, it makes you want to quit reading and start cooking.

Alice Waters cooks in a style that has come to be called "California French"—i.e., fine French cooking adapted to American tastes and to the ingredients California has to offer. A native of New Jersey, Waters did a year's study in France and was initiated there into the delights of French cooking. Returning to America, she opened a restaurant in Berkeley, California, called Chez Panisse, the title coming from a character in Marcel Pagnol's dramatic trilogy: *Marius,*

---

* Dried tuna from the Maldive Islands, it is sold in packets, broken into small chips, but needs to be pulverised further before use. Substitute dried prawn powder or Japanese *katsuibushi*.

**A combination of flour and freshly grated coconut steamed in a bamboo cylinder, the resulting roll, looking something like a white suet pudding but infinitely lighter in texture, is served with fresh coconut milk and curries and is especially popular as a breakfast dish.

Fanny, and *César.* Chez Panisse's format is unusual: Each night a single, five-course menu is offered. In the restaurant's more than 10-year life, menus have seldom been repeated. Alice Waters explains: "When people come to the restaurant, I want to insist that they eat in a certain way, try new things, and take time with the food."

From the beginning, Alice Waters drew inspiration from Elizabeth David's *French Country Cooking* and Richard Olney's *Simple French Food.* Alice Waters's food is simple in the sense that all nonessentials have been stripped away to bring out the best qualities of the freshest ingredients, achieving a cuisine that is sophisticated yet utterly straightforward. Many have been called "inspired transformations of classic French dishes."

The book includes some 120 menus grouped under such headings as "Inspirations and Adaptations," "Seasonal Menus" and "Menus for Special Occasions." They are preceded by a couple of chapters giving the author's personal credo on cooking and her principles of menu construction. Each menu is accompanied by reflective comments on its theme and the ingredients, and is followed by the recipes.

A sampling of menus: *spring*—wild mushrooms on croutons; thin pasta with spring vegetables; charcoal-grilled salmon with grilled red onions, and buckwheat crêpes with tangerines, glacéed fruit butter and eau-de-vie; *champagne dinner*—oysters on the half shell with mignonette sauce; blinis à la russe; sautéed duck livers with celery root; red leaf and radicchio salad, and fresh pineapple sherbet with champagne sabayon and candied rose petals Escoffier; *a dinner for Baudelairians*—*le crépuscule du soir* (puff pastry filled with black caviar, poached quail eggs and cream); *rêve Parisien* (timbale of duck liver with black pepper aspic); *le mort joyeux* (whole roast stuffed pigeon with black mushrooms); *les bijoux* (salad of endive and pink grapefruit) and *les promesses d'un visage* (ice creams with sauces and caramel),

OYSTERS ON THE HALF SHELL WITH MIGNONETTE SAUCE
(Serves 6)

5 to 6 dozen very fresh tiny oysters

¼ cup champagne vinegar

¾ cup dry white wine

2 shallots, finely minced

½ teaspoon cracked black pepper, or to taste

With an oyster knife, shuck the oysters curved side down to save their juices. Loosen the oysters from their muscles with the knife. Mix the champagne vinegar with the white wine, the minced shallots, and the cracked black pepper. Serve the sauce in three or four small bowls so that people may dip their oysters in the sauce if they like. [p. 86]

BETTER THAN STORE-BOUGHT

Helen Witty and Elizabeth Schneider Colchie's *Better than Store-Bought: A Cookbook* (New York: Harper & Row, 1979) specializes in recipes usually left out of general cookbooks. They themselves described the book as "largely a revival of formulas" because they take aim at products nearly everyone buys already prepared and prepackaged. Examples are corned beef, ricotta, cranberry juice, coarse-ground mustard, sour cream, dill pickles, liverwurst and marshmallows.

Their message is that you can save money, delight your taste buds and reduce heartburn or other unpleasant after-effects if you make these products at home. Some of the improvements they cite are liverwurst free of nitrates; dill pickles free of garlic oil or other things that cause heartburn; reduced amounts of sugar in such things as peanut butter, pickled herring, bread, ketchup, Marinara sauce and yogurt; additive-free recipes for bread, sausages, relishes, candied fruits and pudding mixtures; and hamburger buns that have taste, texture and substance. They also promise real savings on such expensive foods as smoked chicken, *caponata*, pickled Jerusalem artichokes, bitter-orange marmalade and *cornichons*.

They do not claim to re-create name brands. And, with refreshing humility, they admit failure with certain delicacies—good hard pretzels, jelly beans, matzos, halvah, home-cured green olives and Turkish delight.

There are no illustrations, but the more than 250 recipes are supplemented by notes on preparation, notes on equipment, a list of mail-order sources of supply and an index.

CORN CHIPS

1 cup warm (100 degree) water

1 egg yolk

1 teaspoon salt

¾ cup masa harina, or as needed*

Corn oil for frying

1. In a mixing bowl, whisk the water, egg yolk, and salt together until thoroughly mixed. Gradually add enough *masa harina* to make a soft dough, just stiff enough not to stick to your fingers.
2. In a heavy skillet, or an electric one, preheat frying oil at least 2 inches deep to 375 degrees.
3. Fit a cooking press or pastry bag with the plate designed to make a flat, ribbed shape and fill it with *masa* dough.
4. Press out into the hot oil a few short lengths of dough, enough to cover only about half the surface of the frying oil. Fry the ribbons, turning them once, just until they are golden brown. Lift the corn chips from the oil with a slotted spoon or skimmer and drain them on a cookie sheet covered with paper towels. Repeat until all the *masa* dough has been used. [p. 117]

---

* *masa harina* is packaged by at least one major cereal manufacturer with nationwide distribution and is to be found in Hispanic markets and in some supermarkets in large cities. Cornmeal cannot be substituted for it.

CHAPTER FIVE

Cuisine
Cookbooks

Americans have become terribly food conscious in the past two decades. At one end of the scale, this has been expressed in a preoccupation with nutrition and diet, on the other, it has meant an intense interest in fine cooking. These factors, combined with the boom in foreign travel starting in the 1960s, have sparked a trendy fascination with various foreign cooking styles. The first such was touched off by Julia Child's *Mastering the Art of French Cooking* in 1961. Succeeding years have seen boomlets of interest in Chinese cooking, Greek cooking, fine Italian cooking, then *nouvelle cuisine* (the new style of French cooking) and lately, Japanese (especially *sushi*), Thai and Vietnamese food.

This chapter attempts to cover all cooking styles identifiable by nation or geographical area. Regrettably, owing to limitations on space, a particular cuisine may not have a separate entry of its own. In most such cases, a discussion of it can be found in a regional cookbook. Indonesia is a case in point; there is no single title on Indonesian cuisine in this list, but it is well covered in books dealing with Southeast Asia. Likewise, the cuisine of Canada is discussed in several books on American cooking. For Australia and New Zealand, the best bet is a book on international cuisine.

UNITED STATES

What is American cooking? Hamburgers, hot dogs and chili con carne? That answer would satisfy some people, but not the folks who write cookbooks and cook. They might beg the question with, "American cooking is cooking done in America." That doesn't tell us much, but it may have to do, because further attempts at definition get pretty murky. Consider chef Louis Szathmary's formulation: "those distinctively American methods, procedures and utensils first used by the Native Americans, and later by the colonists, pilgrims and immigrants, in preparing nourishment and enjoyment the native flora and fauna of the American continent, as well as the crops and animals subsequently domesticated by pre-Columbian Indians and American agriculturalists." This either means Indian cooking, or cooking done in America. In any case, the latter definition fits the literature of American cooking.

James Beard's American Cookery (Boston: Little, Brown, 1972; paperback edition also) comes as close as any to being a definitive book on American cooking. Beard is one of

America's leading cookery experts and writers, and here he has compiled more than 1,500 recipes representing many facets of American cooking—from *boeuf bourguignon* to hominy grits. Recipes are spiced with lively opinions, and regional specialties are well delineated. Beginners should have no problem because the directions are clear and specific, and the text is illustrated with excellent line drawings.

The Fannie Farmer Cookbook first appeared in 1896 and remains among the top ten best-selling cookbooks of all time. Marion Cunningham and Jeri Laber's *The Fannie Farmer Cookbook,* 12th ed. (New York: Knopf, 1979; London: J. Norman, 1981) is, in the words of the authors, "not an encyclopedia but a daily working cookbook with easy, solid recipes that appeal to brides and veterans." The 1,839 recipes were selected to reflect a modern version of Farmer's principles of cooking from scratch, with detailed instructions and nutritional enhancement. It is a well-researched and modern all-purpose cookbook.

Another sound, comprehensive treatment is Melanie de Proft's *The American Family Cookbook* (Chicago: Delair, 1980; St. Louis, Mo.: Fireside Books, 1981, paperback). This book was first issued in 1974 by the Culinary Arts Institute. Recipes are arranged by course with additional chapters on baking, beverages, preserving, outdoor cooking, low-calorie foods, meal planning and so on.

The Better Homes and Gardens Classic American Recipes (Des Moines: Meredith, 1982) is a succinct, profusely illustrated collection that reflects a medley of cultures. Recipes are divided by region, then arranged by main dishes, side dishes, desserts, snacks and appetizers. Classic recipes include Philadelphia pepper pot, Kentucky burgoo, beef pot roast, tacos, beef teriyaki with pineapple, basic beef stew and roast turkey.

Adelle Davis's *Let's Cook It Right,* new rev. ed. (New York: Harcourt, Brace & World, 1970) is a general-purpose cookbook that emphasizes nutrition and the preparation of food in such a way as to retain both flavor and nutrients.

The history of food and eating in America makes fascinating reading. Although there seems to be no definitive study, the following three titles manage a pleasing blend of chronicle and recipes. Evan Jones's *American Food: The Gastronomic Story,* 2nd ed. (New York: Random House, 1981, paperback) is highly readable, and weaves recipes into the text, then prints them again at the end of the book. *The American Heritage Cookbook* (New York: American Heritage/Bonanza Books, 1982), first published in 1964, features the writings of such latter-day luminaries as Cleveland Amory, Russell Lynes and Lucius Beebe. Louis Szathmary's *American Gas-*

BOURBON CORN CHOWDER

Many Chinese restaurants use canned creamed corn in their soups. I have found that works very well in this chowder. You can, of course, use fresh corn scraped off the cob. But if you do use the canned corn and have on hand either canned or homemade chicken stock, I think you will find this a delicious—and quick—soup. It is the kind of soup that can make a lunch if served in a large bowl, with a salad and dessert.

4 tablespoons unsalted butter
¾ cup chopped onion
2½ cups canned creamed corn
¼ cup bourbon
¼ teaspoon grated nutmeg
1 teaspoon kosher salt
Freshly ground black pepper
2 to 3 drops Tabasco sauce
½ cup chicken stock
½ cup heavy cream

Melt the butter in a saucepan. Add the onion and cook until transparent. Stir in the corn.

Heat the bourbon in a small pan. Ignite the alcohol and let it flame for 1 minute. Pour the bourbon, still flaming, over the corn mixture. Stir in the remaining ingredients. Heat thoroughly and serve hot.

Note: if you prefer a thinner soup, add more stock.

Barbara Kafka, *American Food and California Wine* (New York and London: Harper & Row, 1981), p. 40.

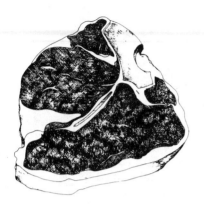

tronomy (Chicago: H. Regenery, 1974) is a portfolio of culinary history and recipes that fit the formula mentioned at the beginning of this section. Examples of the recipes are Brunswick stew, hamburger pie, wild onions and eggs, and oyster shortcake. Special sections include American foods, American methods and conversion of old recipes for today's uses. Illustrations consist of 90 period etchings, woodcuts, prints and phtographs.

At the opposite end of the scale are two books that adopt a trendy, on-the-edge stance. Barbara Kafka's *American Food and California Wine* (New York and London: Harper & Row, 1981) urges us to create our own food using good local ingredients, seasonings from all over the world and the techniques of the past 150 years. She includes 37 recipes, examples of which are smoked salmon mousse and Cajun gumbo. The Metropolitan Home Editors' *New American Cuisine* (New York: Harmony Books, 1981) proclaims sophisticated confidence and innovative joy to be the culinary tone of the 1980s. This new cuisine is based on these principles: freshest ingredients, stylish presentation, and the ingenious and efficient use of time.

REGIONAL

Jean Anderson's *The Grass Roots Cookbook* (New York: Times Books, 1977) has recorded regional recipes much in the manner of a musicologist recording folk music. Her purpose is to save old-fashioned American cooking from extinction. The country is divided by regions; several cooks from each region are selected. All recipes start from scratch.

A readable, well-illustrated tour of U.S. regional cooking is offered in the eight-volume Time-Life series *American Cooking* (New York and London: Time-Life Books, (1968–1971). The titles of the volumes are *American Cooking, Creole and Acadian, New England, Southern Style, Eastern Heartland, The Great West, The Melting Pot* and *The Northwest*.

Raymond Sokolov's *Fading Feast* (New York: Farrar, Straus & Giroux, 1981) is a collection of two dozen essays with recipes, based on the theme that distinctive American regional cooking is disappearing under the onslaught of gradual cultural homogenization. Writing for *Natural History* magazine, Sokolov sought out the last great exponents of such regional specialties as Cajun sausages or Smithfield hams, then wrote about them with a blend of scholarship, wit and pioneer spirit. This is a treasure trove of recipes, but makes no attempt at being comprehensive.

INTERNATIONAL

Craig Claiborne's *New York Times International Cookbook* (New York: Harper & Row, 1971) is a solid introduction to about 50 of the world's cuisines. The arrangement is alphabetical, from Armenia to Turkey, with the recipes for each country organized from appetizer to dessert. There are about 1,000 recipes here, all laid out with step-by-step directions, using American measures.

The following two offerings are brief, comprehensive and beautifully illustrated. *Better Homes and Gardens Classic International Recipes* (Des Moines: Meredith, 1982, paperback) divides the world into 15 areas—Africa, Caribbean, Far East, etc.—and provides each with a culinary introduction. The 300 recipes use easily obtainable ingredients. *The International Cookbook* (Camden, N.J.: Campbell Soup Co., 1980) covers 25 countries in 10 sections, providing each with a cultural/gastronomic introduction and glossary. There are more than 300 recipes in its 300 pages.

The Time-Life International Cookbook (New York: Holt, Rinehart & Winston, 1977) dispenses with introductory notes and goes straight to the recipes, of which there are about 500. Recipes are arranged by course, and each has its title in the original language with an English translation. The index is multilingual.

For a peek at what it all means, try Jessica Kupfer's *The Anthropologists' Cookbook* (New York: Universe Books; London: Routledge & Kegan Paul, 1977). Ethnologists collected these recipes from around the globe (omitting India and China), and they comment on the significance of specific dishes and modes of preparation. Included is a short essay by Claude Lévi-Strauss on the symbolic and structural meaning of food and eating. Recipes use imperial and metric measures, with a table provided for converting to American measures.

The following people provide personal collections of recipes from various cuisines. M.F.K. Fisher's *With Bold Knife and Fork* (New York: Putnam, 1979, paperback) is a series of witty and engaging essays by one of America's foremost writers on food. She gives 140 of her favorite recipes, all using ordinary ingredients. Tom Margittai and Paul Kovi's *The Four Seasons: Splendid Recipes from the World Famous Restaurant* (New York: Simon & Schuster, 1980) collects some 250 inspired recipes from the kitchen of chef Josef Renggli. Some examples are sorrel vichyssoise, salmon escalopes with caviar, and chopped lamb steak with pine nuts. Vincent and Mary Price's *A Treasury of Great Recipes: Famous Specialties of*

VEGETARIANSKI PALACHINKI
Bulgarian Herb Pancakes

3 eggs
1 cup finely chopped fresh parsley
½ cup finely chopped scallions, including 2 inches of the green tops
½ cup finely cut fresh dill leaves
1 teaspoon salt
Freshly ground black pepper
3 tablespoons butter
2 tablespoons vegetable oil

With a whisk or fork, beat the eggs together in a bowl until they are well blended. Stir in the parsley, scallions, dill, salt and a few grindings of black pepper. Taste for seasoning. In a heavy 10- to 12-inch skillet, melt the butter with the oil over moderate heat. When the foam begins to subside, drop about 2 tablespoons of the egg-and-herb mixture into the pan and flatten it into a pancake about 2 inches in diameter. Make about 4 or 5 more pancakes in similar fashion, leaving about an inch between them in the pan. Fry for 2 or 3 minutes on each side, or until the pancakes are golden brown and crisp around the edges. Place the finished pancakes side by side on a heated platter and set aside while you fry the rest, adding more butter and oil to the pan when necessary.

When all the pancakes are done, serve at once as a vegetable accompaniment to meats, poultry or fish.

Michael and Frances Field, *A Quintet of Cuisines*. Foods of the World (New York: Time-Life Books, 1970), p. 90.

the World's Foremost Restaurants Adapted for the American Kitchen (New York, Grosset & Dunlap, 1965) is a lavish production, featuring elegant recipes from 34 great European and 35 great American restaurants, plus a collection of Price household favorites. Of the 700 recipes, most are time-consuming and expensive. Mimi Sheraton's *From My Mother's Kitchen: Recipes and Reminiscences* (New York: Harper & Row, 1979) is a collection of eclectic and ethnic recipes. Her lighthearted reminiscences make for enjoyable reading outside the kitchen as well.

Michael and Frances Field's *A Quintet of Cuisines*, Foods of the World (New York: Time-Life Books, 1970) covers the cooking of 10 countries, which the compilers have lumped into five "mini-cuisines:" the Low Countries (Belgium, Luxembourg and the Netherlands); North Africa (Tunisia, Algeria and Morocco); Poland, Bulgaria and Rumania; and finally, Switzerland. This volume brings together the cuisines left out of the other volumes in the Foods of the World series, of which Field was general editor. The text concentrates more on food and cooking and less on cultural and scenic aspects than is usual for the series. A companion booklet contains 141 recipes.

LATIN AMERICA

The striking thing about the cuisines of Latin America is the way Native American foodstuffs and dishes have affected the cooking styles of the dominant cultures. Jonathan N. Leonard's *Latin American Cooking* (New York: Time-Life Books, 1968) devotes a full chapter to this influence and another to Latin American gifts to the world's larder, such as tropical fruits, vanilla and chocolate. This is a richly illustrated tour of the region, starting with Mexico and the Caribbean and proceeding south to Argentina and Chile. A companion booklet for use in the kitchen contains 106 recipes.

Equally comprehensive, though not as well illustrated, are Cora and Bob Brown's *South American Cookbook* (New York and London: Dover, 1971, paperback), which also contains recipes from Mexico and the Caribbean; Elisabeth Lambert Ortiz's *Book of Latin American Cooking* (New York: Knopf, 1979; London: J. Norman, 1980, paperback Random House, 1981); and Alex D. Hawkes's *The Flavors of the Caribbean and Latin America* (New York: Viking Press, 1978), which was singled out by Craig Claiborne as the best cookbook dealing with the region.

CARIBBEAN

Caribbean cooking is a cosmopolitan mixture of African and European influences modified by such local cultures as the Carib, the Taino and the Arawak. Three books give a comprehensive view of the area's cuisine, showing also how traditions of the separate islands have intermingled to produce something unique. Connie and Arnold Krochmal's *Caribbean Cooking* (New York: Quadrangle, 1975) presents 400 recipes, arranged by course, with historical and ethnic background notes. Features include a list of U.S. stores that carry specialized ingredients; tables of nutritional values; and a glossary.

Available in paperback is Elisabeth Lambert Ortiz's *Complete Book of Caribbean Cooking* (New York: M. Evans, 1983; London, Penguin, 1977). Ortiz has written "complete" books on other cuisines, such as Japanese and Latin American, and this one is a similarly workmanlike job. It brings out the eclectic nature of the foods and cooking methods, and it includes 450 recipes identified by country of origin. Features include a list of mail-order sources of ingredients, an index and a glossary.

Linda Wolfe's *The Cooking of the Caribbean Islands* (New York: Time-Life Books, 1970; London: 1971) is part of the Foods of the World series. It is a superbly illustrated tour of the islands, describing life, food and recipes.

For a classic look at a single cuisine, Carmen A. Valldejuli's *Puerto Rican Cookery* (New York: Pelican, 1983) is hard to beat. It is a translation from a book in Spanish that went through 25 editions under the title *Cocina criolla (Creole Cuisine)*. Unique flavorings such as *adobo* and *sofrito* are lovingly described. The indigenous inspiration of many dishes is emphasized by the Taino petroglyphs that begin each chapter. More than 425 recipes are included, plus indexes in English and Spanish, and a glossary of ingredients.

MEXICO

In a crowded field, Diana Kennedy's *The Cuisines of Mexico* (New York and London: Harper & Row, 1972) stands above the rest in a class by itself. It is the fruit of long residence in Mexico, where Kennedy collected recipes from all over, including those for delicate and subtle dishes quite unlike the stereotype of hot Mexican fare. The book excels in step-by-step instructions on the basics of preparing *masa* dishes, such as tortillas, tamales and *quesadillas*. It contains

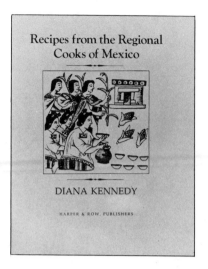

more than 300 recipes, many suitable for beginners; a glossary and pronunciation guide; a list of U.S. sources of ingredients; and a bilingual index. A complementary second book, *Recipes from the Regional Cooks of Mexico* (New York: Harper & Row, 1978), presents 120 new recipes in addition to repeating some of the basics.

A notch below Kennedy, but still serious and comprehensive, are three titles: Elisabeth Lambert Ortiz's *The Complete Book of Mexican Cooking* (New York: M. Evans, 1980, paperback; London: Bantam Books, 1980, paperback); Betty Blue's *Authentic Mexican Cooking* (Englewood Cliffs, N.J. and London: Prentice-Hall, 1978, paperback); and Sharon Cadwallader's *Savoring Mexico* (New York: McGraw-Hill, 1980, paperback). The first two arrange recipes by course, but Cadwallader has written a travel cookbook, where recipes are worked into a running narrative as she considers the 10 regions of Mexico, traveling clockwise from the northeast to the northwest.

In the quick, basic, full-color category, the two best bets are *Adventures in Mexican Cooking* (San Francisco: Ortho Books, 1979, paperback), which does it all in fewer than 100 pages, and Barbara Hansen's *Mexican Cookery* (Tucson, Ariz. and London: H.P. Books, 1980, paperback; New York: Dell, 1981, paperback). Hansen, who writes for the *Los Angeles Times* food section, provides a solid introduction to Mexican food by region, then lays out clear, easy-to-follow recipes by course.

B. Kraig's *Mexican-American Plain Cooking* (Chicago: Nelson-Hall, 1982, paperback) is not what you might think. It's not about how they do it in Texas, New Mexico or California, but about the cooking of Alice de Aguirre, a native of West Virginia, who operated the Hi-Lo Restaurant in Mexico City. Her methods are lovingly described by Kraig, one of her best customers, with the help of black-and-white photos and line drawings. Recipes are arranged by course.

WESTERN EUROPE

Kay Shaw Nelson's *The Best of Western European Cooking* (New York: T.Y. Crowell, 1976) is a collection of recipes that range from *haute cuisine* to folk dishes. Selective rather than comprenehsive, Nelson's book offers choices from an area stretching from Scandinavia to the Iberian peninusla, and from the British Isles to Austria. Arranged by course, the recipes are accompanied by a description of their origin, history and special attraction.

Bon Appetit's Country Cooking (Los Angeles: Knapp Press, 1978) is the result of a collaboration by leading food writers Robin Howe, Nina Froud, Evan Jones and Caroline Conran. Under the editorship of Heather Maisner, they have rediscovered and adapted recipes for 400 European country dishes. Magnificent color photographs make this a remarkably handsome book.

AUSTRIA

Austrian cuisine has more to offer than outstanding cakes and pastries, as Lillian Langseth-Christensen amply demonstrates in her *Gourmet's Old Vienna Cookbook* (New York: Gourmet Books, 1959). Subtitled *A Viennese Memoir,* it includes hundreds of recipes, representing all the traditional courses, interspersed with the colorful recollections of the author. Graphics are nostalgic line drawings and color photographs of finished dishes.

A more conventional cookbook is Gretel Beer's *Austrian Cooking and Baking* (New York: Dover, 1975; London: A. Deutsch, 1954). Though much shorter, it has a varied selection of dishes and a special section on baking.

Olga and A. Hess's *Viennese Cooking* (New York: Crown, 1952) is an English-language adaptation of a standard German language work on Austrian cooking. The section on cakes and pastries is particularly strong.

BELGIUM

Nika Hazelton has produced a handy guide to Belgium in *The Belgian Cookbook* (New York: Atheneum, 1977, paperback). She discourses charmingly on Belgian history, culture and customs, as well as ways of preparing food. Those who know something of Belgian cooking will find familiar specialties like brussels sprouts, Belgian endive and waterzooi (a fish or chicken stew), plus many unusual dishes, in the 137 recipes. Many are appropriate for beginners.

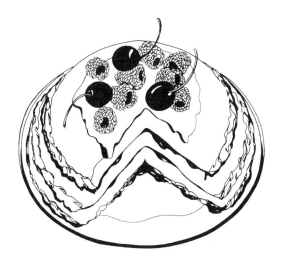

BRITISH ISLES

British cooking is lightly regarded in gastronomic circles, but this view neglects its many virtues. Adrian Bailey's *The Cooking of the British Isles* (New York and London: Time-Life

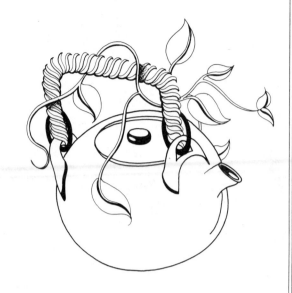

Books, 1969) stresses the variety and high quality of British foodstuffs, and the simplicity of their preparation. The book takes us through England, Scotland, Wales, Northern Ireland and Eire, with ample and pleasing photographs of food, finished dishes and local scenery. Bailey opens with a strong point, the traditional British breakfast, then covers country recipes, tea, beef, cheese, fish, game, and drinking habits. This fine overview is entertainingly written. A companion booklet for use in the kitchen contains 110 recipes.

England

Elizabeth Ayrton's *English Provincial Cooking* (New York: Harper & Row, 1980; London: Penguin, 1977, paperback) uses a systematic regional approach. Proceeding counterclockwise, she gives recipes and background notes in sections devoted to East Anglia, the North, the Midlands, the West Country, the South and Southeast, the Home Counties, London, and then All England. Recipes use imperial and metric measures. A single section of color photos depicts food by region.

Chef-restaurateur Michael Smith resurrects many elegant dishes from the 18th and 19th centuries in his *Fine English Cookery* (New York and London: Faber & Faber, 1980, paperback). Despite the emphasis on elegance, many recipes are relatively simple to prepare and are suitable for beginners; the 250 recipes include many well-known and homely dishes as well.

Though scholarly, Elizabeth David's *Spices, Salt and Aromatics in the English Kitchen* (New York: Penguin Books, 1981, paperback) is never boring or pedantic. The book goes into the history and use of such spices as nutmeg, juniper and cardamom, and highlights the influence of trade with the East in the development of English cuisine. Its 325 recipes are easy to follow.

Ireland

Theodora Fitzgibbon's *A Taste of Ireland in Food and Pictures* (New York: Irish Book Center; London: Pan/David & Charles, 1970, paperback) combines fascinating old photographs with traditional Irish recipes. The photographs (all black and white, and mostly from the 19th century) depict Irish scenes. Recipes range widely from plain tripe and corned beef and cabbage to such grand fare as Wellington steak and Dublin lawyer (lobster in cream, flambéed with whiskey). All have been adapted for the modern kitchen.

Scotland

Scottish food has much in common with that of other Celtic areas, such as Ireland, Wales and Brittany, but it has been strongly influenced by France and Scandinavia. Theodora Fitzgibbon points out similarities (crêpes, oatmeal in cake or cereal form, use of the griddle) while taking note of the Continental flavor of haggis, Lorraine soup and biscuits. Her *A Taste of Scotland in Food in Pictures* (New York: Irish Book Center; London Pan/David & Charles, 1971, paperback) emphasizes the traditional in recipes and 19th-century photographs. A sound, comprehensive approach to Scots cuisine is taken by G. Hay in his *The Commonsense Scots Cookery Book* (Englewood Cliffs, N.J.: Prentice-Hall; Brighton: Angus & Robertson, 1978). Features include color photographs of finished dishes, and chapters on breakfast, high tea and baking day. Recipes are given in imperial/metric measures.

Wales

Theodora Fitzgibbon collected many recipes from old family manuscripts to compile *A Taste of Wales in Food and Pictures* (New York, Irish Book Center; London: Pan Books, 1973, paperback). All are adapted for modern kitchens, and each recipe is faced by a 19th-century photograph of a Welsh scene. Recipes include familiar dishes, such as Welsh rarebit, plus many unusual ones.

FRANCE

Books on French cooking, as a group, outshine all others when it comes to complexity and quality, and in the United States are outnumbered only by those on American cooking. To simplify the discussion, they will be grouped into six categories: general books and *haute cuisine;* books by or about contemporary chefs; everyday French cooking; regional styles; simplified *haute cuisine* and the *nouvelle cuisine.*

In a class by itself is *Mastering the Art of French Cooking, 2* vols. (New York: Alfred A. Knopf, 1961, 1970; London: Cassell, 1963, 1970; Penguin, 1978, paperback). Volume 1 was written by Julia Child, Simone Beck and Louisette Bertholle; Volume 2 is by Julia Child and Simone Beck. Backed by Julia Child's charisma on her program on public television, these books gave new meaning to French cookery for the American kitchen. Food pundits reckon that the first volume was one of the two most influential cookbooks of the past two decades (the other being Hazan's *Classic Ital-*

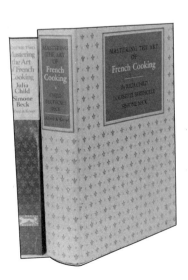

ian Cookbook) in shaping the consciousness of American cooks in the 1980s. It is a very practical modern cookbook and a good collection of classic and regional French recipes. Volume 2 deals with only seven subjects: soups from the garden and the sea, baking, chicken, charcuterie, vegetables and desserts. In all there are 900 recipes, with Volume 2 containing the index for both volumes.

Craig Claiborne and Pierre Franey's *Classic French Cooking* (New York and London: Time-Life, 1970) is an elegantly illustrated disquisition on the theory and practice of *haute cuisine*. They have taken a historical approach, and chapters are devoted to such luminaries as Carême and Escoffier. On the practical side, difficult preparations are illustrated, and the proper selection and "marriage" of foods are discussed. This opulent art seems to be passing into extinction, but the authors have captured its glory days in readable style. A companion booklet contains 100 recipes.

The Best of French Cooking (New York: Larousse; London: Hamlyn, 1978) is a large-format book in which each one of its more than 300 recipes is pictured in color. Recipes range from *haute cuisine* to country cooking, use metric, imperial and American measures, are clearly and simply written and bear both the French name and an English translation.

Certain standard manuals of French cuisine are accessible to inexperienced cooks as well as experts. Following are two of the best. Louis Diat's *Gourmet's Basic French Cookbook: Techniques of French Cuisine* (New York: Gourmet Magazine, 1961) might appeal most strongly to a professional cook, having as it does sections on restaurant and hotel kitchen management, clothing, cutting and carving. Yet it deals with the basics of food preparation and presents more than 1,000 clear, well-laid-out recipes for French specialties. Henri-Paul Pellaprat's *Modern French Culinary Art*, rev. ed. [edited by John Fuller] (Boston: CBI Publishing, 1974; London: Virtue, 1978), was first published in 1935 but remains a practical and comprehensive manual for the experienced cook or for the beginner who wishes to master French cuisine. More than 2,000 recipes are included, plus 300 color pictures and 150 line drawings.

For professional chefs and practitioners, L. Saulnier's *Le Repertoire de la Cuisine*, 13th ed. (Woodbury, N.Y.: Barron's Educational Series, 1976) presents more than 7,000 recipes in brief form. It is a worthy reference book for a high-class caterer. Recipes are arranged in course order.

Raymond Sokolov's *The Saucier's Apprentice* (New York: Alfred A. Knopf, 1976) is a comprehensive and easy-to-understand book on French sauces. The book is an elaborate primer, starting with basic sauces and showing how they are transformed into the classics. Sokolov is a former food editor of *The New York Times*.

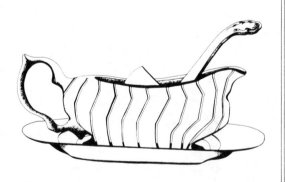

Chefs

Paul Bocuse has been called the world's "greatest living chef." In *Paul Bocuse's French Cooking* (New York: Random House, 1977) he has produced an encyclopedic volume containing more than 1,100 recipes and that is good reading as well. *Paul Bocuse in Your Kitchen* (New York: Pantheon, 1982), which aims at "demystifying French cooking," is an introduction to classic French cooking, using simple ingredients, and including many recipes that the most inexperienced cook can do.

The Master Chefs of France Recipe Book (New York: Everest House, 1982), compiled by Robert Courtine, food and restaurant editor of *Le Monde,* presents recipes from 300 great French restaurants, each of which is depicted by a color photograph or a drawing.

The prolific Elisabeth Lambert Ortiz toured France to compile *Cooking with the Young Chefs of France* (New York: M. Evans, 1981), whose more than 300 recipes embody a contemporary interpretation of traditional cuisine. Drawings illustrate difficult techniques and unusual equipment. Madeleine Peter's *Favorite Recipes of the Great Women Chefs of France* (New York: Holt, Rinehart & Winston, 1979) selects 28 women chefs who own restaurants. Recipes represent various culinary styles, including *haute cuisine, nouvelle cuisine* and home cooking at an elevated level. Most are simple, honest and easy to prepare. The background sketches of each chef make interesting reading.

Alain Senderens is chef-owner of L'Archestrate, a Parisian restaurant of rare excellence and international fame. In *The Three-Star Recipes of Alain Senderens* (New York: William Morrow, 1982) he makes a selection of recipes for amateur cooks. Philip and Mary Hyman have translated and adapted these recipes, inserting American measures and suggesting American ingredients where alternates can be used. Recipes are arranged by course and vary from intermediate level to difficult.

Everyday Cooking

Auguste Escoffier's *Ma Cuisine* (New York: A & W Publishers, 1978) is considered the bible of everyday French cooking, also known as *cuisine bourgeoise.* The book is much easier to use than his classic *Le Guide Culinaire* but still demands a level of skill. The American edition adds U.S. measures and suggestions for alternate ingredients. Jacqueline Gérard and Madeleine Kamman's *Larousse French Home Cooking* (New York: McGraw-Hill, 1980) excels with its format, which sets up each recipe in a clever and economical way and classifies each as traditional, time-saving, modern

SAUMON CRU AUX HERBES
Raw Salmon with Herbs
Christiane Conticini

This delicious hors d'oeuvre is nicest served on individual plates.

1 pound raw salmon—choose a piece from the middle of the body
4 shallots, minced
juice of 1 lemon
2 teaspoons of green peppercorns, crushed
1 tablespoon minced chives
2 tablespoons minced fresh chervil, or 1 tablespoon dried
2 tablespoons mild olive oil, preferably French
1 tablespoon cognac

Peel the skin off the salmon, using a small sharp knife inserted between the skin and flesh, if necessary. Slicing parallel to the backbone, cut the flesh into thin slices. They should look like slices of smoked salmon.

Mix together the remaining ingredients (if the chervil is fresh, cut it into pieces with scissors, don't chop it), then marinate the salmon in the mixture for 30 minutes in the refrigerator. Without draining the salmon, arrange it attractively on individual small plates and distribute the herbs and marinade over the pieces again, but a bit sparingly.

Serve with triangles of thin toast (as with caviar), fresh unsalted butter and lemon wedges.

Madeleine Peter, comp., *Favorite Recipes of the Great Women Chefs of France* (New York: Holt, Rinehart & Winston, 1979), p. 56.

MADELEINES

MET	UK	US	
90 g	3 oz	6 Tb	Flour
	¼ tsp	¼ tsp	Salt
	2	2	Small eggs
90 g	3 oz	⅓ cup	Sugar
	½ tsp	½ tsp	Vanilla essence or orangeflower extract Grated rind ½ lemon
90 g	3 oz	¾ stick	Unsalted butter Icing/confectioners' sugar

Makes 18 small cakes

Melt the butter and let it cool to luke-warm. Set the oven to gas mark 4, 350 degrees F. Sift the flour and salt together. Butter and flour the madeleine moulds. Beat the eggs, using an electric beater if desired, until thick and pale yellow. Add the vanilla or orangeflower extract and gradually beat in the sugar. Continue to beat until the mixture is very light and fluffy. Sprinkle on a third of the flour, lemon rind and butter at a time and fold in carefully with a rubber spatula so as not to lose the airiness of the mixture. Fill the moulds three-quarters full with the mixture.

Bake for 15 minutes. When cool, turn out on to a cake rack and sprinkle with icing/confectioners' sugar.

Shirley King, *Dining with Marcel Proust: A Practical Guide to French Cookery of the Belle Epoque* (New York: W.W. Norton; London: Thames & Hudson, 1979), p. 121.

and original, or money-saving. This is an American translation of *La Cuisine de Jacqueline Gérard*. Its 280 recipes use American, metric and imperial measures.

Shirley King's *Dining with Marcel Proust* (New York: W.W. Norton; London: Thames & Hudson, 1979) is a nostalgic look at the bourgeois food of an earlier era. It contains period illustrations, quotes from Marcel Proust and recipes for food that is generally savory and unpretentious.

Jacques Pepin is a well-known chef and cooking demonstrator with a program on public television. His *Everyday Cooking with Jacques Pepin* (New York: Harper & Row, 1982) concentrates on old-fashioned family food and features detailed color pictures of all techniques and preparations. One of his earlier titles, *A French Chef Cooks at Home* (New York: Simon & Schuster, 1980, paperback), is a fine basic book with a comprehensive selection of recipes.

Regional

Samuel and Narcissa Chamberlain's *The Flavor of France in Recipes and Pictures* (New York: Hastings House, 1978) became an instant classic when it appeared in 1952. It was reissued recently and is a wonderful cook's tour of France. Each recipe is accompanied by a photograph of French scenery from the area where it originates.

Simone Beck's *Simca's Cuisine* (New York: Alfred A. Knopf, 1972) is a selection of menus and recipes mainly from Normandy, Alsace and Provence. Beck, who collaborated with Julia Child on *Mastering the Art of French Cooking*, here gives 200 of her own favorite recipes, many highly original and inspired. A sequel, *New Menus from Simca's Cuisine* (New York: Harcourt Brace Jovanovich; London: J. Murray, 1979), written with Michael James, includes 22 menus ranging from informal suppers to elegant buffets and includes a few contributions from regional America.

Anne Willan's *French Regional Cooking* (New York: William Morrow; London: Hutchinson, 1981) divides France into 12 regions and covers them systematically in this finely illustrated work. Willan is founding director of the École de Cuisine La Varenne in Paris. Recipes use American measures and give metric equivalents.

Richard Olney's *Simple French Food* (New York: Atheneum, 1974, paperback; London: J. Norman, 1981) brings personality and style to cooking instruction. This book specializes in *cuisine bourgeoise*, drawing ingredients from all over France but with the cooking in the style of Provence. This book is well written and is strong on basic ingredients and standard techniques. Suzanne McLucas's *A Provençal Kitchen in America* (Boulder, Colo.: Johnson Books, 1982) handily classifies her 300-plus recipes by degree of difficulty: very easy, intermediate, advanced.

Simplified

Isabelle Marique's *The French Cuisine of Your Choice* (New York: Harper & Row, 1981) presents 225 recipes for simplified classic cuisine designed to speed preparation and lower calories. Esther R. Solomon's *Instant Haute Cuisine: French Cooking American Style* (New York: M. Evans, 1977, paperback) takes 200 recipes, mostly classics, and "translates" them for the American kitchen. In one case, a recipe that calls for 30 separate ingredients and endless preparations has been simplified by substitution of six to seven packaged ingredients and cut to a half hour in preparation time.

Nouvelle Cuisine

Roy Andries de Groot provides a fine introduction to what he calls "Lo-High" cuisine in *Revolutionizing French Cooking* (New York: McGraw-Hill, 1976). Chapter One gives the basics; then he reviews the most important chefs, and their recipes, which have been converted to American measures. *Michel Guérard's Cuisine Gourmande* (New York: William Morrow, 1979; London: Macmillan, 1978) contains in Part One an especially clear explanation of the principles of the new lighter French cuisine, while Part Two—much the larger section—gives the recipes, many original, and all adapted to the American kitchen. *The Nouvelle Cuisine of Jean and Pierre Troisgros* (New York: William Morrow, 1978; London: Macmillan, 1980; 1982, paperback) is for the skilled and sophisticated cook who likes to experiment but wants to stay relatively slim. The two brothers are proprietors of a three-star restaurant in Roanne, France. Here they look at *cuisine minceur*, sparing no expense as they tackle *tête de veau*, young wild boar and pile on the truffles and pâté de fois gras.

GERMANY

If German cuisine brings to mind only potatoes, sauerkraut and sausages, read on for enrichment. Nika Hazelton's *The Cooking of Germany* (New York: Time-Life, 1969) is a sparkling cook's tour of the country organized by region—north,

central, south—documenting both the scenery and fine dishes with lush photographs. Although she notes that "German cooking is far more suited to the average American taste than that of other European nations" due to its stress on basic meat and potatoes, this entry in the Food of the World series contains only 74 recipes, ranging from beginner to intermediate. These plus another 30 recipes are contained in a separate small volume for use in the kitchen.

A classic treatise, Betty Wason's *The Art of German Cookery* (Garden City, N.Y.: Doubleday, 1967), brings together 300 traditional and modern recipes from hors d'oeuvres to dessert, plus sections on baking and German wines and beers. The index lists both German and American names of dishes.

Lüchow's is a legendary New York City restaurant operated by Jan Mitchell, who reveals some of his cooking secrets in *Lüchow's German Cookbook* (Garden City, N.Y.: Doubleday, 1952). The text is enlived by Ludwig Bemelman's droll sketches, and morsels of celebrity gossip between recipes.

Brigitte Shermer Simms's *German-American Cookery* (Rutland, Vt.: Charles E. Tuttle, 1967) takes its title literally by presenting instructions for typical and traditional dishes in both German and English, an undoubted attraction for students of the German language.

GREECE

In the past 15 years, Greek cuisine's soaring popularity has given rise to a number of sound and comprehensive books. These include Eva Zane's *Greek Cooking for the Gods* (San Francisco and London: 101 Productions, 1970; 1980, paperback); Lou Seibert Pappas's *Greek Cooking* (New York and London: Harper & Row, 1973, 1974) and a pair of titles from the Recipe Club of St. Paul's Greek Orthodox Church, *The Art of Greek Cookery* (Garden City, N.Y.: Doubleday, n.d.) and *The Regional Cuisines of Greece* (Garden City, N.Y.: Doubleday, 1981). The last two complement each other and are composed of the prized recipes of experienced cooks, mostly based on simple ingredients but ranging in difficulty from the simplest of vegetables to tricky filo roll spirals.

Somewhat different is Theonie Mark's *Greek Islands Cooking*, new ed. (North Pomfret, Vt.: David & Charles, 1979; London: Batford, 1978). Based on a PBS television series and keyed to the Aegean Islands, its 200 recipes, adapted to American cooks and kitchens, are grouped by seasons of the year, each section moving from appetizers to dessert. Special sections include a historical introduction to Greek cooking, an all-seasons chapter, basic techniques, and comments on coffee and wine.

HOLLAND

Helen Halverhout's *Dutch Cooking* (New York: Rogers Book Service, 1975; Amsterdam: De Driehoek, n.d., paperback) leans heavily toward such traditional dishes as spiced red cabbage, hotchpotch, Limberg pies and buttercakes. The chapter on Dutch food habits is enlightening and amusing. In the recipes, however, it is not clear whether the measures are imperial or American.

ITALY

Waverley Root's *The Cooking of Italy* (New York and London: Time-Life, 1968) reminds us that Italian cuisine is the mother cuisine, the source for all cuisines of Latin Europe. In a witty first chapter he explores the history of cooking in ancient Etruria and Rome. After an overview of modern cooking, and pasta, he tours the provinces, with brilliant photographs of each stop along the way. A companion booklet contains 101 recipes.

Enduring excellence is stressed in Marcella Hazan's *The Classic Italian Cookbook* (New York: Alfred A. Knopf, 1976; London: rev. ed., Norman & Hobhouse, 1982; Macmillan, 1981, paperback) and the sequel, *More Classic Italian Cooking* (New York: Alfred A. Knopf, 1978). Hazan's approach, which established a new standard among gourmet cooks, is characterized by absolute freshness of ingredients, homemade pasta and delicate, irresistible sauces. Many of the 250 recipes are appropriate for beginners, and illustrations include step-by-step photographic layouts for difficult techniques.

A comprehensive approach for the serious student is *Giuliano Bugialli's Classic Techniques of Italian Cooking* (New York: Simon & Schuster, 1982). Bugialli is a well-known cooking instructor in America who has written other books on the subject. This one is keyed to techniques: carving, basic preparations, chopping, grinding, etc. Recipes range from authentic regional dishes to the complex formality of *Alta Cucina*. There are many black-and-white, step-by-step illustrations, with finished dishes pictured in colored endpapers. The book contains more than 500 recipes, with appendices on wines, and an Italian/English glossary.

Two books that have stood the test of time are Elisabeth

David's *Italian Food*, 3rd ed. (New York and London: Penguin, 1970, paperback) and Ada Boni's *Talisman Italian Cookbook* (New York: Crown, 1972; London: Pan Books, 1975, paperback). David's treatment is historical and cultural as well as gastronomic. Particularly interesting among the 450 recipes are the sections on fish dishes, hors d'oeuvres and salads. The Boni book is a translation of an Italian best seller that gives a complete picture of Italian cooking, both traditional and modern.

For a quick but thorough approach, it is hard to beat James McNair's *Adventures in Italian Cooking* (San Francisco: Ortho Books, 1981, paperback). In fewer than 100 pages, McNair covers cooking techniques, kitchen necessities, special equipment and ingredients, then recipes from appetizers to desserts. It features profuse color illustrations and special sections on coffee, menus and suppliers. Similarly brief but complete is *Sunset* magazine's *Italian Cookbook*, 2nd ed. (Menlo Park, Calif.: Lane, 1981, paperback). It concentrates on the basics, and the 175 recipes are all accessible to beginners.

Regional enthusiasts will treasure Anna Martini's *Mondadori Regional Italian Cookbook* (New York: Crown, 1983). The book incorporates lavish color photography in an exhaustive region-by-region consideration of techniques and recipes. General sections include those on beef, cured meats and sausages, cheeses and kitchen equipment. The book contains more than 500 recipes, each designed to serve four. In a lower key, with less lavish production, are Nika Hazelton's *The Regional Italian Kitchen* (New York: M. Evans, 1978: 1983, paperback), which concentrates on recipes not generally known in America, and Wilma la Sasso's *Regional Italian Cooking: From the Alps to the Mediterranean* (New York: Macmillan; London: Collier-Macmillan, 1975, paperback), which packs more than 500 recipes into 270 pages.

Deserving special mention is Edward Giobbi's *Italian Family Cooking* (New York: Random House, 1978, paperback). The 200 recipes are served family style and do for six to eight persons. Craig Claiborne has pronounced this "an excellent, down-to-earth volume" whose recipes are inspired and easy to follow.

SCANDINAVIA

The cuisines of Denmark, Norway, Sweden and Finland have similarities, such as great cold dishes, as well as national specialties, such as Finnish natural foods and Swedish breads. Both aspects are dealt with in two overviews of the region. Madeleine Lundberg's *Scandinavian Cooking* (New York: Crown, 1976) groups recipes in the following categories: smorgasbord, meat dishes, fish dishes, soups, desserts, baking and Christmas fare. Features include scenic color photos and a metric conversion table. Dale Brown's *The Cooking of Scandinavia* (New York: Time-Life, 1968; London: Time-Life International, 1969) is a richly illustrated, country-by-country tour. Difficult preparations are illustrated, and foods and finished dishes are photographed. Chapter topics include cheeses, Christmas feasts and akvavit, the caraway-flavored liquor of the region.

Favorite Swedish Recipes (New York: Dover, 1975; London: Dover, 1977, paperback) edited by Sam Widenfelt (London) and Selma Wilfstrand (New York), is a standard work that has been in print for years both here and in Sweden. It presents 200 recipes and is well illustrated by both color and black-and-white photographs. Elise Sverdrup's *Norway's Delight* (River Edge, N.J.: Vanous, 1980, paperback) covers all types of Norwegian food.

Finnish personality and culture as well as Finnish cuisine are explained in Beatrice Ojakangas's *The Finnish Cookbook* (New York: Crown, 1964). Chapters are arranged by course, with a separate section on baking, and a reading list is included.

SPAIN AND PORTUGAL

Spain and Portugal have distinct cuisines, which in turn are strongly regional. Covering the whole of the Iberian peninsula, Peter S. Feibleman's The *Cooking of Spain and Portugal* (New York and London: Time-Life, 1969, 1970) stresses the differences. As an entry in the Food of the World series, the book is richly illustrated, covering not only food and finished dishes but also the characteristic lanscapes and markets of each region. Certain areas are spotlighted—for Spain, Andalusia, the Levant, Catalonia and the Basque frontier; and for Portugal, the rugged North and the Lisbon regions. The sections on sauces and seafood are excellent. A separately bound booklet contains 105 recipes.

Donald E. Asselin's *Portuguese-American Cookbook* (Rutland, Vt.: Charles E. Tuttle, 1966) presents a variety of traditional recipes adapted to American kitchens. Many are of the long-simmering variety. The text features line drawings, and an index is included.

William H. Emery's *The Flavor of Spain* (Boston: CBI Publishing Co., 1983) states boldly that Spanish cooking does not depend upon the heavy use of garlic and olive oil. Having laid that ghost, Emery covers not only the traditional courses but also goes into Spanish history, customs, provincial cooking styles, and guidelines for shopping. The text is simply written and contains useful charts and line drawings.

Another recent and comprehensive work is Betty Blue's *Authentic Spanish Cooking* (Englewood Cliffs, N.J.: Prentice-Hall, 1981). Blue is a professor of Spanish who has broadened her expertise to include both Mexican and Spanish cooking. The chapters on Spanish customs and cuisine and on fish and shellfish are especially interesting. Features are decorative line drawings, bilingual recipe titles and an index.

Two oldish but highly respected treatments of Spanish cuisine are available in paperback. They are Betty Wason's *The Art of Spanish Cookery* (New York: Cornerstone [Simon & Schuster], 1977) and Marina Pereyra de Aznar's *The Home Book of Spanish Cookery*, rev. ed. (London and New York: Faber & Faber, 1975). Both are comprehensive approaches, but Aznar stresses classic dishes common to both France and Spain.

Gerrie Beene and Miranda King's *Dining in Spain* (Rutland, Vt.: Charles E. Tuttle, 1969, paperback) gives classic recipes from famous restaurants in Spain. Clarita Garcia's *Clarita's Cocina: Great Traditional Recipes from a Spanish Kitchen* (Garden City, N.Y.: Doubleday, 1970) comes from the owner and operator of a celebrated Spanish restaurant in Tampa, Florida.

SWITZERLAND

Nika Hazelton, in *The Swiss Cookbook* (New York: Atheneum, 1973, paperback), has written a guide to the country and people as well as to the cooking. In stressing *au bleu* fish cooking, pasta, fondue and roast veal, she has chosen recipes that represent Swiss cooking rather than transplanted French, German or Italian cooking. Chapter topics include cheese, chocolate, wines and restaurant dining. Cultural note: In contrast to modest portions served at home, restaurant portions are huge. The 250 recipes are arranged by course.

EASTERN EUROPE

Most thorough in scope is Kay Shaw Nelson's *Eastern European Cookbook* (New York: Peter Smith, n.d.; London: Dover, 1978, paperback). A chapter each is devoted to Russia, Poland, East Germany, Czechoslovakia, Hungary,

Rumania, Bulgaria, Yugoslavia and Albania. Given the small space, the recipe selection is limited but represents the best from each country. The 400 recipes are clear and workable, and each section is introduced by a short history of the country and cuisine. Marina Polvay's *All Along the Danube: Classic Cuisines of Eastern Europe* (Englewood Cliffs, N.J. and London: Prentice-Hall, 1980, paperback), by limiting its scope to Austria, Germany, Czechoslovakia, Hungary, Yugoslavia, Rumania and Bulgaria, can afford a more complete recipe selection for each. Christmas recipes are especially notable. The food and history notes between recipes provide additional interest.

In a nostalgic vein is Joseph Wechsberg's *Cooking of Vienna's Empire* (New York and London: Time-Life, 1968), which is part of the richly illustrated Foods of the World series. This book harks back to an era that ended with World War I, although a chapter on up-to-date Austrian cooking is provided. A chapter each is devoted to the regional creations of Hungary, Czechoslovakia and Yugoslavia, and a companion booklet with 100 recipes is provided. Max Knight covers the same ground in *The Original Blue Danube Cookbook* (Berkeley, Calif.: Lancaster-Miller, 1979), but from the unique perspective of his mother's handwritten notes. He presents fine recipes from the old Austrian Empire (including those of individual nationalities), from boiled potatoes to Sacher Torte. Illustrations consist of decorative line drawings.

CROATIA

The ancient kingdom of Croatia is now a province of northwestern Yugoslavia, with its capital at Zagreb, and the Dalmatian coastline is one its most attractive areas. Alojzicje and Ruzica Kapetanovic's *Croatian Cuisine* (San Mateo, Calif.: Associated Publishers, 1978) presents more than 450 recipes whose characteristic ingredients include paprika, green and red peppers, fresh dairy products (especially sour cream), a wide variety of fresh fruits and vegetables, and many freshwater and saltwater fish. Sauerkraut is an important staple, and smoked bacon and onions are key flavoring elements. Dishes are named in both English and Croatian.

CZECHOSLOVAKIA

Two books on Czech cuisine represent a study in contrasts. Pat Martin's *The Czech Book: Recipes and Traditionals* (Iowa City, Ia.: Penfield, 1981) is a slender paperback volume that

PODVARAK
Chicken and Sauerkraut

To Serve 4 or 5

1½ pounds sauerkraut
A 3-pound frying chicken, cut up
Salt
7 tablespoons bacon fat or lard
½ cup finely chopped onions
¼ teaspoon finely chopped garlic
1 tablespoon finely chopped hot chili peppers
Freshly ground black pepper
½ cup chicken stock

Wash the sauerkraut under cold running water, then soak it in cold water 10 to 20 minutes to reduce its sourness. Squeeze it dry by the handful.

Wash the chicken pieces quickly under cold running water, pat them dry with paper towels and salt generously. Over high heat, in a heavy 10-inch skillet, heat 4 tablespoons of the fat until a light haze forms over it. Brown the chicken pieces a few at a time, starting with the skin sides down and turning them with tongs. As each browns, remove to a platter and add a fresh piece to the pan until all the chicken is done. Set aside.

Heat the rest of the fat in the skillet until a light haze forms over it and add the onions and garlic. Cook them for 2 or 3 minutes, or until the onions are slightly translucent. Add the sauerkraut, chili peppers, and a few grindings of black pepper. Cook uncovered for 10 minutes over medium heat. Using the tongs, lay the chicken pieces on top of the sauerkraut and pour the stock over the chicken. Bring the liquid to a boil, then reduce the heat to low and cook, covered, for 30 minutes, or until the chicken is tender. Serve the sauerkraut on a platter with the chicken, either surrounding it or as a bed for it.

Joseph Wechsberg, *The Cooking of Vienna's Empire*. Foods of the World (New York: Time-Life Books, 1968; London: Time-Life International, 1969), p. 164.

devotes as much space to background notes (Czech culture, dates, customs, celebrities) as it does to cooking. Nevertheless, it contains 180 recipes and numerous poster-type color photos. On the other hand, Joza Brizova's *Czechoslovak Cookbook* (New York: Crown, 1965) plunges directly into recipes (soup to nuts, plus baking and candy), with nary a word of orientation. The 700 recipes, names in both English and Czech, use American measures. There are no illustrations.

HUNGARY

George Lang's *The Cuisine of Hungary* (New York: Atheneum, 1971; 1982, paperback) is reputed to be the finest book in English on Hungarian cuisine. Lang, a restaurateur, amateur cook, and historian, brings considerable erudition to his historical and gastronomical notes on the different regions of Hungary, and the 300 recipes do justice to the variety found in this extraordinary and unique cuisine. It is much more than goulash and strudel, although these familiar dishes are adequately covered. The book includes 12 menus for regional and special-occasion dinners.

Plain Hungarian home cooking is the territory of E. Weiss and R. Buchan's *The Paprikás Weiss Hungarian Cookbook* (New York: William Morrow, 1979). Weiss is the proprietor of Paprika Weiss, the famous Hungarian food store in New York City. Here he selects his favorite recipes, "plain basic dishes of the kitchen of my childhood," which number more than 180 and range from soups through lunches, dinners, vegetables, side dishes and desserts.

The following three books are competent and well-rounded collections of Hungarian recipes: Charlotte Biro's *Flavors of Hungary* (San Francisco and London: 101 Productions, 1973, paperback); Lilla Deeley's *Favorite Hungarian Recipes* (New York: Peter Smith, n.d.; paperback, Dover, 1972; London: Dover, 1973, paperback) and Susan Derecskey's *The Hungarian Cookbook: The Pleasures of Hungarian Food and Wine* (New York: Harper & Row, 1972).

POLAND

As one would expect, Polish cooking closely resembles German and Russian cooking, yet Polish cooking shows signs of strong Italian, French and Jewish influence. The Culinary Arts Institute's *Polish Cookbook* (New York: Fireside Books, 1977; 1982, paperback) presents more than 400 recipes prefaced by an introduction to the history, natural resources and daily routines of the Polish nation. Chapters are arranged from appetizer to dessert, with special attention to fish, sausages and smoked meats, sour cream, mushrooms, beets, cabbage and game. All recipes use American measures and cooking equipment.

Two translations from the Polish are Marja Ochorowicz-Monatowa's *Polish Cookery* (New York: Crown, 1958) and Zofia Czerny's *Polish Cookbook* (River Edge, N.J.: Vanous, 1976; London: Collet's Holdings, 1976). Ochorowicz-Monatowa's book was first published at the turn of the century as a "Universal Cookbook" and became the bible of the upper-class housewife. The present version has been adapted to modern kitchens by Jean Karsavina, who pruned down the original 2,200 recipes to a manageable, but unspecified, number. The selection ranges from simple economical country fare to very sophisticated dishes. The Czerny book is a first-class selection of interesting and varied recipes adapted to American measures.

RUSSIA

For completeness and authenticity, it would be hard to surpass A. Krashennikova's *Russian Cooking* (Moscow: Mir, 1975; London: Central Books, 1974; Chicago: Imported Publications, 1974). One reviewer said it looks as though it was written by a committee, but its 750 recipes cover everything from soups to fancy breads. A separate section on food preservation covers preserves, pickles, brines, mushrooms and the like. Measures are metric, but a table of equivalents is given in the front. Sixteen color illustrations are included.

Full-color treatment is provided by Helen and George Papashvily's *Russian Cooking* (New York and London: Time-Life, 1970). This is a gastronomic tour of the USSR, with scenic and cultural sidelights added. Due emphasis is given to the variations and uniqueness of the Baltic states, the Ukraine, and Caucasus and the Central Asian Steppes. Especially noteworthy is the section on Russian Easter pageants and their egg decorations. A companion booklet for use in the kitchen contains 150 recipes.

If diet is the key to longevity, the answer may lie in Sonia Uvezian's *Cooking from the Caucasus* (New York and London: Harcourt Brace Jovanovich, 1976; 1978 paperback). These are recipes from Armenia, Azerbaidzhan and Georgia, where a life-span of 130 years is not uncommon. The core foods in the Caucasian diet are fresh vegetables and herbs, fruits, milk products, nuts, cracked wheat and honey (often replacing sugar). There are no illustrations, but features include a glossary of special ingredients, a U.S. shopping guide and an index. This book originally appeared under the title *Best Foods of Russia*.

MEDITERRANEAN

Paula Wolfert sadly notes that what inspired her to write *Mediterranean Cooking* (New York: Times Books, 1982; London: Pan Books, 1980, paperback) is fast disappearing. She refers to the unique atmosphere of the Mediterranean, a combination of clean air, good humor, love, culture and delicious food. Though the way of life may have succumbed to the rat race, good food is still procurable. Wolfert maintains that ingredients are the key, and they are wild herbs, citrus fruits, olives, dates, garlic, oil, honey, nuts, eggplant, tomatoes, peppers, chickpeas, lentils, beans, yogurt, cheese, pasta, couscous and figs. The recipes use American measures. Features include a list of American sources for hard-to-find ingredients and an index by nationality and recommended course.

The diversity produced from these common ingredients fascinated Kay Shaw Nelson in *Mediterranean Cooking for Everyone* (New York and London: Dover, 1979, paperback). Taking her 220 recipes from Spain, southern France, Italy, Greece, Turkey, Lebanon, Syria, Israel, Egypt and North Africa, she points out that each region has produced distinctive fare from the same materials. Recipes are presented by course, using American measures, with an index by country, dish and ingredient.

Alan Davidson's *Mediterranean Seafood* (Baton Rouge, La.: Louisiana State University Press, 1981; London: Penguin, 1972, paperback) catalogs the fish found in the Mediterranean, describing them and listing the various names by which they are known in seven languages. Part Two covers cooking techniques and recipes.

JEWISH

Jewish cuisine is both traditional and international. For centuries, basic recipes have been handed down from generation to generation, but the repertoire contains variations from many lands. Two basic books that reflect this heritage are Judy Jackson's *The Home Book of Jewish Cookery* (Boston and London: Faber & Faber, 1981, paperback also), which contains recipes from both the Ashkenazi and Sephardic traditions, and Jennie Grossinger's *The Art of Jewish Cooking* (New York: Random House, 1958), which draws its 400 recipes from Jews of many countries. Both books provides notes on Jewish dietary laws and festivals.

More consciously international is Hanna Goodman's *Jewish Cooking Around the World: Gourmet and Holiday Recipes* (Boston: Jewish Publication Society of America, 1974). A well-known lecturer and demonstrator, Goodman keys her text to the Jewish calendar and gives international variations of each dish, including those from China, Europe, North Africa and the Middle East. Three hundred kosher recipes are included, most easy enough for a beginner.

Ruth and Bob Grossman's *The Kosher Trilogy* (Middlebury, Vt.: Eriksson, 1974, paperback) contains three books in one—"Chinese Kosher," "Italian Kosher" and "French Kosher" —each separately introduced and indexed.

Molly L. Bar-David's *Israeli Cookbook* (New York: Crown, 1964; London: Hamlyn, 1965) presents more than 1,000 recipes, arranged by course. The American edition uses American measures and is adapted to American kitchens. Additional chapters consider baking and beverages.

MOROCCO

There is something about Morocco that inspires good cookbook writing. Paula Wolfert, in *Couscous and Other Good Food from Morocco* (New York: Harper & Row, 1973), manages to convey a deep affection for the place as well as to stimulate the appetite with this selection of Moroccan recipes. A native New Yorker who settled in Morocco, Wolfert orients the reader with background notes on 10 important spices and nine secondary aromatics. She gives a map of regional specialties, and she has altered traditional recipes for American kitchens. Illustrated with line drawings of ingredients and techniques and color photos of some finished dishes, this is not a comprehensive study but an effort to expand the reader's horizons with the best of Moroccan cuisine.

A well-rounded approach is taken by Irene F. Day's *The Moroccan Cookbook* (Chester, N.Y.: Music Sales, 1978, paperback). She presents introductory material on the land and the people, and an afterword, "A Master Cook in the Casbah." Familiar Moroccan dishes such as couscous, Bastela [pigeon pie] and Gazelle's Horn [almond-filled pastry] are presented in a chapter called "The Classic Seven." Subsequent chapters are arranged by course.

HOW TO COOK COUSCOUS

In 1711 a Monsieur Mouette visited Fez and wrote the following description of the making of *couscous:*

They take a great Wooden Bowl, or Earthen Pan, before them, with a Porringer full of Flower [flour]; and another of Fair Water; a Sieve; and a Spoon. Then they put two or three Handfulls of the Flower into the Bowl, and pour three or four Spoonfulls of Water on it, which they work well with their Fingers, every now and then sprinkling it with Water, till it all runs into little Lumps like small Pease, and this they call Couscousou. As it rolls up they take it out of the Bowl and put it into the Sieve to separate the Flower that may remain loose; and there are some Women so expert at making it, that it is no bigger than Hail shot, which is the best. In the meanwhile they boil a great deal of good Meat, as Pullets, Beef, and Mutton, in a Pot that is not above a Span open at the Mouth, and so narrow at the bottom that it may sink two Inches within the Mouth of the other, the bottom whereof is full of holes like a Cullender. Into this last pot they put the Couscousou over the other Pot the Meat boyls in, when it is almost Ready, Leaving it so about three quarters of an Hour, close cover'd with a Napkin, and a wet Cloth with a little Flower, being wrapped about the Mouth of the other Pot, that no steam may come out that way, but all ascend to pierce the Couscousou. When ready they turn it out into a Dish, and stir it about, that it may not cling together, but lie loose in Grains: Then they butter it, and lastly pour on the Broth and all the Meat.

Paula Wolfert, *Couscous and Other Good Food from Morocco* (New York: Harper, 1973), p. 134.

MIDDLE EAST

Cookery of the eastern Mediterranean area can be viewed as a number of distinctive cuisines, or as simply regional variations on the same cuisine. The area definition varies, with Iran, Iraq, Syria, Israel, Egypt, Jordan, Lebanon and Turkey being the usual scope, though some treatments also include Greece and North Africa. One of the most comprehensive is Rose Dosti's *Middle Eastern Cooking* (Tucson: HP Books, 1982, paperback), with 225 recipes arranged by course. Color photos illustrate how-to sequences for difficult preparations, and finished dishes. Special sections include a U.S. shopping guide and a glossary of terms. Equal in scope but twice as long is Tess Mallos's *The Complete Middle East Cookbook* (New York: McGraw-Hill, 1980), which Craig Claiborne pronounced "as close as any book could come . . . to the definitive recipes of Greece, Turkey, Armenia, Israel, Lebanon and so on." Harry G. Nickles's *Middle Eastern Cookery* (New York and London: Time-Life, 1970) conducts a well-illustrated tour of nine countries, sustaining the thesis that there is but one cuisine with regional variations. A companion booklet for use in the kitchen contains 121 recipes.

Claudia Roden's *A Book of Middle Eastern Food* (New York: Alfred A. Knopf, 1972; London: Vintage, 1974, paperback) concentrates on Arab and Israeli food. Roden, a Sephardic Jew raised in Egypt, provides background on history, table manners, hospitality customs and Muslim dietary laws. The more than 500 recipes are arranged by course rather than country and include the name in the original language. Eva Zane, who has also written a book on Greek cookery, covers the rest of the Middle East and North Africa in her *Middle Eastern Cookery* (San Francisco and London: 101 Productions, 1974, paperback). Recipes are arranged by country, and each group is prefaced by notes on food lore and eating customs.

Traditional Arab recipes adapted to the modern kitchen are the specialty of Marie K. Rhayat's *Food of the Arab World* (Troy, Mich.: International Book Center, paperback). Originally published in 1959, the book is well illustrated and contains 140 recipes.

ARMENIA

Ancient Armenia was the land of the Tigris and Euphrates rivers, but today the Armenian nation is divided among Turkey, Iran and the Soviet Union. Traditional Armenian cooking is covered exhaustively in Sonia Uvezian's *The Cuisine of Armenia* (New York: Harper & Row, 1974). Recipes are arranged by course, with separate sections on the traditional Armenian industries of wine-making and rose-petal preserves. Rachel Hogrogian's *Armenian Cookbook* (New York: Atheneum, 1975, paperback) is an illustrated book of Armenian recipes.

IRAN

Nesta Ramazani's *Persian Cooking: A Table of Exotic Delights* (Charlottesville, Va.: University Press of Virginia, 1982) is good on the historical and cultural context of Iranian cooking. Ramzani makes a convincing case that such Middle Eastern delights as stuffed vegetables and kebabs may have originated in ancient Persia. The 275 recipes range from the standard items just mentioned to such exotic treats as duckling in pomegranate-walnut sauce, and stewed chicken and tangerines. The section on soups is particularly good, and other features include an extensive mail-order source list. This book first appeared in 1974. Maideh Mazda's *In a Persian Kitchen* (Rutland, Vt., and London: Charles E. Tuttle, 1960) is an interesting collection of Persian recipes, with decorative illustrations.

TURKEY

Venice Lamb's *The Home Book of Turkish Cooking* (New York and London: Faber & Faber, 1973, paperback) presents recipes for such familiar Turkish dishes as dolmas, boreks and koftes, plus a wide variety of others. The author eases the Western cook's task somewhat by suggesting substitutes for hard-to-find items.

AFRICA

Laurens Van der Post's *African Cooking* (New York and London: Time-Life, 1970) presents a colorful panorama of cuisines south of the Sahara. Van der Post chooses to stress Ethiopia, the highlands of East Africa, the areas that were formerly Portuguese Africa, and South Africa. The photos of scenery, foodstuffs and finished dishes are excellent. A companion booklet contains 120 recipes.

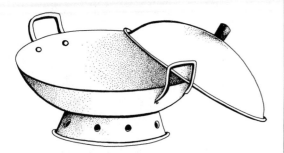

West African cooking adapted for American kitchens is covered in Ellen G. Wilson's *A West African Cookbook* (New York: M. Evans, 1971).

ASIA

In the broadest category, Jeni Wright's *Encyclopedia of Asian Cooking* (New York: W.H. Smith; London: Octopus, 1980) takes us across Asia, from India to Japan, in a country-by-country survey of cookery. The book does justice to the major cuisines, but also touches on some of the lesser-known, such as Burmese, Laotian and Korean. This is a large, handsome paperback, with copious color illustrations of ingredients and finished dishes.

Pearl Buck's *Buck's Oriental Cookbook* (New York: Simon & Schuster, 1974) is a selection of the famous author's favorite dishes from China, Indonesia, Thailand, Burma, India-Pakistan, the Philippines, Indochina, Korea, Malaysia and Japan. Many of the 450 recipes are appropriate for beginners, and those from each country are presented with background notes on how meals are served.

Jacqueline Heriteau's *Oriental Cooking the Fast Wok Way* (New York: New American Library, 1977, paperback) shows how to apply wok techniques to the cuisines of India, Japan and Southeast Asian countries.

NORTHEAST ASIA

China, Japan and Korea are the subjects of *The Oriental Cookbook* (Menlo Park, Calif.: Lane, 1970) by the editors of *Sunset* magazine. This is a good basic book with extensive introductory notes on new products, shopping, use of unfamiliar utensils and menu planning. The format is 8½-by-11 paperback with many helpful black-and-white photos and line drawings. It contains 150 recipes adapted to American kitchens and divided into three chapters by cuisine.

Jane and Charles Richards' *Classic Chinese and Japanese Cooking,* 2nd rev. ed. (San Francisco: City Lights, 1972, paperback) is also aimed at the beginner, but nonetheless includes a range of recipes, from simple to elaborate.

SOUTHEAST ASIA

Most comprehensive in this category is Rafael Sternberg's *Pacific and Southeast Asian Cooking* (New York: Time-Life,

1970). It is concerned with islands of the Pacific rim and thus includes interesting chapters on Hawaii and Tahiti as well as on Indonesia, Malaysia, the Philippines, Vietnam and Thailand. The book is profusely illustrated with photographs of ingredients, finished dishes and typical scenery. The text is easy to read and includes lucid explanations of the use of local spices and special ingredients, such as coconuts. A companion recipe booklet for use in the kitchen contains 127 recipes.

The subtlety of Southeast Asian cuisine is the theme of Rosemary Brissenden's *Asia's Undiscovered Cuisines: Recipes from Thailand, Indonesia and Malaysia* (New York: Pantheon, 1982; London: Penguin, 1972, paperback). Accordingly she provides a clear and helpful introduction to the unfamilar herbs, spices, utensils and techniques involved. Two hundred fifty recipes are given—with American measures— and 15 menus. Features include mail-order sources, a glossary in six languages and suggested alternates for hard-to-find ingredients.

A slightly different combination of cuisines is studied in the *Flavors of Southeast Asia: Recipes from Indonesia, Thailand and Vietnam* (San Francisco and London: 101 Productions, 1979) by Maudie Horsting et al. The basics of Southeast Asian cooking are covered in an introductory chapter. The cuisines are covered in separate sections, each prefaced by a rundown on the mealtime customs, etiquette and rituals.

CHINA

American interest in Chinese cooking boomed at the beginning of the 1970s, with the result that the book buyer can select from among more than 160 titles. Chinese cuisine fits in with the current emphasis on natural foods and physical fitness, and these books uniformly stress natural ingredients, lean meat, poultry or fish, crunchy vegetables and the avoidance of overcooking. The titles below are arranged in order of decreasing scope.

An Encyclopedia of Chinese Food and Cooking, by Wonona Chang et al. (New York: Crown, 1973), is at once a cookbook and a reference book on all aspects of Chinese cookery. More than 1,000 recipes (plus variations) are included, as well as sections on nutritional values of Chinese food, cooking techniques, utensils, and various diets (low-salt, ulcer, etc.). Foodstuffs and other ingredients are carefully identified in black-and-white photos, and there are color plates of finished dishes.

Gloria Bley Miller's *The Thousand Recipe Chinese Cookbook* (New York: Grosset & Dunlap, 1970) is impressively comprehensive and has a clear format. Recipes are drawn from all regions of China, and they pay particular attention to color, taste, shape and nutrition. There are menu suggestions for parties ranging from two to 12 guests.

In the category of introductory texts, the field is crowded. Craig Claiborne and Virginia Lee's *The Chinese Cookbook* (New York: Barnes & Noble, 1983; London: A. Deutsch, 1973; paperback, Sphere, 1974) is outstanding. It can serve as an introduction, or as a standby for the experienced cook. The 240 recipes are accurate and clear. Preparations, utensils and ingredients are amply described, or illustrated with drawings. Regions covered include the North, the Yangtse Valley, and the South.

A more recent and highly readable treatment is Barbara Tropp's *Modern Art of Chinese Cooking* (New York: William Morrow, 1982). A noted China scholar, Tropp characterizes this work as a reflection of one person's taste rather than a comprehensive treatment. Nevertheless, at 623 pages, it should be exhaustive enough for most. Amid sections on techniques and regional styles, Tropp touches on such topics as yin and yang in the kitchen as well as poetry, philosophy and art.

Each of the following titles, given in alphabetical order by author, has found a large audience and has something in particular to recommend it. *The Art of Chinese Cooking* (Rutland, Vt., and London: Charles E. Tuttle, 1956), by the Benedictine Sisters of Peking, had by the mid-1970s gone through 40 printings. It is based on cookery lessons given in Tokyo by American nuns and concentrates on pork, fowl, beef and seafood dishes. Joyce Chen's *Joyce Chen Cook Book* (New York: Barnes & Noble, 1983, paperback) enjoyed tremendous popularity in hardcover during the 1960s, when her cooking show was featured on PBS. The 150 recipes take from Cantonese, Mandarin and Szechwan styles. Grace Zia Chu's *The Pleasures of Chinese Cooking* (New York: Simon & Schuster, 1975, paperback; London: Faber & Faber, 1974, paperback) initially appeared in 1962 and is generally considered to be the first great Chinese cookbook written for an American audience. According to Chu, there are four requirements for good Chinese food: It must appeal to the eye by its coloring, to the nose by its aroma, to the ear by its crunchy sounds and to the mouth by its flavor.

Karen Lee and Aileen Friedman's *Chinese Cooking for the American Kitchen* (New York: Atheneum, 1980) shows how and when to use whatever produce is fresh and available and convert it to Chinese-style cuisine, and how to coordinate a multicourse Chinese dinner. Mai Leung's *The Classic Chinese Cook Book* (New York: Harper & Row, 1976) uses a well-balanced approach, selecting 200 recipes from the four regional cuisines. The section on techniques and implements is well illustrated. Kenneth Lo's *Chinese Food* (New York: Peter Smith, n.d.; London: Penguin, 1972) is a standard work by a respected expert on Chinese cooking who is based in London. Recipes use imperial measures, with a conversion table provided. Nancy Chih Ma's *Mrs. Ma's Chinese Cookbook* (Rutland, Vt., and London: Charles E. Tuttle, 1960) is a best seller that has gone through more than 30 printings. It stresses quick preparation time (10 to 15 minutes) and economy of ingredients. Just about every one of its 200 recipes is illustrated.

N. Sakamoto's *The People's Republic of China's Cookbook* (New York: Random House, 1977) draws its recipes from three publications of the mainland government: *Treatise on Famous Chinese Dishes* (1958–1965), *The Cookbook of Famous Dishes from the Peking Hotel Restaurant* (1960) and *The Masses Cookbook* (1966). The 250 recipes are divided by culinary region and are prefaced by remarks on the evolution of the dishes. Unusual ingredients, techniques and utensils are illustrated by line drawings. Mary Sia's *Chinese Cookbook* (Honolulu: University Press of Hawaii, 1975, paperback) is a perennial best seller in the islands. Recipes number 400 and are eclectic as to region.

Madame Wu's Art of Chinese Cooking (New York: Bantam, 1975, paperback) was written by Sylvia Wu, proprietor of a Los Angeles restaurant. In addition to recipes arranged by regions, special sections include how to prepare a dinner party in 30 minutes, diet programs and a list of Chinese fortunes to insert in homemade fortune cookies.

Regional

The four regional styles of Chinese cooking are the Eastern (Shanghai), the Northern (Peking and Shantung), the Western (Szechwan and Hunan) and the Southern (Canton). Two books specializing in regional styles are Lucille Liang's *Chinese Regional Cooking* (New York: Sterling, paperback; London: Oak Tree Press, 1979), which features line drawings, American measures, and color photos of finished dishes; and Kenneth Lo's *Chinese Regional Cooking* (British title: *Chinese Provincial Cooking*) (New York: Pantheon Books, 1980; 1981, paperback; London: Sphere, 1981, paperback), which selects 60 to 75 recipes from each region. Recipes use imperial measures, with a conversion table provided.

The hot and spicy cuisine of Hunan is explained step by step in *Henry Chung's Hunan Style Chinese Cookbook* (New York: Crown, 1978). Chung is chef-owner of a restaurant in

San Francisco's Chinatown that *The New Yorker* once praised as the "best Chinese restaurant in the world."

Especially attractive to busy beginners will be the quick but comprehensive approach of *Sunset Chinese Cookbook* (Menlo Park, Calif.: Lane, 1979, paperback) and *Betty Crocker's Chinese Cookbook* (New York: Random House, 1981). Each does it all in fewer than 100 pages, and each uses profuse color illustrations. Another good basic book for beginners is Gary Lee's *The Wok: A Chinese Cookbook* (Concord, Calif.: Nitty Gritty Productions, 1970). It contains only 150 recipes, but cooks who master the techniques presented here will be able to improvise to their heart's content.

INDIA

Indian cuisine has jumped in popularity in the U.S. since the early 1970s, and it is no longer necessary to state that it is more than "just curry." Its rich variety is well documented, perhaps most completely in the following four books. Madhur Jaffrey's *Invitation to Indian Cooking* (New York: Vintage, 1975; London: Penguin, 1978, paperback) is already considered a classic because the recipes combine ease of preparation, authenticity, and adaptation to American conditions. Various sections include sources of special ingredients, notes on flavoring and spices, notes on utensils and a glossary. Beginners will love Julie Sahni's *Classic Indian Cooking* (New York: William Morrow, 1980) because the first 95 pages are devoted to the principles of Indian cooking, spices, special ingredients, equipment and techniques. Only then does she continue with 400 pages of recipes, by course. A pictorial approach is taken in M. Pandya's *Complete Indian Cookbook* (London: Hamlyn, 1980; New York: Larousse, 1981), which boasts extremely attractive line drawings and abundant color plates of ingredients and finished dishes. The format is comprehensive, but Americans should note that recipe measurements are given in imperial and metric quantities, with a table of equivalents. Sipra Das Gupta's *The Home Book of Indian Cookery* (New York and London: Faber & Faber, 1980, paperback) includes recipes from all parts of India and is especially good on desserts.

The Time-Life entry for the subcontinent is Santha Rama Rau's *Cooking of India* (New York: Time-Life, 1969). The prose is highly readable and abounds in cultural insights. Regional cuisines are stressed, with chapters on typical foods, vegetarian diets, spices, specialties of minority groups, barbecuing, seafood and festivals. The photography is superb. A companion booklet is included, containing 108 recipes.

JAPAN

Japanese cuisine, with its austere elegance, projects Japanese values as well as techniques and ingredients. Not just a collection of recipes, Shizuo Tsuji's *Japanese Cooking: A Simple Art* (New York: Kodansha, 1980) excels in the practical application of the basic concept of making much out of little while maintaining a high standard of beauty and integrity. A national authority and proprietor of the Tsuji Hotel School in Osaka, Japan, Tsuji devotes his 145-page Part I to a patient discussion of how the Japanese way of thinking applies to cooking approaches, concepts and ingredients. Part II consists of recipes grouped by cooking techniques: deep-frying, one-pot cooking, steaming, etc. There are 16 beautiful and informative color photos and abundant line drawings. It is a handsome book and perhaps the most authentic and well-rounded approach to Japanese cuisine available in English.

Less authoritative but perhaps more accessible is Elizabeth Andoh's *At Home with Japanese Cooking* (New York: Alfred A. Knopf, 1980). Born and raised in the United States, Andoh studied Japanese classical cooking in Tokyo and here creates the basic book she wished were available when she started out. It was developed after years of giving cooking lessons to expatriates in Japan and is tailored to those who want to create authentic Japanese dishes in an American kitchen. She emphasizes use of Japanese techniques and equipment and is strong on explaining easily missed nuances of Japanese style. There are no photographs, but ink drawings illustrate pots, pans and other utensils. Useful appendices include language notes, foodstuff lists, a glossary of Japanese terms and an index. Some recipes are adjusted to Western tastes—e.g., increasing the proportion of meat to other ingredients.

Another comprehensive approach comes from Elizabeth Lambert Ortiz in her *Complete Book of Japanese Cooking* (New York: M. Evans, 1980). Similar to Ortiz's complete books of Caribbean and Mexican cuisine, this volume has recipes ranging from simple to elaborate, with useful illustrations, a Japanese glossary and utensil descriptions. It is available in paperback as well as hardcover.

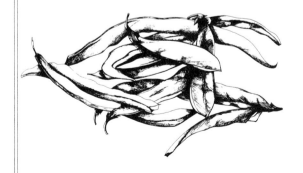

Rafael Steinberg's *The Cooking of Japan* (New York and London: Time-Life, 1969, 1970) applies the formula of Foods of the World series to Japan, with outstanding results. This book combines superb photographs of Japanese food and culture with an approach to cuisine keyed to the seasons of the year, with added chapters on history, preparation, seafood, eating out, elegant meals and ceremonies. It contains 84 recipes (beginner to intermediate level), with a separate booklet for use in the kitchen.

More specialized are Russ Rudzinski's *Japanese Country Cookbook* (Concord, Calif.: Nitty Gritty Productions, 1969), which presents simple, everyday dishes of regional Japan (325 recipes, intermediate level), and Kaichi Tsuhi's *Kaiseki: Zen Tastes in Japanese Cooking* (New York and London: Kodansha International, 1972, 1981), which concentrates on the cooking done for the tea ceremony, and the Zen philosophy it exemplifies. The color photographs are a delight.

PHILIPPINES

Philippine cuisine is the result of many diverse cultural influences, including Malayan, Spanish, American, Mexican and Chinese. Reynaldo Alejandro's *The Philippine Cookbook* (New York: Coward, McCann & Geoghegan, 1982) presents more than 300 recipes, all adapted to the American kitchen, among which are found such traditional delicacies as *adobo* (a rich chicken-and-pork stew) and *ginataan* (meat prepared with coconut milk). Preliminary chapters discuss Philippine customs and cuisine, and then basic techniques. Recipes are presented by course.

SINGAPORE

Zarinah Anwar's *With an Eastern Flavor* (Woodbury, N.Y.: Barron Educational Series, 1978; London: Souvenir Press, 1979) might be described as Indian food with an Indonesian tilt. It contains more than 200 recipes divided into chapters covering areas such as North Indian, South Indian, Indonesian and Singaporean dishes and noodles. Use of color photography is lavish, especially for finished dishes, food as it might appear in the market, and in spice charts.

SRI LANKA

Priya Wickramashinghe's *Spicy and Delicious: Exotic and Tasty Recipes from India and Sri Lanka* (Glastonbury, Conn.: Ind-US, Inc., 1979; London: Hodder & Stoughton, 1981, paperback) has a thoroughgoing and low-key approach. Although it states the "truly indigenous" diet of the area is strictly vegetarian, the book includes recipes for a wide variety of meat and poultry dishes, but many more for fish and other seafood. There are separate chapters for salads and chutneys, savories and side dishes. The recipes use imperial measures with metric conversions.

THAILAND

Thai cooking has been described as a combination of Indian and Chinese cuisines. Jennifer Brennan's *The Original Thai Cookbook* (New York: R. Marek, 1981) takes a comprehensive approach, beginning with an introduction to life in Thailand and continuing through the Thai kitchen, cooking fundamentals, fruit and vegetable carving, menus, courses and beverages. A British edition of the same book is entitled simply *Thai Cooking* (London: J. Norman, 1981). Marie M. Wilson's *Siamese Cooking* (Rutland, Vt., and London: Charles E. Tuttle, 1965) presents interesting dishes well adapted to American kitchens.

VIETNAM

Vietnamese cuisine, though little known, has been proclaimed a "glory of gastronomy" by Craig Claiborne. Highly recommended is Bach Ngo and Gloria Zimmerman's *The Classic Cuisine of Vietnam* (Woodbury, N.Y., and London: Barron's Educational Series, 1979). Jill N.H. Miller, author of *Vietnamese Cookery* (Rutland, Vt.: Charles E. Tuttle, 1968) describes it as a blend of Indian, Malay and French cooking. She presents 150 recipes for soups, desserts and main dishes of pork, beef, seafood, chicken and duck. There are background notes on special ingredients, and suggestions for serving.

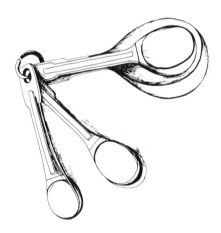

CHAPTER SIX

Cookbooks
by
Type
of
Food
or
Special
Ingredient

Writers are forever drawing up global cookbook categories. The game goes like this. There are two sorts of cookbooks: those you use and those you read. Another would draw the line between books that guide you on a certain cuisine and books that present an author's own approach to cooking.

For the purposes of this book, another distinction seemed apt: There are two kinds of cookbooks: those worth including and those not. Below that, many more categories had to be devised.

The present category lumps together cookbooks that focus on one type of food, such as meat, and those that approach all cookery from the angle of a special ingredient, such as wine. To some extent it jumbles all the other criteria. Here, for example, you will find books that are both usable and readable, those that are cuisine-oriented and those that give you a glimpse of the author's own taste.

Certain trends are discernible. There seems to be no end of books about vegetables (even leaving aside vegetarianism), seafood, herbs and spices, dairy products (especially cheese) and game. On the rise are books about chocolate and soybean products. Conversely, cooking with flowers has been almost completely neglected.

BEER, WINE AND SPIRITS

BEER

Carole Fahy's *Cooking with Beer* (New York: Peter Smith, 1972; Dover, 1978, paperback) covers the whole range of cookery, and it is surprising how many good dishes can be made better by the addition of beer. Three hundred recipes are included, most suitable for beginners. Being English, the author uses as much ale and porter (typical English brews) in these recipes as she does lager. Luckily, in the decade since the book's original publication these heartier beers have become much more available in the United States. Otherwise, recipes calling for them would have to be supplemented with malt or yeast for flavor.

SPIRITS

Intriguing dish names are a feature of this branch of cookery. Consider, for example, "Rum Runner's Spareribs," "Acorn Squash in Heather Dew," and "Ginned Shrimp." Sonia Allison's *Spirited Cooking: With Liqueurs, Spirits and Wines* (North Pomfret, Vt.: and London: David & Charles, 1982) presents more than 125 recipes divided into starters, main dishes and desserts. Three to be recommended are mustardy rabbit in Cointreau sauce, fruited liver with brandy, and veal chops Campari. Illustrations include decorative line drawings and eight beautiful color plates of finished dishes.

Mary Anne and Frank Cullen's *The Eighty Proof Cookbook: An Introduction to Cooking with High Spirits* (New York: St. Martin's Press, 1982, paperback), is arranged by name of liquor, with chapters on scotch, gin, Bourbon, etc. Then within each chapter are recipes broken down by appetizer, vegetable dish, main course and dessert. More than 115 recipes are given, including *guacamole con tequila*, regal brandy paté and Italian rumcake.

A handy little book is the *Mr. Boston Cordial Cooking Guide* (New York: Warner Books, 1982), which contains approximately 170 recipes, from soups to desserts and breads, plus profuse color photos and line drawings. The range of liqueur is limited to those manufactured by Glenmore Distilleries, but that is a wide selection indeed.

A broader range of cordials is covered by Marjorie Chite's *Cordial Cookery* (Maplewood, N.J.: Hammond, 1982, paperback). The 250 recipes are grouped into sections on exotic vegetables (e.g., zucchini anisette), main-dish delights (such as shellfish alla Sambuca) and dessert specialties (e.g., Kahlua mousse).

WINE

Six cookbooks by the California Wine Advisory Board are good buys for those interested in cooking with wines and spirits. The first four below contain 300 recipes each, all collected from California winemakers, some signed by the contributor, and covering the entire menu. They are *Adventures in Wine Cookery*, 2nd ed. (San Francisco: Wine Appreciation Guild, 1980, paperback, *Easy Recipes of California Winemakers* (San Francisco: Wine Appreciation Guild, 1970), *Favorite Recipes of California Winemakers* (Boston: Piper Books [Houghton Mifflin], 1963), and *Epicurean Recipes of California Winemakers* (San Francisco: Wine Appreciation Guild, 1978). (The recipes in this volume are more complicated than the others.) The fifth volume, *Gourmet Wine Cooking the Easy Way* (San Francisco: Wine Appreciation Guild, 1980) consists of recipes from producers of convenience foods, with brand names included. The last volume, Emily Chase's *Wine Cookbook of Dinner Menus* (San Francisco: Wine Appreciation, 1978) stresses complementary wines to be served with different dinner menus.

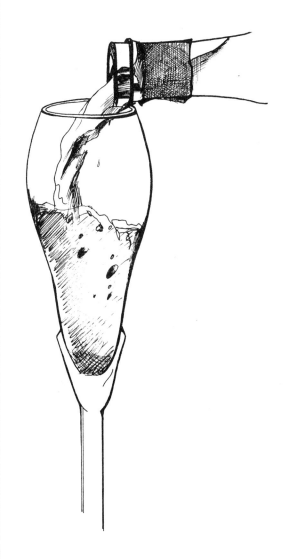

Audrey Ellis's *Wine Lovers Cookbook* (Boston: Merrimack Book Service, 1975) includes recipes for cooking with wine, plus wine choices for all kinds of meals. Claude Morny's *A Wine and Food Bedside Book* (North Pomfret, Vt.: David & Charles, 1972) offers both delightful reading and practical menu hints.

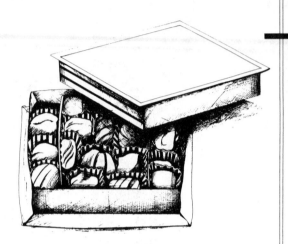

CHOCOLATE

The following books are an embarrassment in diet-conscious America. Each page of them bears wonderfully fattening recipes and anecdotes designed to subvert the will-to-slimness. So let the reader beware.

"On the second day of Christmas my true love will serve me a Mars Bar upon a silver salver." Thus goes one line of a prose poem to chocolate in Helge Rubinstein's *The Ultimate Chocolate Cake: 110 Other Chocolate Indulgences* (New York: Congdon & Weed, 1983). A bit crass? Never mind. This book is a fantasy trip for the hard-core chocolate lover. The 225 recipes are grouped under such topics as savory dishes, hot desserts, cold desserts, cakes, confections and drinks. Quantities are given in imperial and metric measures, with a table of American equivalents.

Maida Heatter's Book of Great Chocolate Desserts (New York: Alfred A. Knopf, 1980) should satisfy the most abject chocoholic. Heatter begins with basic instructions, techniques and equipment and proceeds through chapters on cookies, pastries, pies, desserts, sauces and decorations. The recipes are workable (but must be followed exactly) and include such treats as the marshmallow-frosted St. Louis Chocolate Layer Cake, the Black Forest Cherry Torte and Positively-the-Absolute-Best-Chocolate-Chip Cookies.

A lower key is taken in *Farm Journal's Choice Chocolate Recipes* (Garden City, N.Y.: Doubleday, 1979; New York: Ballantine, 1982, paperback). Two hundred recipes are distributed among chapters dealing with cakes, cookies, brownies, pies, desserts and sauces, fudge and candy. Eight color plates depict finished dishes.

CURRY

Archaeologists have traced the use of curry in India back to 4000 B.C., which must be some sort of record for sustained popularity. In sauces, soups or stews, curries have gained currency in the West, but if yours is not to be a parody of the real thing, you might want to check Helen Lawson's *How to Make Good Curries* (New York: Transatlantic, 1980; London: Hamlyn, 1973). In a lucid and well-organized introduction, Lawson identifies the herbs and spices used in curry powder and explains how they are mixed with other ingredients to form the base for curry. Then separate chapters consider the use of curry in sauces, soups and breads, and with rice, fish, meat, poultry, eggs and vegetables. Eight color plates illustrate finished dishes.

DAIRY PRODUCTS

Annie E. Proulx and Lew Nichols's *The Complete Dairy Foods Cookbook* (Emmaus, Pa.: Rodale Press, 1982) demonstrates how to make everything from cheese to custard in your own kitchen. The 150 recipes are arranged by principal ingredient, such as milk, sweet cream, sour cream, cheese, yogurt, etc., and there are separate sections on equipment and sources of supply. The book is visually interesting, with a combination of black-and-white drawings, engravings and photographs.

Olga Nickles's *The Dairy Cookbook* (Millbrae, Calif.: Celestial Press, 1976, paperback) concentrates on yogurt, cheese, sour cream and milk. There are admirably clear directions on how to make these products at home, plus detailed discussions of more than 100 natural cheeses. Line drawings illustrate the text, which contains more than 300 recipes.

A British publication, Bee Nilson's *Cooking with Yogurt, Cultured Cream and Soft Cheese* (Boston: Merrimack Book Service; London: Pelham, 1973) shows how these products can add interest and variety to everyday dishes. Alternatively, many of the recipes are drawn from cultures whose culinary traditions stress the use of dairy foods. Recipes use imperial and metric measures.

CHEESE

Several good manuals on cheese are available. Evan Jones's *The World of Cheese* (British title: *Book of Cheese*) (New York: Alfred A. Knopf, 1978, paperback; London: Macmillan, 1980) has what must be a definitive lexicon on cheese varieties of the world. Early chapters are devoted to the world of cheese, how to make it or buy it and what cheeses are good with drink. The later chapters consider use of cheese in the

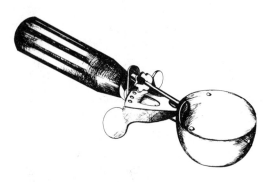

RUTH LOWINSKY'S CAMEMBERT ICE CREAM

Any embellishment of Camembert may strike you as a case of gilding the lily. If it doesn't, you'll find this recipe from Mrs. Lowinsky's *Lovely Food* (London, 1931) delicious and worth the effort. The method is from Jane Grigson's *Good Things*.

1 Camembert, soft and mature but not over-ripe
½ cup heavy cream
½ cup light cream
Cayenne or Tabasco
Salt
Water biscuits

Mash up (or put in a blender) the cheese with the two creams. Season well with cayenne or Tabasco and salt to taste. Freeze until just firm, but not hard. No need to stir. Serve sliced on a bed of cracked ice cubes with water biscuits that have been thoroughly heated.

Evan Jones, *The World of Cheese* (New York: Knopf, 1978; London: Macmillan, 1980), p. 179.

various aspects of cookery, with more than 120 recipes. Endpapers are color photos of popular cheese, with keys for easy identification.

Quite similar is Anita M. Pearl's *Completely Cheese: The Cheese Lover's Companion* (New York: Warner Books, 1979, paperback). Pearl devotes 500 pages to such topics as history, manufacture, national cheese classifications, survey of world cheeses, then cheese in cookery. Illustrations consist of a few black-and-white photos. Vivienne Marquis and Patricia Haskell's *Cheese Book* (New York: Simon & Schuster, 1969, paperback) aims at being a "definitive guide to the cheese of the world . . . how they taste, how they are made, how to select and use them, their history and lore. . . ." It includes 65 recipes from all phases of the meal.

Two books concentrate on cheese in cooking. Prize-winning author Nika Hazelton did a first-rate job on *The Art of Cheese Cookery* (Berkeley, Calif.: Ross Books, 1978, hardcover and paperback). The 250 recipes cover all the standard cookery topics, from appetizers and canapés through entrées and baking to salads, puddings and sandwich spreads. A color photo (with key) pictures 36 cheese varieties. Mary Berry's *Cooking with Cheese* (North Pomfret, Vt.: David & Charles; London: Batsford, 1980) covers the same territory with competence. The more than 200 recipes use imperial and metric measures.

CHEESECAKE

The cheesecake had its origin on the Greek island of Samos as far back as 800 B.C. according to John J. Segreto in *Cheesecake Madness* (New York: Macmillan, 1981). This is but one nugget of trivia he unearths in an entertaining history of the cheesecake, which opens this aptly titled book. The rest of the text is devoted to over 100 cheesecake recipes, plain and fancy, which include such hot numbers as Swiss cocoa marbled cheesecake. Steve Sherman's *Cheese Sweets and Savories: Pies, Quiches, Cheesecakes and Appetizers* (Brattleboro, Vt.: The Stephen Greene Press, 1982; paperback 1983) has a broader scope and boasts 150 recipes but has no illustrations.

COTTAGE CHEESE

The low calorie/high nutrition aspects of cottage cheese are stressed in Richard O. Brennan's *Incredible Edibles: The Complete Cottage Cheese Cookbook* (Houston: Educational Editions, 1981, paperback). This book exhausts the topic of cottage cheese cookery, devoting separate chapters to appetizers, beverages, breads, desserts, main dishes and so on. More than 100 recipes are included.

EGGS

Ann Seranne's *The Complete Book of Egg Cookery* (New York: Macmillan; London: Collier-Macmillan, 1983) is a definitive statement on the subject. Author of 20 other cookbooks, Seranne takes us through the basics of egg cookery, proceeds through breakfast, lunch and dinner, and gives us two chapters on egg desserts, plus recipes for breads, party food and convalescent fare. The text is supplemented with line drawings and includes more than 250 recipes. Lou Pappas's *Egg Cookery* (San Francisco: 101 Productions, 1976, hardcover and paperback) takes us on a cook's tour from "Hors d'Oeuf" to "Breads and Pastries." Pappas's over 250 recipes are easy to follow.

Self-styled "world's fastest omelet maker" Helmer Howard has teamed with Joan O'Sullivan to produce *The Forty-Second Omelet Guaranteed* (New York: Atheneum, 1982). It's the amusing saga of how he earned his title, and it gives lessons on how you can add speed to your repertoire. Narcissa Chamberlain's *Omelette Book* (New York: Alfred A. Knopf, 1952, paperback; New York: McGraw-Hill, 1976; London: McGraw-Hill, 1976, paperback) covers every conceivable sort of omelet, including various national styles from France, Germany, Italy, Spain, China and Russia. Illustrations include both color and black-and-white photos. Bob and Coleen Simmons's *Crepes and Omelets* (Concord, Calif.: Nitty Gritty Productions, 1976, paperback) is really two books in one. From one end it's crepes, from the other, omelets, with each section containing more than 80 recipes. Printed on attractively tinted paper in a short, wide format, it has the look of a gift book.

Paul Mayer's *Quiche and Souffle,* new ed. (Concord, Calif.: Nitty Gritty Productions, 1972, paperback), also uses the tumble concept: Starting from one end it's a quiche book; from the other, a soufflé book. Both sections use the same arrangement of material: history, equipment, basics, then variations with meat, fish, poultry, etc. Included are a total of 135 recipes (60 soufflé, 75 quiche). George Bradshaw's *Soufflés, Quiches, Mousses and the Random Egg* (New York: Harper & Row, 1971; London: André Deutsch, 1973) covers many of the classic egg dishes in 144 pages. The recipes are lucid, and the headnotes give excellent advice. Edie and Tom Hilton's *The Quiche Cookbook* (New York: Crown, 1976, paperback) is based on Edie's experience as a West Coast caterer. The text includes 83 recipes.

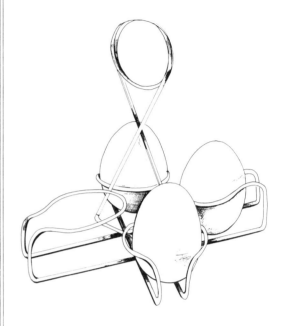

EGGS AND CHEESE

The best of this group is the Time-Life Editors' *Eggs and Cheese* (Alexandria, Va.: Time-Life, 1981; London, 1980). An entry in the Good Cook series, the book is written to a standard format: 90 pages of description and how-to techniques followed by over 200 recipes gleaned from a wide variety of published sources. The color photography is outstanding, particularly in the step-by-step treatment of techniques, which deal in sequence with whole-egg cookery, whole-egg presentation, beaten-egg cookery and cheese cookery. With over 180 recipes, Darlene Kronschnabel's *Ideals Eggs and Cheese Cookbook* (Milwaukee: Ideals, 1982, paperback) touches all the bases in a briefer format, with particularly good chapters on fondues, soufflés, quiches and omelets. The cheese identification and description chart is very handy. Sixteen color photos illustrate finished dishes.

A handsome book, Peter Kump's *Quiche and Paté* (New York: Irena Chalmers, 1982, paperback) handles two disparate topics with great skill. Chapters include short pastry, quiches (savory and dessert) and patés (savory and dessert). The book is graced by attractive line drawings but lacks an index. Kump is the proprietor of a cooking school in New York City, and this book is part of the Chalmers Great American Cooking School series, which has many notable entries.

FONDUE

Alison Burt's *Fondue Cookery* (New York: International Publications Service, 1971; London: Hamlyn, 1971) considers not just the classic Swiss dish (melted Emmenthaler cheese dipped on pieces of bread and accompanied by kirsch) but also unique varieties involving Parmesan cakes, baked chicken, onions and cider. The more than 100 recipes cover general tabletop cooking (e.g., Swiss bread, pancakes, pepper kebabs and paella) and accompaniments such as salads and garlic breads. The book is well illustrated and features a good introduction to fondue party organization.

FLOWERS

An unusual topic is treated delightfully in Mary MacNichol's *Flower Cookery: The Art of Cooking with Flowers* (New York: Fleet Press, 1967; London: Collier-Macmillan, 1972, paperback). The book contains not only many imaginative flower recipes but also headnotes of fact and folklore about flowers plus fascinating quotations from prose and poetry.

Eleanor S. Rohde's *Rose Recipes from Olden Times* (New York: Peter Smith; London: Dover, 1974, paperback) is an illustrated book of recipes showing how to use both the petals and the fruit in cooking.

FRUCTOSE

Fructose, a fruit sugar a third sweeter than table sugar at the same caloric content, became readily available to consumers in the 1970s due to technical advances in its production. Minuha Cannon's *The Fructose Cookbook* (Charlotte, N.C.: East Woods Press, 1979, paperback) shows how these qualities can be used to enhance the reader's health. Fructose also enchances the flavor of many foods and, being hygroscopic, helps retain the freshness of baked goods. The 150 recipes use these characteristics in most phases of everyday cooking.

J. T. Cooper and Jeanne Jones's *The Fabulous Fructose Recipe Book* (New York: M. Evans 1979) is a follow-up on their diet book with a similar title. This book stands on its own, however, with a recapitulation of the principle of the diet, an explanation of the maintenance diet program and scores of recipes.

FRUIT

Solid research and polished writing are the hallmarks of the work of English writer Jane Grigson; and she puts these qualities to good use in *Jane Grigson's Fruit Book* (New York: Atheneum, 1982). Arranged alphabetically by fruit name, segments consist of a descriptive/historical essay in the first person, followed by several recipes. Highly recommended for cooking or browsing. *The Fresh Fruit and Vegetable Book: A Complete Guide to Enjoying Fresh Fruits and Vegetables* (New York: Harper & Row, 1981, paperback) is a useful compendium of information, recipes and advice put out by the United Fresh Fruit and Vegetable Association. It contains tips on how to select products, more than 1,000 preparation and serving suggestions and 250 recipes. The text is accompanied by decorative line drawings and a handy calorie and carbohydrate chart. Television personality Joe Carcione's *The Greengrocer Cookbook* (Millbrae, Calif.: Celestial Arts,

PAVLOVA

A pudding made for Pavlova when she visited Australia in the Thirties. The soft and chewy-centered meringue is not, I think, original to Australia, but comes from the European *pâtisserie* tradition. What is original is the shape, and the idea of mixing cream with passion fruit and Chinese gooseberries. Other fruit can be used—strawberries and passion fruit is another popular combination.

3 large egg whites
175 g (6 oz/¾ cup) vanilla caster sugar
1 teaspoon cornflour (cornstarch)
1 teaspoon vinegar
250 ml (8 fl oz/1 cup) whipping cream
2 passion fruit
extra sugar
2-4 Chinese gooseberries (Kiwi fruit), peeled, sliced.

Use an electric beater if you can and whisk the whites until stiff. Add the sugar, beating until the meringue looks smooth and silky. Then mix in the cornflour and vinegar. Pile or pipe on to a baking sheet lined with vegetable cooking parchment, hollowing out the center to form a nest.

Bake 1¼–1½ hours at mark ½, 130 degrees C (250 degrees F) until firm. When cool, remove the plate.

Pour the cream into a basin. Scoop out the pulp of the passion fruit. If you wish to sieve out the seeds, simmer with a little sugar just to warm the pulp which will then go easily through a sieve: it should in no way be cooked. Whisk the cream, flavoring it to taste with the passion pulp. Pile into the nest, then arrange the slices of Chinese gooseberry on top.

Jane Grigson, *Jane Grigson's Fruit Book* (New York: Atheneum, 1982), p. 132.

1975, paperback) is arranged by season, then by type of fruit. It includes some unusual recipes for exotic fruits.

Excellent line drawings are a distinctive element of Paul Dinnage's *The Book of Fruit and Fruit Cookery* (Boston: Merrimack Book Service, 1982; London: Sidgwick & Jackson, 1981). Articles are arranged A to Z, each consisting of a descriptive write-up and several recipes, which are given in imperial and metric measures.

The following two books concentrate on cooking to the exclusion of description and selection. Mary Norwak's *Cooking with Fruit* (New York: Transatlantic, 1960; London: Dover, 1974, paperback) comprises more than 200 recipes arranged by course, including appetizers, main courses, stuffings, breads and desserts. Recipes use imperial measures. Gail Worstman's *The Natural Fruit Cookbook* (Seattle: Pacific Search, 1982, paperback) is similarly thorough in scope but emphasizes such accompaniments as raw honey, whole-grain flours, noninstant powdered milk, sea salt and the like. It contains 240 recipes and discusses 35 kinds of fruit.

BERRY

Caro Katz's *The Berry Cookbook* (Piscataway, N.J.: New Century, 1980, paperback) is a large-format book with attractive line drawings. In more than 200 recipes she covers black, blue, cran, elder, goose, juniper, mul-, rasp- and strawberries, also giving hints on substitutes.

LEMON

The lemon's versatility is amply demonstrated in Doris Tobias and Mary Merris's *The Golden Lemon: A Collection of Special Recipes* (New York: Atheneum, 1981, paperback). Some innovative ideas from the authors are *poulet au citron* (lemon chicken), lemon Parmesan bread, pork roast with lemon glaze and butterscotch-lemon sauce. Also included are recipes from such luminaries as James Beard and chef André Soltner.

GELATIN

The Knox Gelatin Cookbook (New York: Benjamin Co., 1977, paperback) is a well-produced volume, with plentiful color photos of finished dishes. Recipes are divided into such chapters as basics, appetizers, main dishes (for example, Ham and Potato Medley), salads, desserts, and jams and jellies, plus a brainstorm called Knox Blox.

HERBS AND SPICES

Craig Claiborne is one of our most eminent cookbook writers. *Cooking with Herbs and Spices*, new rev., enl. ed. (original title: *Herb and Spice Cookbook*) (New York: Harper & Row, 1970; 1983, paperback) is an early effort of his that has stood the test of time. Four hundred recipes are arranged under 54 herbs and spices and are accompanied by a wealth of information about basic condiments. The book is generously illustrated.

Monica Mawson's *Cooking with Herbs and Spices* (Northridge, Ill.: Domus Books, 1980; London: Hamlyn, 1978), though only 112 pages, is a highly useful guide to the subject. It contains background information, guides for growing herbs, and many exciting and unusual recipes, which are given in both American and imperial measures. Illustrations include both color and black-and-white photos. Malvina W. Liebman's *From Caravan to Casserole: Herbs and Spices in Legend, History and Recipes* (Miami: E.A. Seemann, 1977) can be read for pleasure as well as for its recipes, which run the gamut from appetizer to dessert; herbs are illustrated with engravings. June Roth's *Salt-Free Cooking with Herbs and Spices* (Chicago: Contemporary Books, 1977, paperback) is based on the premise that the blandness of salt-free food can be corrected by the judicious use of herbs and spices. The over 100 recipes are divided by course, from appetizer to dessert, and information on the sodium content of common foods is provided.

Though not cookbooks, the following volumes deserve mention. Waverley Root's *Herbs and Spices: The Pursuit of Flavor* (New York: McGraw-Hill, 1980) is composed of four contributions: an essay by the late Mr. Root on what herbs and spices have meant to the human race and a geographical survey on how they are used in various regions of the world; a chart by Paula Wolfert on what seasonings to use in some 60 international recipes; an essay by Nika Hazelton on how to use herbs and spices in the kitchen; and an essay on herb gardening by English gardening expert Roy Genders, including an illustrated lexicon of about 100 plant species. The text is unfortunately marred by a too-busy visual design, which in some places interferes with reading.

Tom Stobart's *Herbs, Spices and Flavorings* (New York: Overlook Press, 1982; London: Penguin, 1977, paperback)

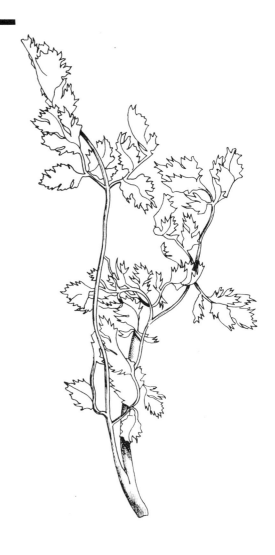

is a useful reference work and a pleasure to read as well. It provides invaluable information, nomenclature in various languages and accurate line drawings.

HERBS

Virginia Bentley's *Let Herbs Do It* (Boston: Houghton Mifflin, 1973, paperback) presents anecdotes and cooking suggestions for 26 herbs, from anise to vanilla. Each has a line drawing, a descriptive write-up and four or more recipes. *Bonnie Fisher's Way with Herbs Cookbook* (New Canaan, Conn.: Keats, 1980, paperback) stresses natural seasonings to go with natural foods for maximum nutrient content. The book is arranged by 52 basic herbal seasonings, from allspice to violet, with decorative line drawings and more than 200 recipes. Alan Hooker's *Herb Cookery* (San Francisco: 101 Productions, 1971, paperback) is ably done, presenting 175 recipes arranged by type of food. The headnotes stress the interplay of herb flavors with natural food flavors. A section on blending herbs at home discusses *bouquet garni*, herb salts, dessert blends, Far Eastern blends and currry powders.

Donald Law's *Herbs for Cooking and Healing* (Los Angeles: Wilshire, paperback; London: Foulsham, hardcover, 1969) explores medicinal as well as culinary uses for herbs. Linda Doeser and Rosamond Richardson's *The Little Garlic Book* (New York: St. Martin's Press; London: Pitakus, 1983) provides a wealth of information on the different varieties of garlic, unusual facts relating to health and medicine, and 20 garlic recipes. This is one of a "little book" series graced with excellent line drawings.

SPICES

A large, wide-ranging treatment, Avanelle Day and Lillie Stuckey's *The Spice Cookbook* (New York: David White, 1964) contains more than 1,400 recipes. Early chapters provide a history of the spice trade and a description and history of individual spices, with tables of how to use them. Arrangement is by type of food, and 29 menus are included.

HONEY

Juliette Elkon's *Honey Cookbook* (New York: Alfred A. Knopf, 1955) lays claim to being the first general book of honey recipes. It is a competent job that has been in print for nearly 30 years. The 250 recipes range from appetizers to desserts with, an interesting chapter on meads, punch and cocktails.

Chapters on beekeeping and bee lore are an added attraction in Arthur W. Andersen's *Bee Prepared with Honey: 140 Delicious Honey Recipes* (Bountiful, Utah: Horizon Publishers, 1975, paperback). Andersen also makes extensive use of line drawings and black-and-white photos.

Recipes from the *American Bee Journal* are the basis for Dadant & Sons, Inc.'s *The Honey Kitchen: The Best Honey Recipes in the World* (New York: Charles Scribner's Sons, 1982). The more than 425 recipes included, some dating from the early 1800s, run the gamut from salads to desserts. Another general approach is Hazel Berto's *Cooking with Honey* (New York: Crown, 1972). At the back of the book is a complete list of honey varieties and their flavors, plus sources of supply. Chapters are arranged by courses, with additional material on baking and beverages. Approximately 400 recipes are included.

Gene Opton and Nancie Hughes' *Honey Feast* (Berkeley, Calif.: Ten Speed Press, 1979, paperback) contains over 110 unusual honey recipes for all phases of the meal, plus a section on special equipment.

MEAT

Faith Medlin's *A Gourmet's Book of Beasts* (New York: Paul S. Eriksson, 1975) tells all about 57 different animals that are slaughtered for the table, with each essay accompanied by one recipe. The book is nicely illustrated in black and white, with photos of animal sculptures and old engravings.

Sonia Allison's *Bistro Book of Meat Cookery* (North Pomfret, Vt., and London: David & Charles, 1980) uses a comprehensive approach, with chapters on beef, lamb, pork, veal, poultry and variety meats. Finished dishes are illustrated by large color plates, and line drawings are used to represent the various cuts of beef, lamb, etc. The 120 recipes use imperial and metric measures.

Two books deal with the quality-price relationship in different ways. Ninette Lyon's *Meat at Any Price* (New York: Transatlantic, 1963) is a translation from the French. Lyon gives recipes for a wide variety of meat dishes, all graded by cost. On the other hand, the *Lobel Brothers Meat Cookbook* (New York: Cornerstone, 1980, paperback) comes to us from the proprietors of a butcher shop on Manhattan's Upper East Side that purveys only the finest meats. Billed as the "world's most famous butchers," Leon and Stanley Lobel also write a food column for the Gannett newspapers. Here they present more than 175 recipes from several world cui-

IGUANA MOLE

3 pounds iguana meat
Boiling water
Juice of 1 large lime

Cover iguana meat with boiling water in kettle to which lime juice has been added. Simmer for 30 minutes, or until tender. Tear meat into long slender strips. Reserve stock.

1 pound fresh, sweet green peppers
1 medium onion, quartered
2 cloves garlic, minced
2 tablespoons vegetable oil
½ tablespoon crushed dried hot red peppers, or more, according to taste

Cut green peppers into quarters; discard seeds and stems. Place quarters—skin side up—on tray under broiler until skins blister; peel off skins; place in blender. Add onion and garlic. Purée. In flameproof earthenware pot, over low heat on stovetop, combine oil, red peppers, and blender mixture. Simmer, stirring occasionally with wooden spoon, while preparing other ingredients.

1½ pounds fresh tomatoes
1 large tortilla, toasted and crumbled
¼ cup seedless raisins
¾ cup ground almonds
½ teaspoon salt
¼ teaspoon anise seed
¼ teaspoon ground cloves
¼ teaspoon ground cinnamon
1 ounce unsweetened chocolate

Plunge tomatoes into boiling water for about a minute; remove skins; cut in half—crosswise—and press out seeds; cut halves into sections and place in blender. Add tortilla, raisins, almonds, salt, anise, cloves, and cinnamon. Purée. Add to earthenware pot. Cut chocolate into slivers over pot. Add 1 cup stock. Simmer 1 hour, thinning with additional stock if desired.

16 large tortillas
4 tablespoons sesame seeds

Wrap tortillas tightly in aluminum foil and heat in preheated 325-degree oven for 20 minutes. Likewise heat meat in tightly covered dish. Serve meat and *mole* on hot tortillas, sprinkled with sesame seeds. Serve with cactus salad and refried beans. Serves 8.

Faith Medlin, *A Gourmet's Book of Beasts* (New York: Eriksson, 1975), p. 48.

sines, including England, France, Germany, the Middle East and America.

LAMB

Both lamb and mutton are covered in Rhoda Nation's *Mary Bought a Little Lamb and This Is How She Cooked It* (New York: International Publications Service, 1975, hardcover; Rutland, Vt.: Charles E. Tuttle, paperback, n.d.). The title may be facetious, but there can be no objection to the thorough and often innovative way she deals with these meats.

Part of the Good Cook series, Time-Life's *Lamb* (Alexandria, Va., and London, 1981) is given the customary skillful and colorfully illustrated treatment. This is a large-format book with 90 pages of instruction on techniques, then a section consisting of 200 already published recipes, really the best of the best from a wide variety of cookbooks. Techniques include grilling, broiling and frying, roasting, poaching and braising, and extension techniques.

Canadian chef Jehane Benoit doubles as the owner of a sheep farm; thus she speaks with unimpeachable authority in *Madame Benoit's Lamb Cookbook* (New York: McGraw-Hill, 1979). The book gives us the basics, then deals in turn with ground lamb, chops and steaks, shish kebab, leg of lamb, shoulder, etc. It includes more than 100 recipes and a number of color plates, plus a chart of lamb cuts. The chapter on lamb variety meats is noteworthy.

BEEF

Beef is America's favorite meat. Beefsteak is considered the Cadillac of cuts, whereas ground beef is the most popular fast food. Marguerite Patten's *The Epicure's Book of Steak and Beef Dishes* (Los Angeles, Calif.: Knapp Press, 1979) presents more than 100 ways of preparing beef, including braising, boiling, broiling, roasting, stewing and casseroles. These are integrated into 22 menus. Techniques are illustrated by line drawings, and many of the finished dishes are pictured in full-page color plates.

Ceil Dyer's *The Chopped, Minced and Ground Meat Cookbook* (New York: Arbor House, 1976, hardcover and paperback) was inspired by the inflation of the 1970s. Through 200 recipes she rings all the changes on this modestly priced meat, from meat loaf through hash international to all-in-one skillet creations. *Betty Crocker's Hamburger Cookbook* (New York: Western Publishing Co., 1973 paperback) presents a surprisingly thorough assortment of ground-beef recipes in only

76 pages. Color photos illustrate many of the finished dishes.

HAM

Monette R. and Robert W. Harrel, Jr.'s *The Ham Book: A Comprehensive Guide to Ham Cookery* (Norfolk, Va.: Donning, 1977, paperback) covers the history of ham and the curing process, provides a guide to selecting, cooking, carving and serving ham, and gives more than 340 recipes from appetizers to desserts. The text is embellished by decorative line drawings.

MEAT EXTENSION

Dorothy Ivens's *Great Dinners with Less Meat* (Englewood Cliffs, N.J.: Prentice-Hall, 1981 hardcover and paperback) considers a variety of meat extenders, including rice, beans, gravy, vegetables, ground meat, pastry and crepes—but always with a care to the complementary flavors and assortment of textures. Included are more than 110 recipes, and attractive line drawings by the author.

The thesis of Nancy Albright's *A Little Meat Goes a Long Way* (Emmaus, Pa.: Rodale Press, 1982, hardcover and paperback) is that, in cutting down on meat, you need not sacrifice flavor or nutrition. Chapters are arranged by type of meat, and extenders include grains, legumes and vegetables. There are 200 recipes but no illustrations.

Marian Burros and Lois Levine's *Come for Cocktails, Stay for Supper* (New York: Macmillan, 1971, paperback) combines quick and easy techniques with meat extension. Designed to deal with the unexpected guest, these recipes are for interesting dishes that can be prepared from foods usually available at home, then cooked and served with a minimum of fuss.

SAUSAGE

Jane Grigson combines a superb writing style with authentic recipes in *The Art of Making Sausages, Patés and Other Charcuterie* (original title: *The Art of Charcuterie*) (New York: Alfred A. Knopf, 1976, paperback; London: Penguin, 1970, paperback). This is a gourmet subject, but the approach is practical and should afford chefs and students an introduction to the way salting curing and cooking pork and other meats is done by professionals. The recipes for terrines, patés and homecooked sausages are very good.

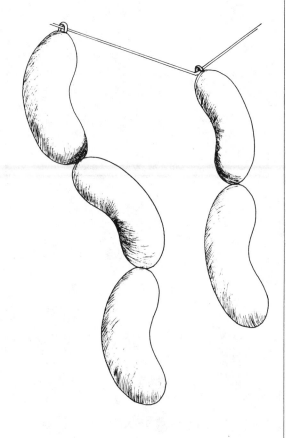

The following are all practical, competent books on home sausage-making. The most readable by far is Richard Gehman's *Signet Book of Sausage* (New York: New American Library, 1976, paperback), whose style is informal and witty. More than 100 recipes are included. Charles Reavis's *Garden Way's Book of Home Sausage Making* (Charlotte, Vt.: Garden Way Publishers, 1980, paperback; London, 1981, paperback) provides detailed instructions for making 32 different sausages, plus dozens of ways of combining them with other ingredients. The book is illustrated by 47 black-and-white how-to photos. Pamela Riddle and Mary J. Danley's *The Complete Sausage Cookbook* (San Francisco: San Francisco Book Co., 1977, paperback) is a little more comprehensive, listing more than 100 types, including meat-extended and meatless varieties.

The emphasis is on making sausage with reduced sugar, salt and fat in Bertie M. Selinger and Bernadine S. Rechner's *The Homemade Sausage Cookbook* (Chicago: Contemporary Books, 1982, paperback). The 100 recipes are divided into six sausage groups, each provided with menu ideas.

For those in a hurry, Yvonne Y. Tarr's *The Super-Easy-Step-by-Step Sausagemaking* (New York: Random House, 1975, paperback) should fill the bill. In 80 large-type pages she presents 15 types of sausages and 11 ways of serving them. No index.

PATÉ

A sense of humor is a helpful ingredient, according to Joyce Van Doorn in *Making Your Own Paté* (Berkeley, Calif.: And-Or Press, 1981, paperback). Under the title "What to Do with Failed Paté," Doorn quotes an ancient saying: "A boisterous laugh is an approved remedy for indigestion and other complaints after a meal." After introductory material on history, correct utensils and ingredients, she presents dozens of recipes for different kinds of paté. The book is embellished with line drawings of pigs and other barnyard animals.

VEAL

Craig Claiborne and Pierre Franey's *Veal Cookery* (New York: Harper & Row, 1978) would be a fine addition to anyone's cookbook library. The recipes range in difficulty from beginner to advanced, but for a cook with the necessary skills, they are practically fail-safe. The step-by-step format is easily understood, and the directions are clear and precise.

VARIETY MEATS

One man's offal is another man's variety meats, or organ meats. These cuts, although relatively inexpensive, are ignored by many people. Just reading Jana Allen and Margaret Gin's *Innards and Other Variety Meats* (San Francisco: 101 Productions, 1974) can lower your discomfort level and might even convert you into a fan. The 262 recipes are arranged by type of cut, such as kidney, heart, sweetbreads, tripe and tongue. Each cut is introduced by a historical sketch.

Time-Life's *Variety Meats* (Alexandria, Va.: 1982) is a plush treatment of the subject, featuring more than 200 recipes from 20 countries. The color photography is exceptional, and the text is thorough. Technique chapters include sautéing and deep-frying, grilling, braising and sausage-making. Recipes use American measures and metric equivalents.

NUTS

Margaret Eastman's *Seed and Nut Cookery* (Brattleboro, Vt.: The Stephen Greene Press, 1982, paperback) contains 99 recipes using 29 easily obtainable seeds and nuts. Examples are caraway cheese soup, cumin chips and pumpkin seed rarebit. Arranged by the type of seed or nut, the book has no illustrations.

A large-format book, Dorothy Frank's *Cooking with Nuts* (New York: Crown, 1979) groups recipes under headings for 13 common nuts, such as almonds, brazil nuts and walnuts. Illustrations consist of 15 black-and-white photos.

A relic of the boom in Carteriana, Cynthia and Jerome Rubin's *Peanut One Goes to Washington: The Peanut Cookbook* (Charlestown, Mass.: Emporium Publications, 1976, paperback) offers 73 serviceable peanut recipes, from appetizers to desserts. The introduction and appendix contain a wealth of information on the peanut.

PASTA

Foodperson extraordinaire James Beard has turned in an excellent performance in *Beard on Pasta* (New York: Alfred A. Knopf, 1983). The book is handsomely produced as well,

NOODLE DOUGHNUTS
Metélt Fánk

To Serve 6 to 8

2 cups Flour	½ liter
3 Eggs, 2 lightly beaten	3
2 Egg yolks	2
½ tsp. Salt	2 ml.
3 cups Milk	¾ liter
½ cup Crushed blanched almonds	125 ml.
½ cup Granulated sugar	125 ml.
½ tsp. Vanilla extract	2 ml.
1 cup Fresh bread crumbs	¼ liter
½ cup Lard, melted	125 ml.
½ cup Confectioner's sugar	125 ml.

Mix the unbeaten egg, the egg yolks and salt into the flour, making a dry dough. Roll out very thin, and cut into broad noodles. Boil the noodles in the milk until all moisture is absorbed. Stir in the almonds, granulated sugar and vanilla. While still hot, pack the mixture into a large buttered baking pan to form a layer about ½ inch (1 cm.) thick. Cool.

Turn out the cooled noodle mixture onto a board and cut it into rounds with a cookie cutter. Dip each round in the lightly beaten eggs, then in bread crumbs. Fry in the melted lard. Drain, sprinkle with confectioners' sugar and set in a warm oven until all of the rounds are fried. Serve hot.

Quoted from Time-Life eds., *Pasta* (Alexandria Va.: Time-Life Books, 1981), p. 159. N.B.: The recipe was excerpted by them from Bennet, Paula P. and Clark, Velma R. *The Art of Hungarian Cooking* (Garden City, N.Y.: Doubleday, 1954).

with decorative line drawings throughout and endpapers that illustrate the many shapes of pasta. He instructs on how to make pasta at home, then with 126 recipes shows how to use it in broth, with vegetables, fish and seafood, how to stuff it, cook it with eggs and cheese, and so on.

Pasquale Bruno, Jr.'s, *Pasta Tecnica* (Chicago: Contemporary Books, 1981) is a step-by-step, how-to book with profuse black-and-white illustrations. There are good chapters on pasta machines, doing it by hand or with a food processor, plus recipes for 11 kinds of *pasta all'ouvo* and six kinds of *pasta secche*.

Sophie Kay's *Pasta Cookery* (New York: Dell, 1981, paperback; Tucson, Ariz., and London: HP Books, 1979, paperback) focuses on homemade pasta and how to serve it. The 200 recipes are arranged by course. The HP Books' edition is a large-format book, utilizing lavish color photography for how-to sections and to picture finished dishes.

The *Sunset Pasta Cook Book* (Menlo Park, Calif.: Lane, 1980, paperback) is a well-illustrated, whirlwind course on making and serving pasta. It covers all phases in fewer than 100 pages.

Time-Life's *Pasta* (Alexandria, Va.: 1981) applies the Good Cook series formula with outstanding results. The first 86 pages are devoted to techniques: making pasta, boiling, poaching and steaming, baking and frying. The later portion of the book is comprised of 192 recipes from published sources. Brilliant color photography is used throughout.

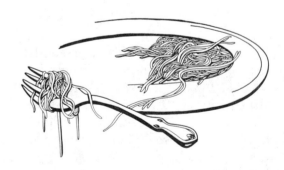

POULTRY

Half of the more than 200 recipes in James Beard's *Fowl and Game Bird Cookery* (New York: Harcourt Brace Jovanovich, 1979, paperback; London: 1980, paperback) deal with chicken. The rest are distributed among turkey, duck, squab, goose, pheasant, quail, partridge, snipe and dove. This book is a proven winner, first published in the 1940s. It is embellished with bird prints and decorative line drawings.

Anita Borghese wrings every imaginable variation out of this versatile bird in *The Great Year-Round Turkey Cookbook* (Briarcliff Manor, N.Y.: Stein and Day, 1982, paperback). The more than 250 recipes include even such things as turkey sausage and hash.

CHICKEN

Carl Jerome's *The Complete Chicken* (New York: Random House, 1978) should prove enlightening for the beginning and experienced cook alike. Jerome was formerly director of James Beard's cooking classes, and the book focuses on technique, stressing fundamentals. The explanations are clear, and the format is easy to use. Chicken sautéed with whole garlic cloves is just one example of the uncomplicated, elegant recipes.

Originally published in Australia, Trevor Wilson's *Great Chicken Dishes of the World* (New York: McGraw-Hill, 1979) is a judicious selection from many countries, but all are adapted to the Western kitchen. The book features excellent black-and-white and color illustrations.

GAME

A big, comprehensive treatment of the subject is Joan Cone's *Fish and Game Cooking* (McLean, Va.: EPM Publishers, 1981, paperback). The book goes systematically through upland birds, waterfowl, small game, big game, fish, etc. More than 350 recipes are given, but there are no illustrations.

Joan Cone takes a lighter approach in *Easy Game Cooking* (McLean, Va.: EPM Publishers, 1974, paperback). The book features black-and-white photos, 125 recipes and separate chapters on game accompaniments and use of microwave ovens. Barbara Hargreaves's *The Sporting Wife* (New York: State Mutual Book, 1980; London: Witterby, 1976, paperback) is an English book with attractive line drawings and many recipes both traditional and unusual.

The following are competent works that would interest persons who enjoy these foods: Bradford Angier's *Home Cookbook of Wild Meat and Game* (Harrisburg, Pa.: Stackpole, 1982, paperback); Robert Candy's *Getting the Most from Game and Fish* (Charlotte, Vt.: Garden Way, 1978, paperback; London, paperback); and L.W. Johnson's *Wild Game Cookbook: A Remington Sportsmen's Library Book* (New York: Benjamin Co., 1968, paperback).

The following books are more specialized. "Dressing the armadillo" is an eye-catching section of Sam Goolsby's *Great Southern Wild Game Cookbook* (Gretna, La.: Pelican, 1980). It is arranged by type of game, then by course. Jan Wongrey's *Southern Wildfowl and Wildgame Cookbook* (Lexington, S.C.: Sandlapper Store, 1976) boasts more than 170 recipes for such delicacies as turkey, squirrel, possum and raccoon. And Audrey A. Gorton's *Venison Book: How to Dress, Cut Up and Cook Your Deer* (Brattlesboro, Vt.: The Stephen Greene Press, 1957, paperback) accomplishes its task with the help of good line drawings and useful charts of cuts.

RICE

East/West is the name of the rice game. This is made quite clear in Phyllis Jervey's *Rice and Spice: Rice Recipes from East to West* (Rutland, Vt., and London: Charles E. Tuttle, 1957, paperback) and in Marian Tracy's *The East-West Book of Rice Cookery* (New York: Peter Smith, paperback; New York and London, Dover, 1976). The latter presents 135 recipes from Europe, America, Southeast Asia and the Far and Near East, arranged by course from hors d'oeuvres to desserts. The versatility of rice is stressed in Robin Howe's *Rice Cooking* (New York: Transatlantic, 1973). This prolific English cookbook author presents a broad selection of dishes based on rice.

SEAFOOD

A.E. Simms summed up the aims of this section neatly, if somewhat pompously, when he wrote: "Chefs, cordon bleus and domestic cooks have here . . . a guide to the exploitation for table pruposes of all the piscatorial riches of the world." He was extolling the virtues of the encyclopedic volume *Fish and Shellfish*, rev. ed. (Boston: CBI Publishers, 1973; London: Virtue, 1979). A translation from the French, this comprehensive manual has an A to Z section on various species of fish and shellfish, then a section containing more than 1,000 recipes, both British and international cuisine, followed by a glossary and two indexes. The text is illustrated by 416 color and black-and-white photographs. This would seem to be an ideal handbook for caterers.

Less grand but still all-embracing is *James Beard's Fish Cookery* (New York: Warner Books, 1967, paperback). The over 700 recipes are grouped by fish, which in turn are separated into saltwater fish, freshwater fish, shellfish and amphibians.

The field of seafood cookery is particularly rich in thorough, workmanlike publications. These include Sarah D. Alberson's *Blue Sea Cookbook* (New York: Hastings House, 1968), which has more than 750 recipes; Walter Kaprelian's *The Captain's Cookbook* (New York: Holt, Rinehart & Winston, 1976), a compilation of over 160 seafood recipes from charter boat captains around America; Mel and Sheryl London's *The Fish-Lovers' Cookbook* (Emmaus, Pa.: Rodale Press, 1980; London: 1981), with more than 300 recipes, and 116 illustrations, including 16 pages in full color; Lou Pappas's *International Fish Cookery* (San Francisco: 101 Productions, 1979, paperback; London: 1980, paperback), with a guide to both fish and shellfish, and 250 recipes grouped by course and cooking method; and Ruth A. Spear's *Cooking Fish and Shellfish* (Garden City, N.Y.: Doubleday, 1980), a large-format book with 400 pages of recipes arranged by type of seafood and cooking technique.

Sunset magazine's *Seafood Cookbook* (Menlo Park, Calif.: Lane, 1981, paperback; London: Lane Books, 1976, paperback) presents 175 recipes in fewer than 100 pages. The six basic cooking techniques are well illustrated, along with a guide to buying and preparing fish. This book should appeal to both beginners and experienced cooks.

FISH

Chef John Clancy and Beatrice Saunders's *John Clancy's Fish Cookery* (New York: Holt, Rinehart & Winston, 1979, paperback) is a simplified, step-by-step course in cooking. Seventy-five recipes are grouped under such headings as "Broiling," "Baking," "Steaming" and "Sautéing." Kenneth N. Anderson's *Eagle Claw Fish Cookbook* (New York: Dorison House, 1978) is an all-in-one manual, providing the basics on how to fish in both salt water and fresh water, how to preserve and prepare the catch, and more than 100 recipes by cooking technique. Time-Life's *Fish* (Alexandria, Va., and London, 1979) applies the Good Cook series format to the subject with completely satisfying results. The 90-page techniques section covers "Poaching and Steaming," "Braising and Stewing," "Baking," "Broiling and Grilling," "Frying" and special presentations. This is followed by 200 recipes gleaned from other cookbooks. The color illustrations are superb. See below for a companion volume.

SHELLFISH

Another addition of the Good Cook series is Time-Life's *Shellfish* (Alexandria, Va., 1982). The photography is excellent as usual, and the 90-page introduction to techniques in-

cludes a handy shellfish cookers' chart with shellfish names down the left-hand side and minutes of cooking according to method across the top. Approximately 200 recipes from published sources are included.

REGIONAL

Jean Nicolas, a former instructor at the Culinary Institute of America, has produced a comprehensive treatise in *The Complete Cookbook of American Fish and Shellfish* (Boston: CBI Publishers, 1980). This is done is a large, textbook-style format, with plenty of useful line drawings. Jane J. Hamm's *The Beach Cookbook*, rev. ed. (Huntsville, Ala.: Strode, 1976) is aimed at the person stuck with cooking while on vacation at the seashore. It aspires to be a "complete seafood book of recipes for the Gulf, or Atlantic, or Pacific area" but sticks to the "fast, easy, tried and true."

Alan Davidson's *North Atlantic Seafood* (New York: Viking Press, 1980; London: Macmillan, 1979; New York: Penguin, 1980, paperback) uses a quasi-scholarly approach. The book begins with a 230-page description-and-identification section, with fish arranged by taxonomic grouping and illustrated by line drawings. Then comes a section containing 10 to 20 recipes from each of 19 North Atlantic countries.

Yvonne Y. Tarr's *The Great East Coast Seafood Book* (New York: Random House, 1982, paperback) uses 400 regional and classic recipes grouped by methods of preparation. There is a short disquisition on catching, boning and filleting fish, and many useful line drawings. Local chef Howard Mitchem's *Provincetown Seafood Cookbook* (Reading, Mass.: Addison-Wesley, 1976, paperback) serves up his recipes with generous helpings of folk history, local color, drawings, old photos and humor—for example, "How to Cook a Sea Serpent." *Classy Conch Cooking* (Miami: Banyan Books) refers not to the local gastropod but to the cuisine preferred by natives of the Florida Keys. The book features alluring scenic photographs, a street map of Key West, and 43 "mouthwatering, taste-tempting, Florida Keys recipes."

Isaac Cronin and Jay Harlow's *The California Seafood Cookbook* (Berkeley, Calif.: Aris Books, 1983, hardcover and paperback) is a cook's guide to the fish and shellfish of California, the Pacific Coast and beyond. It is an A to Z approach, arranged by species name, with 75 species portraits and 150 recipes. Not every fish has a recipe, however, and some alien species have crept into the list, such as Maine lobster. The book is illustrated with fetching line drawings. Barbara Lawrence's *Fisherman's Wharf Cookbook* (Concord, Calif.: Nitty Gritty Productions, 1971, paperback) is a short, wide book, attractively illustrated with color drawings and paintings. Its 104 gourmet fish recipes are arranged by source—i.e., famous San Francisco fish restaurants such as Alioto's and The Tadich Grill.

BLUEFISH

Greta Jacobs and Jane Alexander's *The Bluefish Cookbook* (Chester, Conn.: Globe Pequot, 1981, paperback) is a handwritten labor of love. It offers approximately 50 recipes, many of the sort "you've never dreamed of" for the fabulous *Pomatomus saltatrix,* otherwise known as the bluefish.

SPECIAL

Peggy A. Hardigree's *The Freefood Seafood Book* (Harrisburg, Pa.: Stackpole, 1981, paperback) teaches you to wander the "north edge of the sea," there to find, gather and cook shrimp, lobster, clams, crabs, flounder and more than 140 other delicacies. It includes many useful line drawings.

VEGETABLES

Of the big, all-inclusive type of book, Robert Ackart's *A Celebration of Vegetables: Menus for Festive Meat-Free Dining* (New York: Atheneum, 1979, hardcover and paperback) is one of the best. It does not push vegetarianism but extols vegetables for their own sake. More than 600 recipes are arranged into menus for spring, summer, autumn, winter and basics, with each recipe sensibly headed by preparation time, cooking time and oven temperature (if applicable). Jane Grigson's *Vegetable Book* (New York: Penguin, 1981, paperback; London, 1980, paperback) goes through the list of vegetables A to Z, devoting a descriptive essay to each, and a few recipes from published sources for a grand total of more than 500. Grigson's introduction tells a priceless tale of how England succumbed to the attack of the American "bland" tomato. A similar format is used by Nika Hazelton in *The Unabridged Vegetable Cookbook* (New York: M. Evans, 1976; Bantam, 1980, paperback). A preliminary essay is devoted to each vegetable, its history, nutrition value and ways of keeping and preparing. Recipes total some 350. Time-Life's *Vegetables* (Alexandria, Va., and London, 1979) is part of the Good Cook series. It is hard to imagine a more attractive

CUCUMBERS IN YOGURT
WITH MINT
Doubles/Refrigerates

Preparation: 30 minutes

---

1 cup plain yogurt

---

2 teaspoons fine-chopped fresh mint

---

juice of ½ lemon

Blend the yogurt, mint and lemon juice. Allow the sauce to "work" for several hours in the refrigerator.

---

4 small cucumbers, peeled, seeded and halved lengthwise

Vinaigrette dressing

Allow the cucumbers to marinate in the dressing for 30 minutes, turning them once.

At the time of serving, wipe the cucumber halves with absorbent paper, divide the yogurt among 4 plates and on it float the cucumber, cut side down.

Robert Ackart, *A Celebration of Vegetables: Menus for Festive Meat-Free Dining* (New York: Atheneum, 1979), p. 104.

and effective format. Lush color is used throughout the first 90 pages to illustrate such techniques as boiling and steaming, frying braises and stews, and baking, broiling and grilling. The second section is comprised of 242 "best of the best" recipes from published sources, given in American, imperial and metric measures.

Of the many other vegetable cookbooks, the following deserve a mention: *Best Vegetable Recipes from Woman's Day* (Boston: Houghton Mifflin, 1980) is a collection of 250 recipes representing all phases of the meal. Lois M. Burrows and Laura G. Myers's *Too Many Tomatoes, Squash, Beans and Other Good Things: A Cookbook for When Your Garden Explodes* (New York: Harper & Row, 1976; 1980, paperback; London, 1977, paperback) is arranged by type of vegetable. Teresa Candler's *Vegetables the Italian Way* (New York: McGraw-Hill, 1980) presents over 250 recipes, including many regional specialties, plus a good section on preserving, pickling and freezing. Farm Journal Editions' *America's Best Vegetable Recipes* (Garden City, N.Y.: Doubleday, 1970; New York: Harper & Row, paperback) is subtitled "*666 Ways to Make Vegetables Irresistible*" and covers all phases of the meal. Nancy B. Katz's *The Mostly Vegetable Menu Cookbook* (New York: Grosset & Dunlap, 1982) includes basic recipes as well as many dinner menus. Phe Laws's *Vegetable Cookery: How to Cook Vegetables with Vitality and Verve* (New York: Music Sales, 1980, paperback) discusses 51 different vegetables in 132 recipes and provides a buying calendar. George and Nancy Marcus's *Forbidden Fruits and Forgotten Vegetables: A Guide to Cooking with Ethnic, Exotic and Neglected Produce* (New York: St. Martin's Press, hardcover and paperback) provides a description, history and a few recipes for such things as celery root, fennel, okra, plantain and salsify. *Sunset* magazine's *Vegetable Cookbook* (Menlo Park, Calif.: Lane, 1983, paperback) is a color-illustrated introduction to the subject, covering all courses of the meal in fewer than 100 pages.

GROWING AND COOKING

Lois Burpee's Gardner's Companion and Cookbook (New York: Harper & Row, 1983) uses a warm, chatty approach, with many personal anecdotes and nice black-and-white sketches. The recipe section is arranged by season and includes preserving instructions. Joan Fielden and Stan Larke's *From Garden to Table: A Complete Guide to Vegetable Growing and Cooking* (Toronto: McClelland & Stewart, 1977, paperback) is thoroughgoing and well written, covering the subject vegetable by vegetable.

INDIVIDUAL VEGETABLES

Autumn Stanley's *Asparagus: The Sparrowgrass Cookbook* (Seattle: Pacific Search, 1977, paperback) covers history and growing methods and includes more than 100 recipes from appetizers to desserts. Helen Rosenbaum's *Don't Swallow the Avocado Pit and What to Do with the Rest of It* (New York: Paul S. Eriksson, 1974) has mostly to do with cooking (140 recipes) but also touches on such topics as growing, and use as cosmetics. Inez N. Krech's *Secrets of Vegetable Cookery: Beans and Peas* (New York: Crown, 1981, paperback), part of a series, contains about 50 recipes but no illustrations; Norma Upson's *The Eggplant Cookbook* (Seattle: Pacific Search, 1979, paperback) offers more than 200 international recipes by course; Mary Hamilton's *The Leek Cookbook* (Seattle: Madrona Publishers, 1982, paperback) provides more than 150 recipes embellished by decorative line drawings; Inez N. Krech's *Secrets of Vegetable Cooking: Onions* (New York: Crown, 1981, paperback) covers the subject using approximately 50 recipes; Myra Davis's *The Potato Book* (New York: William Morrow, 1978, paperback) is an amusing and imaginative treatment of the subject, with an introduction by Truman Capote. The book is mainly about cooking, with recipes for all phases of the meal, but also informs us on potato crafts, games and health, and beauty lore. It ends with a tribute entitled *"Poème de Terre."* No index. Judith C. Madlener's *The Sea Vegetable Cookbook: Foraging and Cooking Seaweed* (New York: Crown, 1977, hardcover and paperback) is a field guide to 52 kinds of edible seaweed, from red algae to sea lettuce, covering such topics as identification, taste, use and preparation. The book contains more than 145 recipes and both useful and decorative line drawings; Ann Saling's *Rhubarb Renaissance: A Cookbook* (Seattle: Pacific Search, 1978) tells how to grow, prepare, can, freeze, dry and cook the vegetable, including recipes from quick breads to strawberry rhubarb pie. Margaret Gin's *Tomatoes* (San Francisco: 101 Productions, 1977, paperback; London, 1980, paperback), one of the Edible Garden series, presents more than 120 recipes by course.

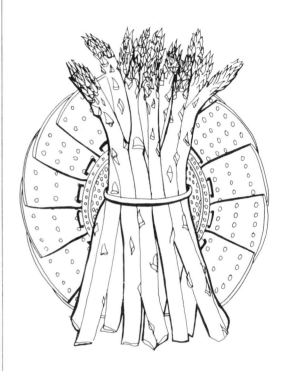

Mushrooms

Monte Mushroom rides again. This cartoon character guides the reader through William G. Flagg's *Mushroom Lover's Cookbook* (South Attleboro, Mass.: Cookbooks, Inc., 1978; Croton-on-Hudson, N.Y.: North River Press, 1982, paperback). The over 112 recipes explore use of mushrooms through all phases of the meal except dessert.

How do different mushroom varieties match with the flavors of various common foods? Jean Granger addresses this question in *Mushroom Matings: The Best of Mushroom Recipes* (San Francisco: Cragmont Publications, 1978, paperback). More than 60 gourmet-level recipes are arranged by course.

Marcelle Morphy's *Mushroom Recipes* (New York: Arco, 1978, paperback) is an international collection. Half of the 200 recipes are devoted to main dishes, such as sole a la Bonne Femme, and the rest to sauces, garnishes, preserves and soup. *Wild Mushroom Recipes*, 2nd ed. (original title: *Oft Told Mushroom Recipes*) (Seattle: Pacific Search, 1973, paperback) is arranged by genus of mushroom, with a few general recipes grouped at the beginning. Produced by the Puget Sound Mycological Society for "hunters of wild mushrooms," the book includes 220 recipes. Kay Shimizu's *Cooking with Exotic Mushrooms* (Woodbury, N.Y.: Barron's Educational Series, paperback; London, 1979) concentrates on such species as shiitake, tree ear, snow puff, wood ear and matsutake. The book has 44 recipes beautifully illustrated by 31 color plates.

The following are collector's or grower's manuals with recipes added. Margaret McKenny's *The Savory Wild Mushroom*, rev. ed. (Seattle: University of Washington Press, 1971, hardcover and paperback) is described as "a guidebook for the cowardly epicure." The text is weighted heavily toward identification and description of mushrooms specific to the Pacific Northwest, with both black-and-white and color photos to aid recognition. A few of the 41 recipes are general, but most are designed for specific wild types.

Nina L. Faubion's *Some Edible Mushrooms and How to Cook Them* (Portland, Ore.: Binford & Mort, 1972) has one chapter on mushrooms as food, containing 88 recipes for both general cooking and preparing specific wild genera. The rest is a field manual for identifying wild species that utilizes line drawings, black-and-white photos and color plates. Alexandra Dickerman's *The Mushroom Growing and Cooking Book* (Santa Barbara, Calif.: Woodbridge Press, 1978, paperback) is a how-to book for cultivating mushrooms at home, plus 130 recipes for use of mushrooms in all phases of the meal, including dessert.

Soybeans and Bean Curds

Soybeans for breakfast, lunch and dinner? Too much of a good thing, perhaps. Yet a tempting case is made for it in Barbara Farr's *Super Soy! Delicious Protein Without Meat* (New Canaan, Conn.: Keats, 1976, hardcover and paperback). The book contains more than 150 recipes for such recherché delights as super waffles with soy sausage (breakfast), soy rice patties (lunch) and vegetable and cheese casserole (dinner). Writing in a similar vein are Mildred Lager and Dorothea Van Grundy Jones in their *Soybean Cookbook* (New York: Arco, 1968, paperback). More than 350 recipes feature soybeans in everything from soup to cakes.

A flourishing subarea of soybean cookery concerns itself with cakes, curds and pastes. Tofu is a high-protein, cheeselike product made from soymilk. At the simplest level is Juel Andersen's *The Tofu Primer: A Beginner's Book of Bean Cake Cookery* (Berkeley, Calif.: Creative Arts, 1981, paperback). It is handwritten, decorated with 19th century cartoons and it contains 25 recipes ranging from breads, sandwiches and snacks through the various courses of lunch and dinner. At the complex end of the scale is William Shurtleff and Akiko Aoyagi's *The Book of Tofu*, Vol. 1 (Brookline, Mass.: Autumn Press, 1975, paperback), which contains 500 recipes drawn from Western and Oriental cuisines, and extensive directions on how to make your own tofu. Gary Landgrebe's *Tofu Goes West* (Palo Alto, Calif.: Fresh Press, 1978, paperback) performs tofu magic on such familiar dishes as spaghetti sauce, *huevos rancheros* and Yorkshire pudding. He even gives us tofu à la king. The text contains 79 recipes and is framed by attractive line drawings.

Tempeh is another fermented soyfood, originating in Indonesia. Described as having a good flavor and a meatlike texture, it may be used in a main course in place of meat, chicken or fish. William Shurtleff and Akiko Aoyagi's *Book of Tempeh* (New York: Harper & Row, 1979, paperback) explains how to make this delicacy, then how to employ it in 130 Western and Indonesian-style recipes.

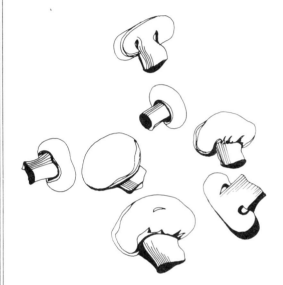

CHAPTER SEVEN

Cookbooks by Course, Process or Technique

Gadgets are a devilishly attractive subject. Or is it just that manufacturers see books about their products as legitimate items in the promotional budget? Whatever the reason, we are blessed with a varied and alluring literature on such machines as microwave ovens, electric cooking pots and food processors.

Another inexhaustible topic is the almighty importance of food as an aspect of health, be it physical or spiritual. Establishment science has laid down broad principles for a healthy diet, but within them there is plenty of scope for special pleading on behalf of such things as strict vegetarianism, natural foods, honey and sea salt. Similarly, it would seem that eating soybean products is one of the royal roads to spiritual well-being.

Take away the main course of a meal and what have you got? A good subject for a book. Those little befores and afters, those side dishes can be chatted about endlessly. Appetizers, hors d'oeuvres, salads, breads, garnishes, soups —all come in countless permutations.

The wonderful thing about techniques is they are so technical. They can be broken down, photographed step by step, practiced by the numbers, gotten up to speed and then shown off—or, if the truth be told, skipped over with the cozy feeling that they can be mastered later, when time permits.

Hors d'Oeuvre Artistry
by JULIA WEINBERG

APPETIZERS

These books cover all sorts of tidbits that are, as the French put it, "hors d'oeuvres," or outside the main courses. Coralie Castle and Barbara Lawrence's *Hors d'Oeuvres, Etc.* (San Francisco: 101 Productions, 1973, paperback) dwells at length on spreads and toppings for sandwiches and canapés (including 132 recipes), then goes to other openers, such as patés and pastry dishes (empanadas, pirashki, etc.). Fondues, hot pots and Chinese buffet dishes are also included in the 600 recipes. Renny Darling's *Great Beginnings and Happy Endings: Hors d'Oeuvres and Desserts for Standings Ovations* (Beverly Hills: Recipes-of-the-Month Club, 1981, paperback) writes that many of her hors d'oeuvres are to be distinguished from entrées or main dishes only by the size of the portion. Of the book's 375 recipes, most are simple to prepare and relatively inexpensive. Margon Edney and Ede Grimm's *The Elegant Hors d'Oeuvre* (San Diego: Tofua Press, 1977) deals with both conventional and microwave cooking, and the more than 100 recipes include quite a few low-calorie or light hors d'oeuvres.

Gloria Edwinn's *Just for Starters*, subtitled *A Treasury of 350 of the World's Best Hors d'Oeuvres and Appetizers* (New York: Viking Press, 1981), discusses dips and spreads, cold hors d'oeuvres, hot hors d'oeuvres and filled pastries and shows how to put together a survival kit for emergencies such as unexpected guests. For serious cooks only, Charles Mok's *Practical Hors d'Oeuvre and Canape Art* (Boston: CBI Publishers, 1978,) is a textbook with many color photographs that give a good idea of artful presentation and color compatibility in food preparation. Rose Naftalin's *Grandma Rose's Book of Sinfully Delicious Snacks, Nibbles, Noshes and Other Delights* (New York: Random House, 1978) continues in the vein of her outrageous dessert book, with such items as apple squares with a sweet butter, rum and sour-cream crust. She offers a wide variety of appetizers as well.

A local, then national success, the Rockdale Temple Sisterhood's *In the Beginning: A Collection of Hors d'Oeuvres*, new rev. ed. (Cincinnati: Rockdale Ridge Press, 1982, paperback) has run through 12 previous editions. Specializing in elegant-looking, easy-to-prepare items, the 360 recipes are embellished by attractive line drawings. This book can be purchased slipcased together with a sequel titled *And Beginning Again: More Hors d'Oeuvres for Cooks Who Love In the Beginning*. Julia Weinberg's *Hors d'Oeuvres Artistry* (Piscataway, N.J.: New Century, 1982, paperback) was originally titled *Big, Beautiful Book of Hors d'Oeuvres*. It presents 225 "out of the ordinary" recipes for such occasions as holidays, tea parties, ladies' club luncheons, etc. There are 12 color plates of assembled hors d'oeuvres. Time-Life's *Hors d'Oeuvres* (Alexandria, Va.: 1982) has a graceful, informative and lavishly illustrated treatment of the subject. The step-by-step sequences are superb. An 80-page technical section covers classic sauces and aspics, then vegetables, poultry and meat, fish and shellfish, eggs, and crepe, pastry and bread classics. The second section consists of 200 previously published recipes from many countries and epochs.

JEWISH

A fundraising effort for Jewish organizations, Marilyn Stone's *The Chosen: Appetizers and Desserts* (Gainesville, Fla.: Triad Publishing Co., 1982, paperback) offers the best recipes from 120 Jewish cookbooks. There is a list of contributors, and each of the approximately 400 recipes is attributed.

ROQUEFORT CHEESE PIE
Yields 10 to 12 wedges

Tastes as good as it looks! A luscious layer of Roquefort and cream cheese spread over a pastry circle holds tasty bits of anchovies, eggs, green pepper and black olives encircled by a colorful ring of pimiento.

1 pie stick
8 ounces cream cheese
4 ounces Roquefort cheese
2-ounce can flat anchovy fillets, drained and chopped
6 hard-cooked eggs, with yolks and whites chopped separately
½ cup chopped green pepper
Black pitted olives, sliced
Whole pimiento, sliced into thin strips

1. Prepare the pie stick as directed on the package. Roll out dough to a 9-inch circle. Place on a baking sheet. Flute the edges, prick the bottom and bake as directed. Allow to cool.
2. In a mixing bowl combine the cheeses and blend thoroughly. Spread the cheese mixture evenly on the pastry circle.
3. Place the chopped anchovies in the center of the pie. Around the center, create concentric circles of chopped egg yolks, green pepper, chopped egg whites and olive slices. Finally, rim the pie with the pimiento strips.
4. Refrigerate until firm. To serve, slice into wedges.

Julia Weinberg, *Hors d'oeuvres Artistry* (Piscataway N.J.: New Century, 1982), p. 140.

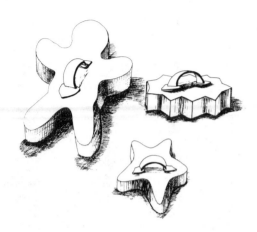

BAKING

(For bread baking, see "Bread.")

Strictly business is William J. Sultan's *Practical Baking,* 3rd rev. ed. (Westport, Conn.: Avi Publishing Co., 1981, paperback). A good baker's manual or classroom text, it covers seven major baked goods: bread and rolls, sweet yeast dough products, biscuits and muffins, fried products, pies and pastry, cake specialties and cookies. A similar title is Joseph Amendola's *Baker's Manual for Quantity Baking and Pastry Making,* 3rd rev. ed. (Rochelle Park, N.J. and London: Hayden Book Co., 1972). An instructor at the Culinary Institute of America, Amendola provides basic and advanced techniques for a wide range of baked products. The text abounds in charts, graphs, line drawings and black-and-white photos.

Somewhat lighter in approach is Joseph Amendola and Donald E. Lundberg's *Understanding Baking* (Boston: CBI Publishers, 1970, paperback). This is a self-learning book with clear explanations of why things happen and how to prevent mishaps. All aspects of baking are examined.

Less forbidding but still comprehensive are the following books: Dolores Casella's *World of Baking* (New York: David White, 1968, paperback) is unusually thorough, providing copious notes with each of the more than 300 recipes. Topics start with cake, frostings and fillings, and proceed through cookies and pies on to sourdough and miscellaneous items. Tables include equivalent measures and substitute ingredients (for example, yogurt for buttermilk). Elise W. Manning's *Farm Journal's Complete Home Baking Book* (Garden City, N.Y.: Doubleday, 1979) is brightly produced with generous margins, 17 color photographs and numerous black-and-white illustrations. The over 450 recipes cover the basics—yeast breads, cakes, cookies and pies. Diane Harris's *Woman's Day Book of Baking* (New York: Simon & Schuster, 1978) is aimed at the beginner. It presents a simple method of learning about the basics, then applies the lessons to yeast breads, quick breads, coffee cakes, cakes and cookies. The over 500 recipes are illustrated with eight full-page color photographs. Paula Peck's *Art of Fine Baking* (New York: Simon & Schuster, 1961; 1970, paperback) gives the reader 500 from-scratch recipes for cakes, frostings, decorations, puff paste and strudels, cookies, pies and tarts, plus pastry appetizers and hors d'oeuvres. Techniques are illustrated with drawings. A briefer but still satisfactory approach is used in Natalie Sylvester's *The Home-Baking Cookbook* (New York: Grosset & Dunlap, 1973, paperback). It is an attractive handwritten book, with 150 recipes and many decorative and useful line drawings.

ETHNIC STYLES

Karen Berg's *Danish Home Baking* (New York: Dover, 1960, paperback) covers the usual baking topics with a Danish tilt. Each chapter is introduced with Danish modes and manners regarding the particular item under discussion. Included are 119 recipes in English with Danish subtitles. Elizabeth David's *English Bread and Yeast Cookery* (New York: Viking Press, 1980; Penguin, 1982, paperback; London: Allen Lane, 1971; Penguin, 1979, paperback) is a history book, reference book and cookbook all in one. A stellar performance, this book enhances the author's already lustrous reputation. The first half considers matters historical and technical, and the second holds recipes for countless breads, buns, tea cakes, fruitcakes, dumplings, doughnuts, pancakes and pizzas. The entire book is written in a fine and witty style. Sara Kasdan's *Mazel Tov, Y'All: A Bake Book for Happy Occasions* (New York: Vanguard, 1968) is a Jewish baking book written in a vivid, funny style. The more than 100 recipes are embellished with amusing line drawings.

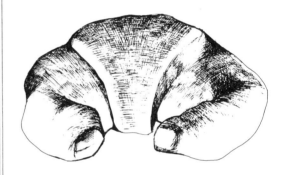

NATURAL STYLE

Martha Katz's *The Complete Book of High-Protein Baking* (New York: Ballantine, 1977, paperback; London, 1978) covers the usual topics, with particular attention to the protein content of ingredients. Katz's motto is "Eat bread and salt, and speak the truth." The over 200 recipes are illustrated with decorative and useful line drawings. Gail Worstman's *The Whole Grain Bake Book* (Seattle: Pacific Search, 1980, paperback) shows how to use whole grains successfully in a wide range of baked goods, including breads, muffins, rolls, pretzels, pizza and bagels, not to mention cakes, cookies and pastries. The book contains more than 130 recipes. Patricia Mayo's *The Sugarless Baking Book* (Brookline, Mass.: Autumn Press, 1979, paperback; Boulder, Colo.: Shambhala Publications, 1983, paperback) is billed as the natural way to prepare America's favorite breads, pies, cakes, puddings and desserts. The over 70 recipes emphasize such ingredients as soymilk, almond milk, cashew milk and tofu sour cream. Rose Hoffer and Muriel Warrington's *Everybody's Favorite (Orthomolecular) Muffin Book* (New Canaan, Conn.: Keats, 1980, paperback) gives 70 muffin recipes, stressing such ingredients as nuts, yogurt, seeds, whole grains, eggs, honey, bran and fruit. (*Orthomolecular* means "supplying the molecules of the body with the nutrients each needs.")

SOURDOUGH

A cheerfully written piece is Don and Myrtle's *Complete Sourdough Cookbook* (Caldwell, Idaho: Caxton, 1972, paperback). Intended for use on the trail, at camp or in the kitchen, the book is spiced with poetry in the style of Robert W. Service (for example, "Sweet Tooth Tilly and Sourdough Sam"). It contains many authentic sourdough recipes from the Old West, plus some of the tamer sort, such as applesauce tea loaf, and timelier items, such as sourdough pizzas.

BREADS

As in other areas of cookery, James Beard covers the subject of bread with completeness and panache. His *Beard on Bread* (New York: Alfred A. Knopf, 1973; Ballantine, 1981, paperback) offers 100 of his favorite recipes, plus variations. The list includes yeast breads, coffee cakes, rolls, flatbreads, and filled and fried breads; headnotes describe how each will look, taste and best be used. No space or words are wasted in *Better Homes and Gardens All-Time Favorite Bread Recipes* (Des Moines, Ia.: Meredith, 1979). In approximately 100 large-format pages, 200 recipes are given for yeast breads, sourdough breads, quick breads and bread fix-ups. Techniques are illustrated by line drawings, and finished products with fine color photographs.

Zen philosophy informs Edward E. Brown's *Tassajara Bread Book* (Boulder, Colo.: Shambhala Publications, 1970, paperback; London, 1972, paperback). This different angle makes for interesting reading, but the book stands on its own as a natural-foods book, with more than 100 recipes on sourdough, yeast breads, nonyeast and quick breads, desserts and pancakes. The drawings to illustrate techniques are particularly good. Tassajara, by the way, refers to a California commune. Dolores Casella's *A World of Breads* (New York: David White, 1966, paperback) surveys all kinds of breads in some 600 recipes. Instructions are clear but require a little experience to be immediately useful. Another all-embracing effort, Bernard Clayton, Jr.'s, *The Complete Book of Breads* (New York: Simon & Schuster, 1974) offers 500 recipes in a clear, concise format with timings in the margin. For fanatics, there's a chapter on how to build an old-fashioned, outdoor adobe oven. A British original,

Patricia Jacob's *The Best Bread Book* (Los Angeles: Corwin, 1975; London: Hamlyn, 1981) does an excellent job on the basics of baking, then treats finishes and toppings, wholemeal breads and rolls, white breads and rolls, tea breads and buns. The over 50 recipes are classifed as either "easy," "moderately difficult" or "experienced" only and are give in imperial, metric and American measures.

Ellen Johnson's *The Garden Way Bread Book* (Charlotte, Va. and London: Garden Way Publishers, 1979; paperback) is a baker's almanac, arranged by the month, and offers 140 recipes embellished by black-and-white photos and line drawings. Mel London's *Bread Winners* (Emmaus, Pa.: Rodale Press, 1979) is a collection of over 200 prize recipes from a group of remarkable American home bakers. No shortcuts and no scientific methods are used in Ada L. Roberts' *The New Book of Favorite Breads from Rose Lane Farm*, 2nd rev. ed. (New York and London: Dover, 1981, paperback). There are 30 recipes from the kitchen of a Kansas farmer's wife, with copious commentary, decorative line drawings and even a few poems. Small but inspiring is Georgia and Cecilia Scurfield's *Home Baked: A Little Book of Bread Recipes* (New York: Transatlantic, 1972, hardcover and paperback; London: Faber & Faber, 1956; 1971, paperback). Making your own bread looks easy and enjoyable here. After an introduction to the basics, the 53 recipes are divided into two sections, British and international. Stella Standard's *Our Daily Bread* (New York: Berkley, 1976, paperback) touches on all aspects of home breadmaking, dividing the 450 recipes into two basic groups—those using white flour and those using whole-grain breads. There are useful nutrition charts but no illustrations. *Sunset* magazine's *Breads*, 3rd ed. (Menlo Park, Calif.: Lane, 1977, paperback) is lavishly illustrated with color photos and is surprisingly complete for such a brief treatment (96 pages). The approximately 176 recipes include yeast breads, sourdough, sweet and festive breads, breads to be made in a hurry and even some bread sculpture.

Time-Life's *Breads* (Alexandria, Va. and London, 1981) an entry in the Good Cook series, is a delight to use. The 88-page techniques section is skillfully and beautifully illustrated. Topics include basic yeast breads, enriched yeast, special yeast (sourdough) and bread without yeast. The second section offers 201 recipes from a variety of published sources.

CORNELL FORMULA

Clive M. and Jeannette B. McCay's *The Cornell Bread Book: 54 Recipes for Nutritious Loaves, Rolls and Coffee Cakes*, rev.

ed. (New York: Dover, 1980, paperback; London, 1981, paperback) features the "do-good loaf" derived from Professor McCay's work in animal nutrition at Cornell University. The formula he developed includes soy flour, nonfat dry milk and wheat germ.

INTERNATIONAL

Bernard Clayton, Jr.'s, *The Breads of France* (Indianapolis: Bobbs-Merrill, 1978) is a beautiful collection of classic and regional breads. The recipes (many gleaned from French bakers) are lucid and well presented, often reflecting such fine differences as the influence on French bread of the *pain italien* of Provence, Switzerland and Germany. Lovers of exotic breads will not be disappointed with Florence Laffal's *Breads of Many Lands* (Essex, Conn.: Gallery Press, 1975, paperback). The over 100 recipes offer many such items as Swedish kryddskorpor (rye husks), Nigerian agidi (cornmeal dumplings wrapped in banana leaves) and Indian paratha (unleavened wheat flour, often filled). Lois Sumption and Marguerite L. Ashbrook's similarly titled *Breads from Many Lands* (New York: Dover, 1982, paperback) contains recipes from such places as America, England, France, Germany, Italy, India and Mexico, plus many more. Barbara H. Taylor's *Mexico: Her Daily and Festive Breads* (Claremont, Calif.: Creative Press, 1969, paperback; recipe supplement, 1969, paperback) offers us a peek at Mexico through black-and-white photos and quotations and well as through recipes. Breads include those both corn- and wheat-based, and a much-needed glossary at the end keeps the names straight.

SOURDOUGH

Rita Davenport's *Sourdough Cookery* (New York: Bantam, 1977, paperback; London: HP Books, paperback) ranges from "San Francisco sourdough bread" to sourdough tuna fritters. The book includes over 200 recipes, and in the HP Books edition, lots of color photographs, both full-page and how-to. Timothy Firnstahl's *Jake O'Shaughnessey's Sourdough Book* (San Francisco: San Francisco Book Company, 1976, hardcover and paperback) takes its name from a saloon in Seattle that re-creates an 1890s atmosphere, complete with sourdough bread and other victuals. This is a competent piece of work that is embellished by lots of black-and-white photos and drawings.

BREAKFAST/BRUNCH

Brunch as a commercial phenomenon is distinctly American and is a development of the past 20 years. So says Terence Janericco in *The Book of Great Breakfasts and Brunches* (Boston: CBI Publishers, 1983). This is a fine book for a caterer, as it contains more than 250 recipes for breakfasts, brunches and even a few lunches. A sampling of topics includes beverages, eggs, quiche, chicken, pancakes, breads and basic sauces. Finished dishes are illustrated in 16 color plates.

Brunch is defined as a "festive breakfast" in Pauline Durand and Yolande Languirand's *Brunch: Great Ideas for Planning, Cooking and Serving* (Woodbury, N.Y.: Barron's Educational Series, 1978, paperback). The subject is introduced through a discussion of the classic French menu, then guest and selected other menus. The over 200 recipes are then grouped under all phases of the meal, from drinks through desserts. American and metric measures are used, and the text is enlivened with amusing sketches. Pat Jester's *Brunch Cookery* (New York: Dell, 1981, paperback; London: HP Books, 1980) offers over 200 recipes arranged by course, plus lavish color illustrations (in the HP Books edition). Ruth Macpherson's *Discover Brunch: A New Way of Entertaining*, new ed. (Maplewood, N.J.: Hammond, 1977) is arranged by month, with three menus for each month. The 235 recipes use American measures, and a metric conversion table is provided.

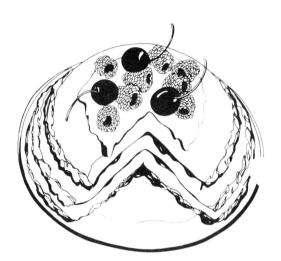

CASSEROLE

In the 1970s the marketing of electric slow cookers brought one-pot cookery into vogue. Georgia and Grover Sales' *The Clay-Pot Cookbook: A New Way of Cooking in an Ancient Pot* (New York: Atheneum, 1977, paperback) takes the idea back to its origins, the unglazed terra-cotta pot. The authors claim the clay pot is more versatile and faster than conventional cooking pots, although it is somewhat difficult and cumbersome to use because of its weight. The method is to dampen the pot, then heat it in a fast, high oven, making use of quick-cooking steam. More than 100 recipes are given, covering all courses.

For a brief but well-illustrated approach, it is hard to beat *Sunset* magazine's *Casserole Cook Book* (Menlo Park, Calif.: Lane, 1980, paperback; London: Lane Books, 1976). Ap-

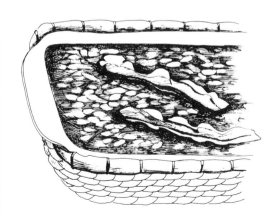

proximately 175 recipes are given in fewer than 100 pages, covering such topics as hearty favorites, meatless entrées, ethnic cuisine, calorie counters, stovetop specialties and super side dishes.

Marian Tracy's *New Casserole Cookery* (New York: Penguin, 1968, paperback) is a collection of recipes (using imperial and American measures) for a wide variety of casserole dishes, including desserts. The recipe collection in Myra Waldo's *Casserole Cookbook: Choice Dishes from Around the World* (New York: Macmillan, 1963, paperback; London: Collier-Macmillan, 1963, paperback) is both international and practical and contains many unusual dishes.

CHAFING DISH

The Swiss are everywhere given credit for creating fondue. Well, it's true. Here finally is a thumbnail history of the dish, and a description of the traditions that accompany its native consumption. In addition, Ed Callahan's *Fondue Cookbook*, rev. ed. (Concord, Calif.: Nitty Gritty Productions, 1975, paperback) offers more than 100 recipes, ranging from the sybaritic Fondue Royale (made with truffles and champagne) to the humble Bernie's Fondue (made with chicken livers and chopped onions). For more on fondue, see also "Cheese," in Chapter 6.

The Culinary Arts Institute provides a generic approach to this type of cookery in *Wok, Fondue, and Chafing Dish* (New York: Delair, 1980, paperback). An introduction covers techniques for all three topics; then the over 250 recipes are arranged by course. The book is embellished by attractive green-tinted drawings, plus eight full-page color photographs of finished dishes.

More in the professional line is John Fuller's *Gueridon and Lamp Cookery: A Complete Guide to Side-Table and Flambé Service*, 2nd ed. (New York: Radio City, 1975; London: Barrie and Jenkins, 1975), which gives much space to questions of equipment, staffing, special handling and the ins and outs of preparation. Although the 75 recipes require some skill, the book might be of some use in the home. A classic in the field is Herbert Kinsley's *100 Recipes for the Chafing Dish* (New York: Arno Press, n.d.). A reprint of the 1894 edition, this book may be of interest mainly to collectors, although, of course, the recipes are still workable.

COLD DISHES

A book of summer dishes, Helen Hecht's *Cold Cuisine* (New York: Atheneum, 1981) considers such topics as cold soups, entrée salads, entrée mousses and dishes in aspic, plus desserts and accompaniments. It includes more than 350 recipes, and sample menus.

Including both hot and cold dishes is Elizabeth David's *Summer Cooking* (New York and London: Penguin, 1955, paperback). There's a lot here—no wonder it's been around for nearly 30 years and still is going strong. The 1,000 recipes are light, easy to prepare and are based on the availability of seasonal meat and vegetables; topics run from hors d'oeuvres straight through to cool summer sweets. The British kitchen terminology may be unfamiliar to some American readers.

Molly Finn's *Summer Feasts* (New York: Simon & Schuster, 1979) leans toward the elaborate, with lots of good vegetable recipes. It makes good use of summer possibilities but surely would come in handy year round.

DEEP-FRYING

Deep-fat frying at home is the topic of Barbara Methven's *Mini-Fryer Cookery* (New York: Crown, 1978). It is oriented toward an appliance called a mini-fryer and offers a consumer's guide to the various brands on the market. The mini-fryer is a versatile gadget, as attested by the 211 recipes, which range right on through the meal from appetizer to dessert.

DESSERTS

Best Desserts Ever (New York: Larousse, 1979) is described by the publisher as a collection of "100 desserts assured of success." Just looking at the color photographs (one for each dish) makes your waistline expand. But success is assured because of the careful formatting and step-by-step instructions, which include metric/imperial and American measures, preparation and cooking times, and tips on making ahead. Preliminary chapters present basic techniques and tricks of the pastrymaker's trade. The bias here is French, but the desserts should appeal to everyone. Time-Life's *Classic Desserts* (Alexandria, Va., 1980) is second to none in

BURNT CREAM
Crème Brûlée

This recipe was taken from *The Ocklye Cookery Book* (1909) by Eleanor L. Jenkinson.
To serve 4 to 6

2½ cups heavy cream, or 1¼ cups (300 ml.) heavy cream mixed with 1¼ cups light cream	600 ml.
4 large egg yolks, well beaten	4
¼ to ⅓ cup superfine sugar	50 to 75 ml.

Bring the cream to a boil, and boil it for about 30 seconds. Pour it immediately into the egg yolks and whisk them together. At this point, return the mixture to the pan and cook it without allowing it to boil, until it thickens and coats the spoon. Pour the mixture into a shallow baking dish. Refrigerate it overnight.

Two hours before the meal, sprinkle the chilled cream with the sugar in an even layer, and place it under a broiler preheated to the maximum temperature. The sugar will caramelize to a sheet of brown smoothness; you may need to turn the dish under the grill to achieve an even effect.

Time-Life, eds., *Classic Desserts* (Alexandria Va.: Time-Life Books, 1980), p. 91.

the photography department. The six how-to chapters are a minicourse in dessert cookery, followed by 209 recipes from published sources.

Anita Borghese's *Just Desserts* (Briarcliff Manor, N.Y.: Stein and Day, 1979, paperback) creates an appetite for justice with more than 400 recipes covering all phases of dessert cooking. Recipes are arranged both by major ingredient (cheese, chocolate) and form/technique (crêpe, puff pastry, soufflé).

Aimed at both the professional chef and the amateur, Dominique D'Ermo's *The Chef's Dessert Cookbook* (New York: Atheneum, 1976, paperback) offers over 450 recipes embracing both classic French cuisine and "American-born" dishes. The how-to section should enable amateurs to get through most of the recipes, which are arranged by type of dessert, plus a chapter on low-cal desserts.

Dieters, cast aside all hope if you dare consult *Maida Heatter's Book of Great Desserts* (New York: Alfred A. Knopf, 1974; Warner, paperback, n.d.). The recipes are all rich and fattening, and what's more, often unusual and intriguing. Where else would you find Gin Ice Cream, or Chocolate Applesauce Torte with Kumquats? The 300 recipes are pitched above the beginner level.

The traditional, step-by-step approach of *McCall's Superb Dessert Cookbook* (New York: Random House, 1978) will appeal to beginners. One notable entry: the recipe for Ratner's famous marble cheesecake.

Originally published by the International Wine and Food Society, Margaret Sherman's *Sweet Puddings and Desserts* (North Pomfret, Vt.: David & Charles, 1971) offers an excellent selection of recipes, using both American and imperial measures. Illustrations include color photographs and line drawings.

Eugene and Marilynn Sullivan's *The Wilton Book of Classic Desserts* (Chicago: Wilton, 1970) is an international collection of recipes, many concocted from nine basic mixtures, which can be made into many dishes and which are clearly explained here.

In a class by itself is Juel Andersen's *Tofu Fantasies* (Berkeley, Calif.: Creative Arts Books, 1982, paperback). Billed as a "cookbook of incomparable desserts," it gives 20 recipes, each embellished with amusing line drawings and funny personal anecdotes. And the recipes do indeed defy comparison—e.g., Wild River Whisky Cake.

LOW-CALORIE DESSERTS

Juel Andersen's *Unforbidden Sweets: More than 100 Classic Desserts You Can Enjoy Without Counting Calories* (New York: Arbor House, 1982) keeps the count down to 200 per serving in most recipes, and in some down to 100. Andersen covers all the usual topics, though—even some show-stopping lavish party desserts.

Carol Cutler's *The Woman's Day Low-Calorie Dessert Cookbook* (Boston: Houghton Mifflin, 1980) counts calories for the total and each ingredient in over 200 recipes. Chapters include hints for lo-cal, fruit- and gelatin-based dishes, plus the standard topics.

DINNER

Need to get dinner on the table in under an hour? Madeleine Kamman's *Dinner Against the Clock* (New York: Atheneum, 1973) presents a system for accomplishing just that through wise buying, clever organization and a sound knowledge of technique. Chapters consider types of food and are keyed to the quickest traditional methods of preparing them. These, combined with sample menus marked "Everyday" and "Company," take the bother out of planning and preparing meals in a hurry. The 275 recipes are backed by advice on equipment, shopping and menu planning.

DRIED FOODS

Deanna Delong's *How to Dry Foods* (Tucson, Ariz. and London: HP Books, 1979, paperback) doesn't neglect cooking. The book has a 63-page section containing over 100 recipes for preparing dried fruits, vegetables, meats and fish. The first half is dedicated to the techniques of drying fruits, vegetables, herbs and spices, nuts and seeds, and meat and fish, with a special section on baby foods. This is a large-format book with handsome color illustrations.

Time-Life's *Dried Beans and Grains* (Alexandria, Va.: 1983) applies the Good Cook series format to this subject. There are 80 pages of cooking techniques, followed by a section offering approximately 200 recipes from published sources. Both photography and writing are excellent.

Two collections of bean recipes deserve mention. Valerie Turvey's *Bean Feast: An International Collection of Recipes for Dried Beans, Peas and Lentils* (San Francisco: 101 Productions, 1979, paperback) contains over 220 recipes divided into soups, salads, eggs, meat, vegetables and miscellaneous. Norma Upson's *The Bean Cookbook: Dry Legume Cookery* (Seattle: Pacific Search, 1982, paperback) is an international collection of more than 200 recipes embellished by high-contrast prints.

ELECTRIC COOKERY

Under this rubric we lump books on electric frying pans, slow-cooking pots and convection ovens. Helen M. Cox's *The Multi Cooker Book* (British title: *The Multi Cooker Recipe Book*) (Boston: Faber & Faber, 1980, hardcover and paperback; London, paperback) is a collection of over 200 recipes for the Sunbeam electric frying pan. Recipes are varied and interesting and use imperial/metric measures. A table of American equivalents is given.

Millions of Americans purchased crockpots in the 1970s, buying also the attractive idea that a few ingredients tossed into the pot before the morning commute could be transformed into a delicious stew by eventide. Mable Hoffman's *Crockery Cookery* (New York: Bantam, 1975, paperback; another edition, Tucson, Ariz.: HP Books, 1975, paperback) doesn't try for novelty but does adapt most basic stew recipes for the crockpot. The 257 recipes contain some international entries, such as teriyaki, chicken marengo, sweet-sour cabbage and canard bourgignon. Martha Lomask's *Low, Slow, Delicious: Recipes for Casseroles and Electric Slow-Cooking Pots* (Boston: Faber & Faber, 1981,; London, 1980) offers over 230 recipes in a good, businesslike format illustrated by 16 full-page color photographs. Recipes use imperial/metric measures, and an appendix gives characteristics of the various pots available in the marketplace.

A convection oven uses a noiseless fan to circulate heated air constantly around the inside of the oven. The advantages claimed for this method are that the same food can be cooked in a third the time needed for a conventional oven, at 25 to 50 degrees lower temperature, using conventional ovenware, and that more than one item can be cooked at a time. Jack D. and Maria L. Scott's *The Complete Convection Oven Cookbook* (New York: Bantam, 1981, paperback) provides over 230 kitchen-tested recipes for Farberware turbo-ovens, while Carmel B. Reingold's *Convection Oven Cookbook* (New York: Harper & Row, 1980, hardcover and paperback) is a large-format book that capitalizes on her more than 20 years' experience in the field.

FOOD PROCESSOR

Finally, an equipment cookbook that emphasizes the food, not the machinery. Jean Anderson's *New Processor Cooking* (New York: William Morrow, 1983) concentrates on real

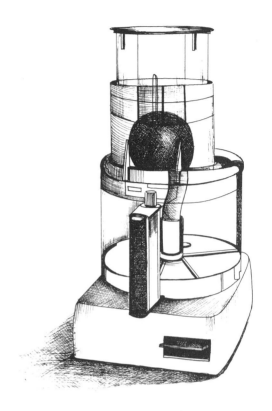

food, not countless purées. Examples of some fine recipes are Pennsylvania Dutch sweet-and-sour potato salad, Maryland stuffed ham, veal strips with mushrooms and cream, and grapefruit-orange marmalade.

A comprehensive approach is found in Yvonne Y. Tarr's *The Great Food Processor Cookbook* (New York: Random House, 1976, paperback), which contains more than 400 recipes and discusses several makes of machines. Particularly useful is a chapter-long yield chart that tells you how much measured yield you can expect from various quantities of raw food, and includes settings and timings for different food processors. The 24 chapters cover all courses of a meal as well as special topics such as outdoor cooking and baby and health foods.

Mary M. Hemingway and Suzanne de Lima's *Food Processor Magic: 622 Basic Recipes and Techniques* (New York: Hastings House, 1976) is similarly wide-ranging when it comes to recipes and techniques, but discussion is limited to the Cuisinart machine.

"Gourmet delights" are the concern of Judith Gethers's *The Fabulous Gourmet Food Processor Cookbook* (New York: Ballantine Books, 1981, paperback). The 250 recipes are restricted to such delicacies as spreads, pâtés and dips; mousses; soufflés and quiches; stocks and soups; sauces and butters; breads, biscuits and rolls; and pies, pastries and cakes. The book is strong on reader aids, including a table that provides quick reference data on the processing of each kind of foodstuff; a table of yield equivalents; a dictionary of food processor parts for several different makes; and a glossary of cooking terms.

The following three are brief, but well-rounded efforts, all profusely illustrated with color photographs. Consumer Guide Editors' *Food Processor Cookbook* (New York: Simon & Schuster, 1977, hardcover and paperback) offers more than 200 recipes that include gourmet dishes, ethnic specialties and familiar American standards. The Cuisinart is the featured machine, but a final chapter gives test reports on several other makes. *Better Homes and Gardens Food Processor Cook Book* (Des Moines: Meredith, 1979) is divided into four sections: a food processing primer; a 19-page food processing chart that lays out preparations, timings and settings for all manner of foods; a chapter on how to adapt familiar recipes to the new technology; and, finally, a section of more than 200 recipes, covering all phases of the meal. Sunset Editors' *Sunset Food Processor Cookbook* (Menlo Park, Calif.: Sunset-Lane, 1974, paperback) goes over much the same material in 80 pages with more than 150 recipes. Special features are a "Mexican Buffet for 12," "Seasonings with Herb Butters" and "Sausages from Scratch."

FROZEN FOODS

All the latest gadgets are covered in Charlotte Erickson's *The Freezer Cookbook*, 2nd ed. (Radnor, Pa.: Chilton, 1978, hardcover and paperback) which is written for anyone who owns a home freezer. Techniques use the microwave oven, slow cooker and food processor. The over 700 recipes are flagged by little images of these machines in the margin and are arranged by course and main ingredient.

Nell B. Nichol's *Farm Journal's Freezing and Canning Cookbook*, rev ed. (Garden City, N.Y.: Doubleday, 1978) approaches the subject from both ends. It teaches how to freeze and can, then gives more than 1,000 recipes to use with the results. Handy endpaper charts answer questions on when to can fruits, when to freeze vegetables and how to gauge quantities. The Culinary Arts Institute's *The Canning and Freezing Book* (New York: Delair, 1975, paperback) is narrower in scope but very thorough in its treatment. Most interesting are the frozen dishes that are ready to eat on reheating. The large-format book has eight full-page color photos.

Freeze-and-reheat recipes are explored more thoroughly in Audrey Ellis's *Cooking for Your Freezer* (New York: Transatlantic, 1970, paperback; London: Hamlyn, paperback), Marika H. Tenison's *Deep Freeze Cookery* (New York: Beekman Publishers, 1979; London: Hart-Davis [2nd rev. ed], 1979; Mayflower, 1980, paperback) and Myra Waldo's *Cooking for the Freezer* (Garden City, N.Y.: Doubleday, 1975, paperback).

GARNISHES

Edible flowers carved from fruits and vegetables are the subjects of Julia Weinberg's *Gourmet Bouquet* (Piscataway, N.J.: New Century, 1978, paperback; London: Butterick, 1978, hardcover and paperback). Subtitled *"Decorative Centerpieces to Eat and Enjoy,"* the book takes you through the operations of slicing, carving, cutting, skewering, shaping and serving, with lucid text and profuse black-and-white photos and line drawings. Twelve color plates illustrate finished pieces. Garnishes are a recognized art in Japan, as evidenced in Bob and Yukiko Haydock's *Japanese Garnishes: The Ancient Art of Mukimono* (New York: Holt, Rinehart & Winston, 1980; London: J. Piatkus, 1980). Arranged by food, the chapters consider apples, carrots, cucumbers, eggs, oranges, radishes, tomatoes, turnips, squash and miscellaneous items.

Few books are illustrated as thoroughly as this one. There are 250 how-to line drawings, 50 black-and-white photos of finished garnishes and four color plates depicting 36 garnishes.

LUNCHEONS

Beverly Barbour's *Easy, Elegant Luncheon Menus* (Radnor, Pa.: Chilton, 1980) contains hundreds of recipes distributed among more than 100 menus. Quantites are given for four, six and 24 portions, and menu categories include Superior Salads and Sandwiches, The Elegant Egg, For the Calorie Conscious, Seasonal Favorites and Ethnic Fare from Everywhere. Finished luncheons are pictured in 12 color plates.

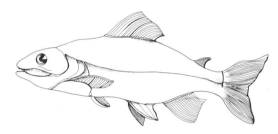

MARINE

More comprehensive than the rest is Phyllis Bultmann's *Two Burners and an Ice Chest: The Art of Relaxed Cooking in Boats, in Campers and Under the Stars* (Englewood Cliffs, N.J.: Prentice-Hall, 1977, paperback; London, 1978, paperback), which covers equipment, food supplies, recipes (breakfast, lunch, dinner, cocktails, pot luck and meals for guests), then easy recipes, plus charcoal, fish, convenience foods, soups and carry-along.

Strictly for boats, the best is Michael Greenwald's *The Cruising Chef* (Blue Ridge Summit, Pa.: TAB Books, 1977 hardcover and paperback), which provides basic suggestions on organizing the galley. The recipes are varied but emphasize fish and make frequent use of the pressure cooker. Sallie Townsend and Virginia Ericson's *The Sea Cook: Or How to Have Superb Meals Afloat Without Becoming a Galley Slave*, 2nd ed. (New York: T. Y. Crowell, 1977, hardcover and paperback) is competent and comprehensive.

Jan Silver's *Heavy Weather Cooking* (Camden, Maine: International Marine, 1980, paperback; London, 1980) is based on a sensible premise: "To minimize perils of acrobatic feats during rough weather, the safest thing to do is to refrain from cooking." She emphasizes snacks and make-aheads.

SHRIMP CREOLE

Shrimp cooked in a tomato creole sauce goes especially well with rice. With frozen shrimp there is about ½ cup liquid added from the juices that cook out during thawing and cooking. If your shrimp has been thawed and drained, you may have to add back this amount of liquid.

3 tablespoons cornstarch
¼ cup chopped onion or 1 tablespoon instant minced onion
½ cup chopped green pepper
½ teaspoon salt
½ teaspoon paprika
½ teaspoon chili powder
⅛ teaspoon instant minced garlic or 1 clove garlic
⅛ teaspoon pepper
½ teaspoon leaf basil or marjoram
3½ cups (1-lb. 12-oz can) undrained tomatoes
3 cups (12 oz) frozen uncooked shrimp

In 1½- or 2-quart casserole, combine all ingredients; mix well. COOK, covered, 12 MINUTES or until shrimp are done and mixture boils, stirring occasionally during last half of cooking time. Serve over rice. 4 to 5 servings.

Litton Industries, *Exciting New World of Microwave Cooking* (New York: Van Nostrand Reinhold, 1976; London, 1974), p. 57.

MICROWAVE OVENS

Litton Industries has set a high standard in its series of books on microwave cooking. One of the earliest was *An Exciting New World of Microwave Cooking* (New York: Van Nostrand Reinhold, 1971, hardcover and paperback). Developed by Litton home economists, the 500 recipes cover all meals and courses but stress main dishes. There are many tips and suggestions for special use, and the color photography is excellent. Another of the series, Litton's *Microwave Cooking: Adapting Recipes* (New York: Van Nostrand Reinhold, 1979), is cleverly formatted, with conventional recipes pictured on three-by-five cards, and the necessary changes entered in handwriting. The index lists ingredients and recipes, plus popular recipes which though not included, can be adapted using the guidelines provided. Approximately 100 recipes are included, and the color photography is exceptional. A poster-sized chart (folded in a pocket) gives setting guides for all popular makes of microwave oven. In the same format is Litton's *Microwave Cooking: Everyday Dinners in Half an Hour* (New York: Van Nostrand Reinhold, 1980). It's a quick and easy guide that offers more that 180 recipes. More Litton books are discussed below under specific categories.

The following are comprehensive introductions to microwave cookery. *Betty Crocker's Microwave Cookbook* (New York: Western Publishers, 1977, paperback; another edition, New York: Random House, 1981) is a large-format book that includes a staggering variety of dishes in its over 350 recipes. Picture these (and you can in 180 color photos): gingerbread pot roast, fish fillets with shrimp sauce, beer-barbecued turkey drumsticks, pecan squash, carrot apple cupcakes and double chocolate fudge cake.

Pat Jester's *Microwave Cookbook: The Complete Guide* (Tucson, Ariz.: HP Books, 1982, paperback) is divided into thumb-indexed sections by course, each preceded by a Q-and-A passage. Recipes number in the 100s, and more than one serving size is measured. Sylvia Schur's *The Tappan Creative Cookbook for Microwave Ovens and Ranges* (New York: New American Library, paperback 1977; another edition 1981) is a useful adjunct to the Tappan manual, offering more than 480 recipes for all meals. Maria L. and Jack D. Scott's *Mastering Microwave Cooking* (New York: Bantam, 1976, paperback) is a cookbook and a consumer's guide to microwave ovens, many of which are pictured in black-and-white photographs. The 242 recipes are arranged by course. Richard Deacon's *Microwave Cookery* (New York: Bantam, 1978, paperback; another edition, Tucson, Ariz.: HP Books,

1977, paperback; London, 1979, paperback) is a sequel to and in some respects an update of his 1973 introduction to the subject. In a large format, the HP Books edition is billed as a "complete guide to success with your microwave" and features profuse color illustrations. The introduction discusses variable-power ovens and temperature probes, and provides a five-day sequence of cooking lessons. The over 215 recipes are arranged by course.

BAKING

Val Collins's *Microwave Baking* (North Pomfret, Vt., and London: David & Charles, 1980) caters to a complete range of baking needs, including bread, cakes, puddings and savory dishes, plus techniques for combining microwave with the conventional oven and the freezer. Readers will be thrilled, Collins says, by "near instant results." The over 300 recipes are given in imperial/metric measures and are illustrated with 32 color plates and useful line drawings. A table of equivalent American measures is provided.

BRIEF GUIDES

Better Homes and Gardens Microwave Cookbook (Des Moines, Iowa: Meredith, 1976) is a large-format book offering over 200 recipes in fewer than 100 pages with a generous number of color illustrations. Recipes are divided into three segments: by course, by meal and microwave plus (using range, freezer and barbecue). Quite similar in format and number of recipes are the Culinary Arts Institute's *Microwave Cookery* (New York: Delair, 1977, paperback) and *Sunset* magazine's *Microwave Cook Book*, 2nd ed. (Menlo Park, Calif.: Lane, 1981, paperback; London: Lane Books [1st ed.], 1976, paperback).

FRUITS AND VEGETABLES

A Litton book, *Microwave Cooking: Fruits and Vegetables* (New York: Van Nostrand Reinhold, 1981), is a complete, well-illustrated guide, with recipes arranged by type of food. Litton's claim that the book is "like having a cooking school in your home" is backed up the clearly written general instruction section, good charts—especially the one laying out seasonal availability—and the removable "Microwave Oven Power Level Setting Guide." Val Collins's *The Microwave Fruit and Vegetable Cookbook* (North Pomfret, Vt., and Lon-

don: David & Charles, 1981) proceeds comprehensively by phases of the meal, including many unusual and delicious recipes: chilled artichoke soup, baked avocado with walnut cheese, apple and cream cheese flan. There are over 200 recipes, using imperial/metric measures, and 32 color plates. Phe Laws's *Vegetable Magic with Microwave* (New York: Music Sales, 1977, paperback) presents the required steps to achieve perfectly cooked fresh vegetables in a matter of minutes. This is a valuable guide, with many creative recipes and tips, but also space provided for timings of individual ovens.

INTERNATIONAL

Phe Laws's *International Gourmet Cooking with Microwave* (New York: Music Sales, 1981, 1976, paperback) offers over 200 recipes arranged by country, including most European cuisines and Latin American, Polynesian, Indian, Southeast Asian and oriental cuisines.

MEATS

Microwave Meats Step by Step (New York: Van Nostrand Reinhold, 1979) is another entry in the fine Litton series. There is an extensive section on selecting, storing and preserving different cuts of meat and includes superb color photographs. Recipes are grouped by types of meat: beef, veal, pork, lamb, liver, sausage and poultry.

NATURAL FOODS

Natural-foods cookbooks are a mixed bag, some implying that their particular approach to diet will promote perfect health and extend the life-span. Others state, more modestly, that they are concerned with basic foods that are unrefined, fresh, not highly processed and that have no additives, leaving the reader to decide the value thereof. Two of the best of this latter approach are Jean Hewitt's *The New York Times Natural Foods Cookbook* (New York: Avon, 1972, paperback and large-format paperback; London: Souvenir Press, 1980, paperback) and its sequel, *The New York Times New Natural Foods Cookbook* (New York: Times Books, 1982). The first sprang from a *Times* campaign to solicit recipes from readers that emphasized foods not highly processed. Of the 3,000 received, 750 are included in the first volume. The book is not vegetarian (though vegetarian main dishes are not ignored) but does promote such choices as whole grains rather than refined ones, and honey and molasses over sugar. The recipes are varied and contain some international classics. The sequel extends this philosophy to another 800 recipes that include baking, chicken and fish but not beef.

In the same mode is Charles Gerras's *Natural Cooking the Prevention Way* (New York: New American Library, 1972, paperback; London, 1980, paperback), a compilation of health-food recipes from the readers of *Prevention* magazine. Particularly good on breakfast recipes, salads and dips, the book also covers meat, fish and poultry. Noted food writer Marian Burros's *Pure and Simple: A Cookbook* (New York: William Morrow, 1978; Berkley, 1982, paperback) is subtitled *"Delicious Recipes for Additive-Free Cooking."* The goal requires some advance organization, but once that's done, it's easy. Her suggestions include making your own biscuit mix in batches, storing your own Shake'n Bake and preparing your own granola. There's a handy key to how far in advance each recipe can be assembled and cooked.

One of the best comprehensive approaches comes from England, George Seddon and Jackie Burrow's *Natural Foods Book* (Chicago: Rand McNally, 1980, paperback; London: Mitchell Beazley [British title: *Wholefood Book*], paperback, 1980). This is a very-large-format book with 300 illustrations, in both color and black and white. The 1,000 recipes run the whole gamut of foods and courses.

Sharon Cadwallader and Judi Ohr's *Whole Earth Cookbook* (Boston: Houghton Mifflin, 1972; New York: Bantam, 1973, paperback; London: Houghton Mifflin, 1973, paperback) offers 200 recipes that were tested in the Whole Earth Restaurant at the University of California's Santa Cruz campus. It emphasizes soups, salads, vegetables, breads and desserts, and though not a vegetarian book, it includes sections on nonmeat protein dishes and grains. *Sharon Cadwallader's Complete Cookbook* (San Francisco: San Francisco Book Co., 1977,) contains more than 900 recipes arranged by course, plus suggested menus.

"Organic John" Calella, a San Francisco radio personality, promotes his "Salade Mandala" in *Cooking Naturally* (Berkeley, Calif.: And-Or Press, 1978, paperback), which he calls an "evolutionary gourmet cuisine of natural foods." He sets out 13 rules for combining fats, proteins, starches, sugar, acids and alkalai to achieve "socio-nutrition" in harmony with the environment. The book utilizes mainly raw

GARBANZO SESAME PASTE DIP
HUMMUS B'TAHINI
(Serves 4 to 6)

1 cup garbanzos
4 cups water (more water as needed to keep garbanzos covered)
⅓ cup lemon juice
2 to 3 large cloves garlic, crushed and minced
⅓ cup tahini (sesame paste)
1 to 1½ cups garbanzo stock OR water
1 tsp. sea salt
2 tbsp. olive oil OR vegetable oil
¼ to ½ tsp. chili pepper, ground
1 large sprig parsley

Cover garbanzos with water. Soak overnight (optional step). Place garbanzos in a heavy saucepan. Bring to boil over high heat. Cover. Reduce heat to medium low. Simmer 3 to 4 hours until tender (easily mashed with a fork). To pressure-cook: place garbanzos in pressure cooker with water. Cover. Bring to full pressure. Cook at full pressure 1 hour. Remove from heat. Cool. However cooked, drain and reserve stock for later use. Mash garbanzos with a foodmill, fork, or your fingers, ½ cup at a time. Do not use blender—it will burn out at this task.

Add to garbanzo paste. Mix until a smooth paste is formed. Add more stock or water to the mixture as needed to make it dip-like in consistency. Place in a bowl. Chill 2 to 3 hours or overnight.

Pour over top of dip.

Sprinkle red pepper around edge of bowl and in a cross pattern across the center. Place 1 sprig of parsley on side. Serve with pita (Arab bread), carrots, radishes, celery, cabbage, cauliflower, or other crisp vegetables. Excellent snack or appetizer for a party. Good served with vegetables, a main dish and pilaf for dinner.

Sigrid M. Shepard, *Natural Food Feasts: From the Eastern World, China, Japan, India, Indonesia, Middle East* (New York: Arco, 1979), p. 93.

and cooked vegetables and fruits in various combinations. Marjorie Ford et al.'s *Deaf Smith Country Cookbook* (New York: Macmillan, 1973, paperback; London: Collier-Macmillan, 1974, paperback) uses only natural foods and is especially strong on breakfast dishes, recipes for camping and baby foods. The title refers to a part of Texas where a particularly fine strain of wheat is grown that was named for Deaf Smith, a hero of the Texas Revolution of 1835.

Pamela Hannan's *Runner's World Natural Foods Cookbook* (Mountain View, Calif.: Anderson World, 1981, paperback) presents over 750 recipes "for people who care about their health" and want to extend their life-span. This is to be accomplished, in great part, through a sugarless diet. Part I explains the diet; Part II gives recipes by course, including baking.

The Gayelord Hauser Cook Book (New York: Putnam, 1955, paperback) is one of the pioneer books of recipes for health and beauty. There are menus for gaining weight as well as for reducing, and there are excellent sections on salads and salad dressings. Jean Kinderlehrer's *Confessions of a Sneaky Organic Cook* (New York: New American Library, 1971, paperback) angles at "making your family healthy when they are not looking." Her recipes aim at taking the "square" stigma off healthy foods, and they include unusual cakes and desserts. Eleanor Levitt's *Natural Food Cookery* (New York: Peter Smith, 1971; Dover, 1979, paperback; London, 1980, paperback) was originally titled *The Wonderful World of Natural-Food Cookery*. Though not vegetarian, it is very good on cereals, grains, seeds and nuts. The 650 recipes are comprehensive in coverage, and supplementary material includes tables of vitamins, sources for them, a glossary of health-food terms and a list of items natural-food people generally avoid.

BACKPACKING/CAMPING
Aubrey Wallace's *Natural Foods for the Trail* (Yosemite, Calif.: Vogelsang Press, 1977) offers recipes for backpackers, from gorp to tuna casserole (canned and dried).

BLENDER
Frieda Nusz's The *Natural Foods Blender Cookbook* (Milwaukee: Keats, 1972, paperback) is two books in one, its 200 recipes divided into the sections "Wheat- and Sugar-Free" and "Blender Busy." Within these categories, recipes are arranged by food item, not by course.

BREAKFAST

Eating simply, sanely and well are the objectives of Diane S. Greene's *Sunrise: A Whole Grain, Natural Food Breakfast Cook Book* (Trumansburg, N.Y.: Crossing Press, 1980, hardcover and paperback). After an introduction on grain mills and flour, the over 200 recipes are divided among such topics as porridge, pancakes, yeast breads and accompaniments—custards, yogurts, sauces, spreads and toppings. There are protein and mineral charts, and a cereal glossary.

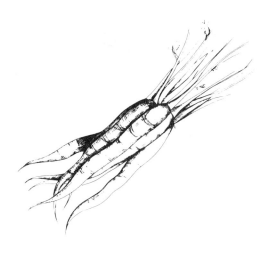

LOW-COST

Charles Gerras's *Low-Cost Natural Foods* (Emmaus, Pa.: Rodale Press, 1982) focuses on such economical items as dried beans, grains and pasta. Charts are provided for these ingredients, and recipes are arranged by course.

ORIENTAL

There's plenty of variety in Sigrid M. Shepard's *Natural Food Feasts: From the Eastern World* (New York: Arco, 1979, paperback), which includes more than 800 recipes from China, Japan, India, Indonesia and the Middle East. The book is embellished by innumerable line drawings.

QUICK AND EASY

Sharon Claessens's *The Twenty-Minute Natural Foods Cookbook: Over 300 Kitchen-Tested Recipes* (Emmaus, Pa.: Rodale Press, 1982) is divided by course and then into three groups: "Make It Fast," "Make It Easy" and "Make It Ahead." No illustrations.

PANCAKES

Just plain pancakes is the forte of James E. Banks's *Uncle Jim's Book of Pancakes*, 2nd ed. (Palmer Lake, Colo.: Filter, 1979, hardcover and paperback). Banks eschews fancy crepe desserts, waffles, fritters and omelets. Here we have are 17 recipes divided into two categories: buttermilk pancakes and sourdough pancakes.

PASTRY

These three volumes are for practicing pastry chefs and serious students. Leonard J. Hanneman's *Pâtisserie: Professional Pastry and Dessert Preparation* (New York: Van Nostrand Reinhold, 1971; London: Heinemann, 1971) covers a wide range of baked goods in a well-illustrated format. William Sultan's *Modern Pastry Chef,* 2 vols. (Westport, Conn.: AVI Publishing Co., 1977, hardcover and paperback) covers in Volume 1 ingredients, procedures, then the baking of quick breads, yeast-raised products, doughnuts, pies, puff paste and *choux* paste and *gateaux.* This is a solid textbook format with lots of useful line drawings, and recipes measured for 100 diners. Volume 2 includes such topics as pancakes, crepes and fritters, custards, puddings, mousses and soufflés, French pastries, tarts and strudels. Joseph Lambeth's *Lambeth Method of Cake Decoration and Practical Pastries* (New York: Radio City, 1980 repr. of the 1934 ed.) is a folio volume on decorating commercial pastries. Each design is illustrated, mostly in black and white, but 20 color plates are included.

For amateur pastry fans comes Gaston LeNotre's *LeNotre's Book of Desserts and Pastries* (Woodbury, N.Y.: Barron's Educational Series, 1977; London, 1981), a showcase for the creative talent and well-honed skills of a master baker. Recipes have been adapted for the home baker by his daughter, Sylvie Gille-Naves. The detailed instructions and hints from the master alone are worth the price of admission.

Bernard Clayton, Jr., is a teacher and the author of two best-selling books on bread baking. His *The Complete Book of Pastry, Sweet and Savory* (New York: Simon & Schuster, 1981) is equally thorough and precise. There are successful chapters on the basics of pastry, pies, cream-puff dough, turnovers and others plus outstanding chapters on ingredients, equipment, leavening and sources of supply.

GERMAN

Margit S. Dutton's *The German Pastry Bakebook* (Radnor, Pa.: Chilton, 1977) covers Ruhrkuchen, Obstkuchen and Flachekuchen; Biskuit; Torten; Brandtieg; Strudel; Blatterteig; Hefeteig; and Kleingebäch, plus chapters on utensils, ingredients, toppings, frostings, fillings and sources of supply.

PIES

A classic work is Louis P. DeGouey's *The Pie Book: 419 Recipes* (New York: Peter Smith, 1949; New York: Dover, 1974, paperback). Topics include technical data; pastry and crust recipes; pie recipes; chiffon pie recipes; and topping, garnishing and glazing. Patricia A. Ward's *Farm Journal's Best Ever Pies* (Garden City, N.Y.: Doubleday, 1981) offers introductory chapters all about pies and the secrets of pastry making, then groups more than 375 recipes under fruit pies, cream pies, custard pies, refrigerated and frozen pies, and savory dish pies.

VIENNESE

Lilly J. Reich's *The Viennese Pastry Cookbook: From Vienna with Love* (New York: Macmillan, 1978, paperback; London: Collier-Macmillan, 1979, paperback) sometimes emphasizes the unusual—e.g., apple fritters in wine dough—but the 200 recipes included cover 50 different kinds of torten, yeast pastries and hot desserts, plus icings and fillings. This is a collection of family recipes, but the subject is well introduced, and there is a list of mail-order sources.

PRESSURE COOKERY

Natural food and pressure cookery go hand in hand. The popularity of one has led to a revival of interest in the other because it allows the use of fresh foods without spending hours over a hot stove. Roy Andries de Groot is an eminent cookbook writer whose *Pressure Cookery Perfected* (New York: Summit Books, 1978, hardcover and paperback) makes a gourmet tool of this appliance. Clear and creative, the recipes are especially notable for the variety of delicious one-dish meals. Home economist K.F. Broughton is an English expert on pressure cooking. Her *Pressure Cooking Day by Day* (New York: International Publications Service, 1975; London: Kaye & Ward, 1970; 1976, paperback; another edition, Pan, 1977, paperback) includes both basic instructions and a wide range of recipes, most interestingly some cakes and bread to be cooked under pressure. Alma P. Ralston's *Pressure Cooking* (Concord, Calif.: Nitty Gritty Productions, 1977, paperback), a small, wide volume with tinted, textured paper, is most appropriate, perhaps, for gift-giving. The text is clearly written and well illustrated with prints and line drawings. After introductory chapters on history and how to use, the over 100 recipes are arranged by course.

POT ROAST OF VEAL IN CALIFORNIA CHARDONNAY

For 4
Cook under pressure at 10 lb for 45 minutes (or at 15 lb for 33 minutes)

Up to 4 Tbs olive oil
A 3-lb. (1.4 kg) nicely shaped, boneless piece of entirely lean rump of veal
4 medium yellow onions, peeled and sliced
1 medium green pepper, coarsely chunked
Enough chopped fresh leaves of parsley to fill 1 cup (2.5 dl)
Salt, to your taste
Freshly ground black pepper, to your taste
1½ cups (3.75 dl) of a fine-quality California Pinot Chardonnay dry white wine

When the noble, white grapevine of Europe, the Pinot Chardonnay, was transplanted to California, it took root with such a thriving intensity and vigor that some of the greatest American white wines have been made from this magnificent grape. At its best, the wine is strong, sometimes slightly smoky, with a superb character and personality and a refreshing, fruity quality that goes almost perfectly with veal. Here, we cook the veal in Pinot Chardonnay and, of course, we drink the same wine with the meal when it is served. The timing in this recipe is for a 3-pound roast—for other weights, allow 15 minutes per pound at 10 pounds pressure, or 11 minutes per pound at 15 pounds pressure.

You will need a large pressure casserole of at least a 6-quart capacity. Heat it, without its base rack, to medium-high frying temperature, lubricate its bottom with 3 tablespoons of the oil and, when it is good and hot, quickly and thoroughly brown the roast on all sides. If necessary, add the fourth tablespoon of olive oil. When the job is well done, turn off the heat. Turn the pot roast around so that its best-shaped end is uppermost. Now pack in around it the onions, green pepper, and parsley, with salt and pepper to taste. Pour over and around the meat the Pinot Chardonnay. Put on the lid, bring the pressure up to 10 pounds and cook for exactly 45 minutes.

When the timer rings, turn off the heat and allow the pressure to reduce gradually of its own accord. Serve the veal, sliced fairly thinly, with its magnificent natural sauce of puréed onions and white wine, accompanied by three vegetables such as green beans, Brussels sprouts and lima beans.

Roy A. De Groot, *Pressure Cookery Perfected* (New York: Summit Books, 1978), p. 123.

RELISHES AND PICKLES

Amusing and well illustrated, Ruby and Jack Guthrie's *A Primer for Pickles and A Reader for Relishes* (San Francisco: 101 Productions, 1974, paperback; London, 1980, paperback) offers 100 recipes for pickling and preserving fruits and vegetables, catsups, chutneys, relishes, sauces and sauerkraut. There is extensive how-to information on pickling and canning, plus directions on how to raise your own raw materials in a backyard garden. Betsy McCracken's *Farm Journal's Homemade Pickles and Relishes* (Philadelphia: *Farm Journal*, 1976, paperback) contains a formula for the perfect cucumber pickle, plus 99 others for tangy vegetables, spicy fruits and peppy sauces.

SALADS

Salads are a virtuous topic, appealing to dieters, natural-foods people and just about everybody else. There seems to be no objection to them. Perhaps this is why there are so many good, big books on the subject. Barbara Gibbons's *Salads for All Seasons* (New York: Macmillan, 1982) offers 180 recipes that embrace not just greens but also hot and cold, potatoes, pasta and rice, plus fruit and gelatin, and main-course-sized. Kay Shaw Nelson's *The Complete International Salad Book* (New York: Bantam, 1981, paperback) gives us a global tour with all the familiar salads, plus such unusual preparations as Albanian mint and Bulgarian walnut salads. Another book of international scope is Rosalie Swedlin's *A World of Salads* (New York: Holt, Rinehart & Winston, 1981, hardcover and paperback; London: Elm Tree, 1980). The nearly 200 recipes cover greens, beans, mixed vegies, pasta, and rice and fruit, and purées.

Gorgeous color photos are just one of the attractions of Time-Life's *Salads* (Alexandria, Va., and London, 1980). An entry in the Good Cook series, it combines a 90-page how-to section that is crisply written and well formatted, with a recipe collection consisting of 207 best-of-best recipes from previously published sources. Sonia Uvezian's *The Book of Salads* (San Francisco: 101 Productions, 1977, paperback) is an attractively produced book with tinted line drawings and over 180 recipes on the usual topics from greens through pasta and rice to molded gelatin creations.

BRIEF

Two large-format books do a competent job in fewer than 100 pages. *Betty Crocker's Salads* (Racine, Wis.: Western Publishing Company 1977, paperback) comprises over 60 recipes on tossed-green, fruit, vegetable and main-dish salads. Illustrations include line drawings and eight color photographs. Ann Lerman's *Big Green Salad Book* (Philadelphia: Running Press, 1977, hardcover and paperback) does more than the title implies, with chapters on fruit, potatoes, rice and pasta, and molds, as well as on green salads. The 127 recipes are embellished by line drawings.

SALAD AND SOUP

Two interesting hybrids are *Rodale's Soups and Salads Cookbook and Kitchen Album* (Emmaus, Pa.: Rodale Press, 1981), which offers 300 recipes in 23 soup-and-salad categories, and Marilee Matteson's *Small Feasts: Delectable Meals with Soups, Salads and Sandwiches* (New York: Crown, 1980), which has recipes organized into menus grouped into several sections according to which element of the trio is stressed: soup, salad or sandwich.

SANDWICH

A book that has endured because of its variety and thoroughness is Arnold Shurcliffe's *The Edgewater Sandwich and Hors d'Oeuvre Book* (New York and London: Dover, 1975, paperback). This reprint of the 1930 edition gives 750 recipes taken from the repertoire of the Edgewater Beach Hotel and other hotels and restaurants.

A more recent effort is Diane Harris's *The Woman's Day Book of Great Sandwiches* (New York: Holt, Rinehart & Winston, 1982), which offers more than 250 recipes divided among the categories "Breads, Spreads and Trimmings"; "Hearty Cold Sandwiches"; "The Perfect Hamburger and Other Hot Sandwiches"; "America's Regional Bounty"; and "International Specialties." In the last category are two of the most delicious entries: the French *croque-monsieur* (grilled ham and cheese sandwich, served hot with a pickle) and the Swiss *Gefülltes Brot* (a French loaf stuffed with a forcemeat based on either chopped cooked ham, rare beef, roast veal, or chicken livers).

If you wish to amuse your palate, dip into Time-Life Editors' *Snacks and Sandwiches* (Alexandria, Va. and London:

Time-Life Books, 1980). Ninety pages of instructions are followed by 205 previously published recipes for *amuse-gueule* (French for snacks; literally, "palate amusers") and sandwiches.

SAUCES

Marjorie P. Blanchard's *The Easy Harvest Sauce and Purée Cookbook*, rev. ed. (Charlotte, Vt.: Garden Way Publishers, 1982, paperback) is intended for those who own a food processor, squeezer-strainer, food mill or blender. The over 170 recipes include 20 vegetable purées, 14 fruit, berry or nut purées and 22 traditional sauces. Features include many black-and-white photos and decorative line drawings.

SOUPS

For soundness and variety it's hard to beat Time-Life's *Soups* (Alexandria, Va., and London, 1980). The 90-page techniques section considers purées, compound broths, panades (bread and soup combinations), cold soups and full-meal soups. The 212 recipes are selected from published sources, and the color photographs are superb. Kay Shaw Nelson's *The Complete International Soup Cookbook* (Briarcliff Manor, N.Y.: Stein and Day, 1980) has recipes arranged by type of soup (clear, bisque, chilled, etc.) rather than by country but lives up to its title nonetheless. Yvonne Tarr's *The New York Times Bread and Soup Cookbook* (New York: Times Books, 1972; New York: Ballantine, 1980, paperback) offers more than 600 bread and soup recipes grouped by area: New World, Mediterranean, Northern Europe, Eastern Europe, Near and Far East. Another combination book, *Better Homes and Gardens Soups and Stews Cookbook* (Des Moines, Iowa: Meredith, 1978; New York: Bantam, 1980, paperback), ranges from appetizers to meal makers, plus stocks, noodles and dumplings from scratch. The over 200 recipes are embellished by good full-page color photographs and decorative color drawings.

Concise in style but international is scope is Coralie Castle's *Soup*, rev. ed. (San Francisco: 101 Productions, 1981, paperback; 1st ed., 1971, paperback). The 250 recipes offer a wide variety, including clear, vegetable, Romanic, oriental, "meal in a bowl," cold soups, fruit soups and those based on canned soups. In large format, Ann Lerman's *The Big Blue Soup Book* (Philadelphia: Running Press, 1978, hardcover and paperback) presents over 100 recipes on stocks, "big" soups, vegetable soups, seafood soups and fruit soups.

VEGETARIAN

Inventive and easy-to-follow recipes are a hallmark of Anna Thomas's *The Vegetarian Epicure*, Books I and II (New York: Alfred A. Knopf, 1978, hardcover and paperback; Book I, London: Penguin, 1973, paperback). In Book I, Thomas proves the point that "gourmet" recipes need not necessarily have meat. In Book II, with more than 250 recipes, she takes the concept worldwide. The recipes will interest practiced cooks but are also workable by beginners. In the same spirit is Judy Ridgeway's *The Vegetarian Gourmet* (Englewood Cliffs, N.J.: Prentice-Hall, 1980, hardcover and paperback; London: Ward Lock, 1979) which includes such dishes as nut rarebit on toast and polenta tomato casserole. The over 320 recipes are embellished by decorative line drawings and six color plates.

A more traditional approach is found in Barbara Echols's *Vegetarian Delights: A Hearty Collection of Natural Foods Recipes* (Woodbury, N.Y. and London: Barron's Educational Series, n.d.). Included are an introduction to vegetarianism, a trip to the natural-foods store and tips on food additives, then basic recipes and chapters on rice and grains, dried foods, eggs and cheese, plus much more. Rose Elliot's *Vegetarian Dishes from Around the World* (New York: Pantheon, 1982, hardcover and paperback; London: Collins) offers over 250 recipes from 30 countries. From a yogic retreat comes JoAnn Levitt et al.'s *Kripalu Kitchen: A Natural Foods Cookbook and Nutritional Guide* (Summit Station, Pa.: Kripalu Publications, 1980, paperback). The over 350 recipes follow these guidelines: Avoid processed or refined foods, meat, fish and eggs, stimulants and depressants; use simple combinations, allow appestat to function, and chew thoroughly. Mollie Katzen's *The Enchanted Broccoli Forest: and Other Timeless Delicacies* (Berkeley, Calif.: Ten Speed Press, 1982, hardcover and paperback) is a handwritten book offering over 220 recipes in many different ethnic cooking styles. Many are unusual, but the arrangement is along conventional lines: soups, salads, bread, entrées, etc.

BRIEF/FAST

Sunset magazine's *International Vegetarian Cookbook* (Menlo Park, Calif.: Lane, 1983, paperback) takes vegetarianism around the world in fewer than 100 pages, with lots of color photographs. The over 200 recipes cover salads and vegetables, soups and stews, grain, pasta and legumes, eggs and cheese, pancakes, crêpes and tortillas, breads and desserts.

Four months' worth of vegetarian meals are laid out in Martha R. Shulman's *Fast Vegetarian Feasts* (New York: Dial Press, 1982, paperback), whose subtitle, *Delicious, Healthful Meals in 45 Minutes,* sums up the intent of the book. The menus are given first; then more than 200 recipes are grouped into chapters on soups, grains, pasta, tacos, etc.

EASTERN

Exotic spices and exciting flavor combinations are characteristic of the recipes in *Madhur Jaffrey's World-of-the East Vegetarian Cooking* (New York: Alfred A. Knopf, 1981). She gathered this collection of 600 from home and restaurant cooks all over Asia and the Middle East. The recipes are models of chatty exposition and are grouped under such topics as vegetables, beans and dried peas, rice and other grains, eggs, milk products, noodles, etc. Examples of unusual recipes are Iranian *koo-koo* (a spongy-textured omelet-like delicacy); Indian-style cream of lentil soup, spiced with roasted cumin seeds; and North Indian-style brown rice with spinach roots, spiced with cumin and coriander. Manju S. Singh's *The Spice Box: A Vegetarian Indian Cookbook* (Trumansburg, N.Y.: Crossing Press, 1981, hardcover and paperback) is notable for its chapter on how to prepare betel *(paan)* for chewing.

PARTIAL VEGETARIAN

Jean Hewitt's International Meatless Cookbook (New York: Times Books, 1980) is by any standard a good collection of international recipes. Although red meat is excluded, there are plenty of recipes for fish and chicken among the 300-plus included here.

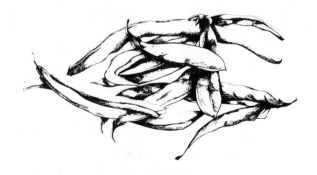

CABBAGE KIMCHEE
(Cabbage Pickle)

(makes 2 quarts)

1 pound Chinese cabbage (about ½ large head)
1 pound white radish
3 tablespoons salt
2 tablespoons finely minced fresh ginger
1½ tablespoons minced garlic
5 scallions, cut into fine rounds, including green
1 tablespoon cayenne or hot Korean red pepper
1 teaspoon sugar

If you are using a small, whole cabbage, cut it in half lengthwise, and cut it across at 2-inch intervals. If you are using half of a large cabbage, cut it in half again lengthwise, and then crosswise at 2-inch intervals.

Peel the white radish, cut it in half, lengthwise, and then cut it crosswise into ⅛-inch-thick slices. In a large bowl put 5 cups water and 2 tablespoons salt. Mix. Add the cabbage and radish to this water and dunk them in a few times, as they have a tendency to float. Leave the vegetables in the salty water. Cover loosely and set aside for 12 hours. Turn the vegetables over a few times.

Put the ginger, garlic, scallions, cayenne, sugar and 1 tablespoon salt in another large bowl. Mix well.

Take the cabbage out of its soaking liquid with a slotted spoon (save the liquid) and put it in the bowl with the seasonings. Mix well.

WILD FOODS

"Banqueting on nature's bounty" is the polar opposite of gourmet dining because, in the lingo of the books discussed here, it means eating what you can gather from the wild with your own two hands. Angier Bradford's *Feasting Free on Wild Edibles* (Harrisburg, Pa.: Stackpole, 1972, paperback) combines two earlier volumes, *Free for the Eating* and *More Free for the Eating Wild Foods*. In it are 500 ways of preparing 337 wild fruits, greens, roots, tubers, nuts and beverages that may be gathered in backyards, fencepost corners, open fields and by lakes and streams.

Gail Duff's *The Countryside Cookbook* (New York: Van Nostrand Reinhold; London: Prism Press, 1982) offers recipes and remedies to be made with more than 50 wild foods. Arranged by season, the wild foods are identified by illustrations (some in color), descriptions, and Latin and vernacular names, supplemented by three or four recipes.

Christopher Nyerges's *Wild Greens and Salads* (Harrisburg, Pa.: Stackpole, 1982, paperback) contains "hundreds of recipes for turning wild greens into healthy, hearty soups, salads, omelets and breads." Examples are stir-fried amaranth, cattail stew, root coffee, and prickly pear ice cream.

Billy Joe Tatum's Wild Foods Cookbook and Field Guide (New York: Workman Publishers, 1976, hardcover and paperback) has an exceptionally thorough plant-guide section with the usual identifying criteria and good details on exactly which parts are used and how. Three hundred thirty recipes are included.

Put this cabbage mixture into a 2-quart jar or crock. Pour enough of the salt water over it to cover the vegetables (about 2 cups). Leave 1 inch of empty space at the top of the jar. Cover loosely with a clean cloth and set aside for 3 to 7 days. In the summer, *kimchees* mature with much greater speed; in the winter, the process slows down unless the central heating is ferocious. Taste the pickle after 3 days to check on the sourness. When it is done to your liking, cover the jar and refrigerate.

To serve, remove just as much of the *kimchee* solids as you think you'll need for a meal—a cupful is enough for 4 people—and put it in the center of a bowl. The *kimchee* liquid in this pickle is left behind in the jar and may be used to flavor soups and stews. Serve this cabbage *kimchee* with any Korean meal.

Madhur Jaffrey, *Madhur Jaffrey's World of the East Vegetarian Cooking* (New York: Knopf, 1981), pp. 378-379.

Shopping
for
Food
and
Equipment

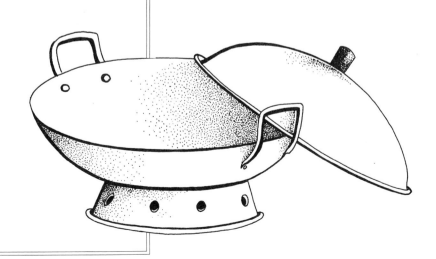

Shopping is hard work for some and a delight for others. Some shun the experience, while others are natural hunters and gatherers. The second group will take to these books with enthusiasm, being aficionados of the sport, so to speak. But natural nonshoppers, being tortoises in the race for bargains, may have the most to gain: These books will help them acquire shopping techniques, learn to plan, and cut their shopping time to a minimum.

One group of books concentrates on the techniques of shopping. Supermarkets are seen as the opposing team in the life game called food shopping. In a sense, supermarkets make the rules of the game, but there are ways of meeting them on their own ground and winning the contest through minimizing expense while getting the quality merchandise everyone wants.

A second group of books concentrates on what food to buy. They may identify, through gorgeous color photographs, all manner of food, so the shopper will know what an often exotic food should look like and therefore be more discriminating. Or they may selectively identify foods the authors think the shopper should be buying for reasons of quality, nutrition or other criteria.

A third group of works deals with equipment. Some are catalogs, others recommend levels of outfitting depending on nature of the kitchen, while still others are preoccupied with a minimum list of specific items that a self-respecting cook should have.

FOOD SHOPPING: QUALITY AND NUTRITION

COOKS' INGREDIENTS

Adrian Bailey et al.'s *Cooks' Ingredients* (New York: William Morrow/Bantam Books, 1980) shows you what they look like, in vivid color and usually in actual size. This is mainly a photographer's book, so the credit must go to Phillip Dowell, who did the marvelously (sometimes excruciatingly) lifelike photographs.

This book could be a tremendous aid to the discriminating shopper. Some 2,000 food items are pictured side by side with other members of their class—e.g., a beef tongue appears alongside a lamb's tongue and a veal tongue; a beef heart appears alongside a pig's heart, a lamb's heart and a chicken's heart. The format gives you a perspective that words can't.

The eight pages on pasta will banish any confusion you

may have experienced distinguishing *tagliatelli* from *tagliarini* or *ziti* from *elicoidali*. Want to sharpen your bean identification skills—say, how to tell the split yellow pea from the split skinless chick-pea? Check the four pages of photographs of dried peas, lentils and beans.

Each food variety is provided with a caption giving its common name, its taxonomic term and often a comment such as, "One of the most tasty of several varieties of dried peas. Its texture is floury but it retains its shape when cooked."

Bailey, assisted by coauthors Elisabeth Lambert Ortiz and Helena Radecka, provides details of the origin, nature, properties and culinary applications in a 100-page textual supplement to the photographs. Cooking directions are of a general nature and do not include recipes.

The visual approach has its limitations, as on the page titled "Other Alcoholic Drinks," in which the reader is presented with a drinker's-eye view of numerous potations. It is impossible (and maybe not even desirable) to tell gin from vodka, or arrack from ouzo, without the aid of the other senses.

THE SMART SHOPPER'S GUIDE

The promise of this book is a savings of 25 to 40 percent on your food bill, while improving the taste and nutrition of what you eat. Joan Bingham and Dolores Riccio's *The Smart Shopper's Guide to Food Buying and Preparation* (New York: Charles Scribner's Sons, 1982) balances the lure of bargains against nutritional value. Accordingly, to achieve the desired results, the smart shopper must invest time and effort not just in the shopping end of the continuum but also in the nutritional analysis and cooking ends, too.

Part One, which makes up about 15 percent of the book, is devoted to overall shopping strategies and psychological tips. Careful planning and a curb on impulse buying are essential elements, combined with seasonal shopping, choosing the right market, market-hopping to maximize savings on specials, couponing and comparison pricing.

The bulk of the book is then divided along nutritional lines, beginning with a chapter on nutritional basics, the four food groups, etc. Parts Three through Seven consider in turn the following groups: vegetables and fruits; grains, nuts, seeds, dried beans and peas; dairy products and eggs; meat, poultry and fish; fats and oils; and sugars and syrups. Within each section, the most common foods are treated to separate discussions, covering what to look for when shopping, general preparation tips, and facts on availability, storage,

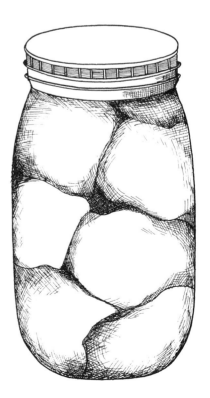

amount to purchase and nutritional content. Each part has a group of easy-to-follow recipes (including sauces), which add up to 60 for the entire book.

The following example typifies their style:

POMEGRANATES

This fruit, which is used to make grenadine, should be heavy for its size, and have a thin purple or deep red skin. Eat pomegranates, seeds and all, or squeeze them for their delightful juice.

Availability: October and November

Storage: Will keep, uncovered, in the refrigerator for a few days.

Amount to Purchase: One per service.

Nutritional Content: Potassium.

Sections on packaged foods, and especially "health foods," help the reader distinguish between products that offer value and those that are a waste of money.

It is a good bet that the savings the authors claim can be achieved provided the reader is willing to take it on as a sort of hobby, or minor obsession.

THE SUPERMARKET HANDBOOK

This is a modern treasure map for supermarket shoppers who seek nutritional gold amid a jungle of packaged goods. Nikki and David Goldbeck's *The Supermarket Handbook: Access to Whole Foods* (New York: New American Library, 1974, paperback) is a guide to the least processed, least adulterated, least "improved" foodstuffs available in your local supermarket. Necessarily, along the way they guide you away from the "nonnutritive, chemically laden nonfoods." Although it was completed a decade ago, the basic advice offered by the Goldbecks is still sound, and many of the details about specific brands stand up to this day.

The book is organized around a hypothetical shopping tour of the market, starting with eggs and dairy products and working through to jams and desserts. Each chapter features a basic discussion of the food, what is is, its different forms and varieties, how it is processed and the effect of the processing on its nutritive value. At the end of each section, the authors offer a list of exemplary brands—i.e., those that best satisfy the nonprocessed, nonadulterated criteria. The Goldbecks are thorough. They even devote a short chapter to "foodless foods"—snacks—which would seem to represent the antithesis of their values. They are, however, able to find virtue in such things as roasted soybeans, popcorn, halvah and baking chocolate. The first section ends with a useful chapter on reading food labels and interpreting food-dating codes.

Part Two is a guide to preparing at home the sorts of foods most subject to adulteration and processing in the prepackaged varieties. These include soups, sauces, breakfasts, baby foods, candy and some baked goods. There are more than 75 recipes for such things as chicken soup, blender mayonnaise and Nikki's brownies.

Although written in a crusading spirit, the book is not strongly debunking in tone but instead aims to help the reader by pointing out good products, wise precautions and home methods of preparing wholesome substitutes for the most highly processed products.

THE NEW YORK TIMES GOURMET SHOPPER

The title of this book is misleading in that it sounds like a guide to expensive, "gourmet" foods. This is not the case, although it certainly does discuss expensive items. Moira Hodgson's *The New York Times Gourmet Shopper* (New York: Times Books, 1983) advises the reader on what is good about a wide variety of foods and how to discern this in the marketplace. The best may be the most expensive, but not always.

Hodgson is a former restaurant and food critic for *The New York Times* and is the author of several cookbooks. This is a personal book in the sense that she relies on her own taste when deciding which is best among, say, 150 different brands of mustard. She articulates her criteria well, so the reader should have no difficulty distinguishing what might be her own idiosyncrasies.

The book's objective is to enable the reader to select the best ingredients for the cooking job at hand. It is a small encyclopedia divided into 11 chapters, covering the basic cupboard, fish, poultry, meat, dairy products, grains, flour and rice, pasta, dried peas and beans, vegetables, fruit, chocolates and nuts. Within the chapters, topics are discussed one by one, with general remarks on what it is, where it comes from and standards of excellence. In crowded fields, Hodgson groups items by types, brands or cost, then speaks frankly about what is good and what is not. Many sections have two or three recipes (serving four) for a total of 275.

The writing is informal and anecdotal. For example, under "Greens," she notes, "In the spring the Irish have always

liked to eat soup made from young nettles. It cleans the blood, they say, after the sluggish months of winter. Indeed any soup, salad, or vegetable dish made from fresh greens is more than welcome when the last snow seems to have gone and the price of leafy vegetables is no longer a bad joke."

HOW TO BUY FOOD FOR ECONOMY AND QUALITY

This is a collection of government pamphlets published under the title *How to Buy Food for Economy and Quality: Recommendations of the United States Department of Agriculture* (New York: Dover Publications, 1975, paperback). They are available separately from the Government Printing Office, but this format is certainly convenient.

There are 13 chapters, each entitled "How to Buy," and covering dairy products, cheese, eggs, dry beans, peas and lentils, vegetables, potatoes, canned and frozen vegetables, fresh fruits, canned and frozen fruits, beef roast and beefsteak, poultry, lamb and meat for your freezer.

The strong points of these pamphlets are several: The text is brief, authoritative and simply written. Care is taken to define marks of quality and to explain criteria inspectors use in assigning grades (AA, A, B). Grade shields are pictured and explained. Shopping guides are provided for fresh fruits and vegetables that clearly define types available in markets and tell what to look for and what to avoid. Excellent use is made of charts—for example, the one giving characteristics of many popular varieties of cheese. After locating the name, the reader can learn at a glance the kind of milk used in manufacture, ripening or curing time, flavor, body and texture, color, the form of retail packaging and common uses.

Particularly good are the black-and-white photographs, which are set in series and illustrate the differences in appearance among the various grades (Prime, Choice, Good, etc.) of beef and lamb. Of course, the various cuts of meat are also pictured for easy identification in the market, and diagrams are provided to show what part of the carcass the cuts come from.

These pamphlets are a good value and would be hard to beat in a brief format. What is lacking in them is the personal point of view and informality of commercially published shopping guides. Moreover, brand-name merchandise is not discussed. Given the topics, this is not terribly important, but it automatically excludes a most fascinating aspect of shopping—how to decide among the various brands on the shelf.

MEAL MANAGEMENT

Faye Kinder and Nancy Green's *Meal Management*, 5th ed. (New York: Macmillan, 1978; London: Collier-Macmillan) is a textbook for housewives, or anyone else who aspires to the title of domestic meal manager. It is a dully written tome, with points to remember (for later testing) in every paragraph. Thus it is not a once-over-lightly treatment of the subject intended for leisure reading. On the other hand, it is excellent for what it sets out to do—present a lot of material in concentrated form with scholarly apparatus. It is ideal for someone who *has* to absorb this material quickly.

The authors selected the title *Meal Management* for its amplitude, covering as it does all the "decision-making and all of the hand- and footwork that meals entail." There are three orientation chapters dealing with concepts and goals of meal management, food, and laws that regulate food supply. Food buying is discussed in the eighth chapter. Then a chapter each is devoted to the four goals of meal management—achieving nutritional adequacy, matching meals to the budget for food, achieving meals the family wants and likes, and matching meals to available time. The remaining chapters are devoted to kitchen management and serving meals, including styles of service, settings, etiquette and special occasions. Omitted are instructions about recipes, cooking and kitchen utensils.

The book is crammed with charts, graphs and tables, and appendices include a format for menus, purchasing guides, a temperature chart of food and control of bacteria, frozen-food storage guides and metric conversion tables.

Meal Management is a rationalization of all the tasks ancilliary to cooking at home presented in a thorough, well-organized manner.

GOOD FRUITS AND HOW TO BUY THEM

This unpretentious little volume fulfills the promise of its title in a businesslike way. Erston V. Miller, a plant physiologist, and James I. Munger, a chemist, are the authors of *Good Fruits and How to Buy Them* (Pittsburgh, Pa.: Boxwood Press, 1967, hardcover and paperback). Despite their credentials, this is not a technical book but one meant to guide ordinary persons in their everyday purchases.

Even the cover is put to good use, with separate listings of fruits that do not ripen after picking (e.g., apricots, plums, grapes) and those that do (e.g., apples, pears, peaches). Of the 18 chapters, the authors devote 16 to types of fruit most frequently seen in North America. These include apples, apricots, avocados, bananas, blueberries, cranberries, rasp-

berries, blackberries, cherries, citrus fruits, grapes, muskmelons, peaches, pears, pineapples, plums, strawberries and watermelons. One chapter is devoted to lesser-known tropical fruits, and one to the history of a few natural hybrids, such as the pink grapefruit and the Gros Michel banana.

In their consideration of each fruit, the authors dwell chiefly on three factors: varieties (recognition of and quality differences between, if significant), season (when to maximize quality and minimize price) and appearance (what it tells you about maturity and taste). Each chapter is concluded with a short history of the fruit. Black-and-white photographs of popular varieties are included.

Two useful charts are provided, one for judging muskmelons (cantaloupe, crenshaw, honeydew and persian), and another that is a seasonal buying guide for other fruits, identifying the months advantageous for buying, those in which you should buy with caution and the off-season.

According to the authors, the toughest test of a shopper's skill at fruit selection is encountered with melons, particularly cantaloupes. They advise, "One of the most important signs of maturity in the cantaloupe is the 'full-slip' at the stem-end. This simply means that the fruit was mature enough to 'abscise' or detach itself from the vine without taking any portion of the stem with it. A 'half-slip' cantaloupe shows a portion of the stem, usually half of it attached to the fruit. This melon was only half mature when picked. When ripened it will be mediocre. Avoid a cantaloupe with any part of the stem attached to it."

CUT YOUR GROCERY BILLS IN HALF!

Barbara Salsbury and Cheri Loveless's *Cut Your Grocery Bills in Half! Supermarket Survival* (Washington, D.C.: Acropolis Books, 1983) is not a quick-and-easy system. It's more like a college course in shopping, complete with homework projects and exams.

Salsbury, a consumer advocate and the author of four previous books, boasts that she once supported a family of four on an annual income of $5,000 (she doesn't specify when this took place) and that the reader can learn to spend less than half of what other families of four spend on groceries, getting popular brands in the bargain. This is backed up by a publisher's guarantee of a refund if you do not cut your grocery bills dramatically *after following the instructions*.

The catch is, the instructions involve quite a bit of homework *and* legwork. It is plausible, though, that a dedicated shopper could get the promised results.

A basic principle is self-knowledge. Through brief tests,

the reader establishes his or her preferences and weaknesses. The shopper can then identify suitable stores and plan his or her expeditions to limit vulnerability. The most universal weakness is impulse buying, a trait most supermarkets are prepared to exploit.

To head this off, the wise shopper must read the supermarket ads, identify the weekly loss leaders and specials, then plan the weekly menus around them. If the specials are seasonal, the shopper can achieve savings through bulk buying.

According to Salsbury and Loveless, it is not enough to go to the one store that offers the best specials. If you do that, you are liable to succumb to the grocer's strategy, which is to capture your loyalty for his store. The authors maintain that it is absurd to suppose that one store (within your preference range) can post prices that on the average are consistently lower than those of its competitors. It follows that profits lost on specials must be made up elsewhere. A shopper who wants to cut the grocery bill in half must visit several stores and take advantage of all the specials.

An objection to this is that the cost of the extra gasoline would more than offset the savings on groceries. The authors answer that planning your menus around the specials makes all the difference. If you make up a menu, then look for specials that might fit, you probably won't make significant savings. Working the other way around increases your efficiency enormously, they say. In other words, good planning is the key.

The book is clearly wirtten, and the text is backed up with a plethora of charts, graphs, self-tests and work sheets, ample evidence that there are no shortcuts here to easy savings.

STRETCHING THE FOOD DOLLAR

Janet Spiegel's *Stretching the Food Dollar: Getting Better and More Nutritious Meals for Less Money* (San Francisco: Chronicle Books, 1981, paperback) is an era-of-limits approach with a touch of elegance. She takes the text of her homily from Coco Chanel, who said, "Some people think luxury is the opposite of poverty. It is not. It is the opposite of vulgarity." It is not expense but style that makes the difference. Spiegel aims to infuse a little style into what would seem to be a dreary business: practicing domestic economy, limiting your diet to what you really need, fighting waste. In a phrase, learn to prepare luxurious, nutritionally balanced meals with inexpensive ingredients.

She divides the subject into six subtopics: a nutrition

SLIVERS OF CHICKEN IN NESTS

2 cups (or less) cooked chicken, cut in slivers

¼ lb. butter

2 tbsp. dry vermouth or dry sherry

grated rind of 1 lemon

juice of 1 lemon

½ cup milk

½ cup sour cream

salt to taste

¼ cup freshly grated Parmesan cheese

1 lb. vermicelli (or very thin spaghetti)

Cook the pasta in plenty of boiling water for 7 or 8 minutes, or until just tender. Meanwhile, heat the butter over medium heat and add the chicken. Cook and stir gently for 3 minutes. Remove with slotted spoon. Add wine, lemon juice, and lemon rind, and cook 1 minute, stirring. Lower heat and add milk and sour cream, stirring. Return the chicken to the sauce, cover pan and keep it warm. (Do not allow the sauce to boil.) Correct the seasoning. Drain the pasta when done and arrange on individual plates, making a nest in each one for the sauce. Divide the sauce among the plates and top with grated Parmesan cheese. Steamed zucchini is a good accompaniment. Serves 4.

Janet Spiegel, *Stretching the Food Dollar: Getting Better and More Nutritious Meals for Less Money* (San Francisco: Chronicle Books, 1981).

primer, planning ahead, shopping seriously, reducing waste, reorganizing your kitchen and pantry, and recipes. The first three topics speak for themselves. Under "reducing waste," she introduces several concepts, such as most vitamins are water-soluble (so eat more homemade soups because the vitamins are in the water), don't overcook (eat more vegetables raw) and don't discard dark outer leaves (shred them into a salad, or eat them on the spot). She includes more than 100 recipes grouped under such hortatory titles as "Eat More Soup" and "Eat Less Meat." One of her ideas for reducing meat portions is to use slivers (julienne or matchstick pieces) of meat combined with complementary vegetable protein.

WAKE UP AMERICA!

John Taylor's *Wake Up America!* (Reseda, Calif.: J & J Publishers, 1980, paperback) is intended as a shopper's guide to better nutrition. The author contends that the best way to improve the nutritional content of American meals is to educate the average shopper to buy more nutritious food. Better nutrition, he believes, brings in its train a whole series of personal benefits, such as feeling better, working better and improved all-around health. His enthusiasm for a superior diet is rooted in his experience as a competitive cyclist of the six-day bicycle-racing sort.

Before taking the reader on a shopping tour of the supermarket, he lays down five general rules for better nutrition: 1. Do not buy food that does not build health. 2. Choose your food carefully. 3. Store your food properly. 4. Cook all food slowly in good-quality cookware. 5. Eat your food in pleasant surroundings. At the bread rack he recommends stone-ground whole wheat, at the dairy case raw milk and plain yogurt, and at the egg shelf, fertile eggs.

Most of Taylor's advice is fairly predictable: Stay away from refined sugar ("sweet death"), highly processed foods, food additives and hydrogenated vegetable oil. But he has unconventional views on the role of cholesterol in heart disease, contending that the high incidence of atherosclerosis in the United States is more a result of our high-carbohydrate diet than high cholesterol intake.

He includes much useful information on the selection of various foods, such as fruits and vegetables. He is skeptical of "health foods" but is a great believer in "organic" vitamins, presenting an exhaustive listing of vitamins and minerals available to the general public, with a discussion of sources, deficiency symptoms, dosage advice and toxic symptoms. Taylor's dietary advice is rounded out with chapters on exercise and meditation.

This is a book for the dedicated diet/health watcher and is a useful compendium of contemporary trends in self-improvement through better eating.

SUPERMARKET NUTRITION

Although written for the average consumer, this is a solid, textbook approach to getting the most nutrition at the least cost while keeping calories to a minimum. Dorothy A. Wenck is a home economist for the University of California Cooperative Extension. Her book *Supermarket Nutrition* (Reston, Va.: Reston Publishing Co., 1981) explains how to accomplish this through shopping in ordinary supermarkets. Like other writers in the field, she believes that the easiest way to improve nutrition is to buy more nutritious foods in the first place.

She lists several enemies of good nutrition. Some, such as inflation, misleading advertising and food quackery, the shopper has little control over. Others, such as poor planning, impulse buying, fad diets, haphazard eating patterns, senseless snacking and laziness, the shopper can do something about. These are the sorts of problems that can be ameliorated through an educational program such as this book embodies. Undoubtedly, if individuals improve their nutrition habits, those larger, seemingly uncontrollable problems will shrink proportionately.

Wenck's views on basic nutrition come from establishment science. Her interpretations and recommendations are balanced, safe and middle-of-the-road. There are no miracle cures here, no rejuvenation claims, no quick-and-easy diets; she finds such claims deplorable and singles out food faddists, product entrepreneurs and additive alarmists for special censure.

She notes that you can pay high prices for food labeled "natural," "organic" or "health food" and still get no better nutrition or safety than that provided by ordinary foods. Moreover, the natural toxicants in some foods far outnumber those put there by pesticides or additives. She writes:

> Consider the strawberry, for example. A ripe strawberry, just as it is picked, contains, among many other things: acetone, acetaldehyde, methyl butrate, ethyl caproate, hexyl acetate, methanol, acrolein, and crotonaldehyde. Every one of these natural substances is poisonous! [p. 49]

Her point is that they don't occur at hazardous levels, and the same is true of additives and contaminants, provided one is not allergic to them.

The best defense against the enemies of nutrition, she says, is to buy plain, unprocessed food and cook it at home. After a wide-ranging discussing of nutrition, she devotes the latter half of the book to techniques of purchasing foods from the four food groups in ways that maximize nutrition and minimize expense.

KITCHEN EQUIPMENT

THE COOK'S CATALOGUE

Equipment freaks will delight in this volume, while the rest of the world may find it merely indispensable when outfitting a kitchen. *The Cook's Catalogue* (New York: Harper & Row, 1975) was compiled by Barbara Poses Kafka and edited by James Beard, Milton Glaser and Burton Richard Wolfe.

The editors have selected and evaluated approximately 4,000 pieces of kitchen equipment and utensils. Of these, 1,700 are illustrated and 200 are supplemented by recipes demonstrating their use. Beginning with 10,000 items ordered from manufacturers worldwide, the editors applied the criteria of efficiency, design, material quality, economics and aesthetics to come up with the best.

Entries are grouped in the following categories: measuring and cleaning tools; knives, sharpeners and cutting boards; cutting instruments other than knives; grinders, crushers, mashers, refiners and extractors; multipurpose machines, beaters and bowls; stovetop cooking utensils; oven casseroles and pots; roasting and broiling pans, appliances and tools; baking pans for batters; pastry baking; pans and preparations and other tools; and specialty cookware— for seafood, eggs, ice cream, cooking at the table, health foods, coffee, tea and wine.

Each chapter is provided with a descriptive overview, and in some cases a history and evolution of the equipment. Entries contain such basic data as a black-and-white picture, a description, dimensions, how the implement is used and an explanation of why this particular model was selected. Prices are given as of June 1975, and this perhaps is the most outdated aspect of the book, because much of the equipment has a classic quality to it. Items range from simple skimmers, ice picks and teapots to complex deep-fryers and food processors, but it is evident that as much thought and care has gone into the selection of some of the $2 items as to those costing $200.

Care has been taken to make this book readable. Much of its charm lies in the wealth of incidental information and

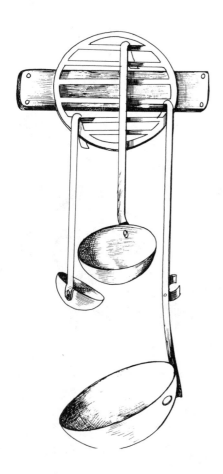

cooking lore in the explanations of how these tools are meant to work. These explanations often throw unexpected light on the logic behind various techniques and preparations.

KITCHEN APPLIANCE COOK BOOK

Better Homes and Gardens Kitchen Appliance Cook Book (Des Moines, Ia.: Meredith, 1982) combines a primer on the use of small kitchen appliances with a full complement of recipes, ranging from appetizers through desserts. A chapter each is devoted to the microwave oven, the crockery cooker, the electric skillet, fondue pots, the food processor, the blender, the crepe pan and the wok. Of the approximately 300 recipes, most are easy to prepare and require a short cooking time. An obvious exception are those for the crockery cooker, many of which require all-day cooking.

The chapter on microwaving is typical of the concise but thoroughgoing approach used in this volume. Of the 60 pages allotted to the subject, four discuss the theory of microwave cooking and its implications for the selection of dishes and utensils, safety tips, timings, recipe conversions and special uses. Then follow 125 recipes divided among appetizers, main dishes, vegetables, savory soups and sauces, sandwiches, desserts and using the microwave oven in conjunction with the kitchen range, the freezer and the barbecue.

The most complex and versatile of all these small appliances is the food processor. Fortunately, the explanatory pages devoted to it here are models of clarity, giving not just a primary orientation but also dealing in turn with hot foods, the steel blade, chopping, puréeing, mixing, kneading, beating, whipping, slicing, julienne basics, the shredding disk and the plastic blade.

The use of graphics is uniformly excellent, with lots of half- and full-page color photographs, backed up by color how-to drawings, and useful charts (such the one on microwaving frozen vegetables).

THE LIVING KITCHEN

Sharon Cadwallader's *The Living Kitchen* (San Francisco: Sierra Club Books, 1983) is a small manual in the back-to-basics mode. It does not concentrate on the selection of better utensils but instead aims at the overall upgrading of the kitchen as the center of family life.

Cadwallader, a resident of Santa Cruz, California, is the author of the *Whole Earth Cookbook* and a syndicated food column for Chronicle Features. She is also a frequent contributor to *The Christian Science Monitor*.

It is her thesis that over two centuries of American life the kitchen declined from being the center of family life to "a small sterile spot where no one wanted to spend much time." In the 1970s she detected a reversal in that trend, exemplified by renewed interest in diet, new ideas about family roles, and architectural concern with informal and natural kitchen designs. This book is her contribution to that trend, which she sees as restoring the kitchen to its original function, "the center for nourishment, both physical and emotional."

She has a well-rounded approach, dealing first with the fundamentals of nutrition, which she explains along conventional lines, stressing whole foods, the four food groups and economy. The 14 recipes in this section are designed to meet basic dietary needs in the most economical fashion.

Chapter Two is a practical guide to kitchen gardening, including layouts that would supply not only herbs but common vegetables as well. Chapter Three is a guide to preserving vegetables and fruits, with ample directions, and with recipes for such things as orange marmalade and rhubarb conserve. Chapter Four, "The Economical Kitchen," discusses food shopping and storage, stressing the advantages of owning a freezer or renting freezer storage space. Chapter Five considers the physical layout of kitchens, giving three ready-made designs for increasing capacity: the Pullman Kitchen, the Efficiency Kitchen and the Family Kitchen. Chapter Six tells how to personalize a kitchen, with decorating hints and ways to increase its versatility.

The Living Kitchen is usefully illustrated with black-and-white drawings and is replete with the necessary charts, conversion tables and index.

THE KITCHEN BOOK

Terence Conran's *The Kitchen Book* (New York: Crown; London: Mitchell Beazley, 1977) is an exhaustive study of kitchens—their history, use and design. It is not, however, a scholarly book, but one that invites browsing and that delights the eye with a profusion of color photographs and drawings. The text is secondary in this book to a succession of intriguing charts, graphs, technical drawings and design layouts.

Like other specialists in the field, Conran noticed in the 1970s a comeback of the kitchen. "We are returning," he wrote, "to an almost medieval situation, where the kitchen is, once again, the hub of the home. It is not only the place where we cook, eat and entertain, it is also the place where we do our laundry and other household chores, and it is certainly the place where the children gather and play. It really ought to be renamed the 'living room,' because that is what it is." (pp. 6–7)

The core of the book is the central sections dealing with styles of kitchens (farmhouse, urban, minimal, etc.), planning your kitchen (starting with your life-style and ending with an equipment survey) and such things as problem kitchens, movable kitchens, stocking kitchens and an analysis of the author's own five kitchens (country home, town home, cottage, restaurant and office kitchens). At the front of the book is a short historical section, then a fascinating look at the kitchens used by a host of food professionals in England, France, the United States and Sweden, including such luminaries as Gaston Le Nôtre, James Beard, Elizabeth David, Robert Carrier and Raymond Oliver. A chapter on caterers directs the reader's thinking to the quantity cook's kitchen layouts, use of space, selection of pots and pans and methods of storage.

The final fourth of the book is devoted to kitchen utensils, featuring a collection of keyed drawings that identify all the necessary implements, gadgets, pots, pans and small appliances. Terence Conran runs a chain of stores called Habitat (branches in the United Kingdom, France, Belgium and the United States; in this country known as "Conran's") that purveys most of this equipment, but he includes here an extensive list of equipment sources located across the United States.

THE PROFESSIONAL CHEF'S KNIFE

When not kissing his fingers and exclaiming, *"Voilà!"* the chef is most often pictured chopping, dicing or splitting something with a large knife. This chef's trademark is his most basic tool, and so frequent and versatile is its use that it might as well be grafted to his hand. The Culinary Institute of America's *The Professional Chef's Knife* (Boston: CBI Publishing Co., 1978) devotes some 60 pages and 200 black-and-white photographs to the care and use of this blade.

The book is meant as a text for professionals, but any person who wields a kitchen knife with some frequency could profit from reading these pages.

The chef's knife has a characteristic triangular shape with a nearly straight back, a curved cutting edge and a projecting heel. It comes in four popular sizes: 14, 12, 10 and eight inches. The long blade is considered best for bulk work

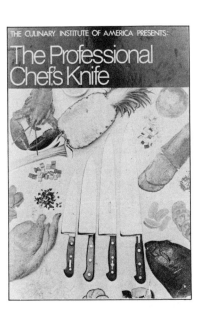

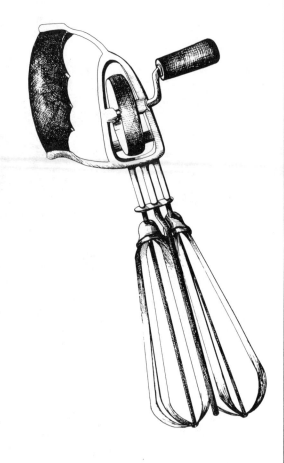

(such as chopping large amounts of parsley) or slicing large pieces of cooked meat. The middle two are thought of as all-purpose (good for any dicing, chopping or mincing), while the short blade is a favorite choice for a *first* chef's knife and is preferred for detailed work (such as mincing shallots).

Two thirds of this book are taken up with description, selection, care, storage, safety, sharpening, stance and gripping techniques, and not one word or picture seems wasted. Of the cutting techniques, perhaps the most interesting pages concern fish fileting and the depiction of many classical meat cuts in actual size.

PIERRE FRANEY'S KITCHEN

Pierre Franey is a journalist, former chef and a self-described "man of food." In *Pierre Franey's Kitchen* (New York: Times Books, 1982) he selects the 101 implements he considers right and necessary for the home kitchen of the serious cook.

Franey came to the United States from France in 1939 to cook for Henri Soulé's Restaurant du Pavillon at the World's Fair. Franey remained to take part in the founding of New York's Le Pavillon Restaurant, eventually rising to the head of the kitchen. In the 1970s he became a columnist for *The New York Times*, writing "The 60-Minute Gourmet," which culminated in his book of the same title, and *Kitchen Equipment*. He also collaborated on *Craig Claiborne's New New York Times Cookbook*. Along the way Franey acquired a home in East Hampton whose kitchen needed a complete revamping, and this experience provides a framework for the present volume, which was cowritten by Richard Flaste.

Of course, this is no mere catalog of equipment. It is a well-illustrated and interestingly written manual on how to use each item of equipment, plus 140 recipes selected to demonstrate the use or show the strengths of each item. Not every item has a recipe if its use is sufficiently unspecialized—a paring knife, for example—but each has a carefully wrought explanation of why it was selected, and the basic techniques to master.

Asked what sort of cookware he relies on most, Franey says he uses tin-lined copper. When it comes to pots, he most often uses 11-inch- and nine-inch-wide sautéeing pans, and for stews, cast iron. He considers high-carbon, stainless-steel knives essential, and as for tabletop appliances, he uses the food processor quite a lot. One item of professional equipment he uses at home is a restaurant stove, mainly because of the high heat generated by the burners, which suits his style of cooking. Among exotic equipment on his list is a *couscoussière,* a kind of steamer used to make the North African cereal staple.

As an aside, Franey includes a bare-bones list of 44 items that a "capable home kitchen" could scrape by with.

THE WELL-EQUIPPED KITCHEN

Time-Life's *The Well-Equipped Kitchen* (Alexandria, Va.: Time-Life Books, 1978, paperback) lists 173 items whose possession earns a kitchen the right to be described as well equipped. Of these, 105 are thought to be essential, a bare-bones set of tools for the serious cook. The remaining 68 would enable a cook to meet practically any contingency.

Items are divided into three categories: *Tools* includes implements for measuring, cutting (and sharpening), grating and grinding, draining and straining, stirring and lifting, mixing, and a kit for bakers; *Cookware* involves pots and pans, frying pans, ovenware, batter and dough containers, and molds; *Miscellany* deals with such things as funnels, openers and pasta machines. One is not let off with a mere 105 items, since many of them come in sets, such as cookie cutters, sauté pans and gratin dishes. Furthermore, table service and flatware are not covered.

This is little more than a pamphlet, yet each item is pictured in black-and-white and adequately explained in 75 words or so. For cookware, there is a handy guide to materials (aluminum, crockery, etc.), with columns describing their characteristics, what they are suitable for, how to care for them and cooking comments. "A Checklist for the Cupboard" sets down the working aids needed in the kitchen under three categories: Preparation, Cleaning and Storage.

No prices or sources are given.

KITCHEN DETAIL

The subject of Herbert Wise's *Kitchen Detail* (New York and London: Quick Fox, 1980) is New American Cuisine. His approach is unusual but logical: Having selected a cuisine, one designs a kitchen around it, fitting out appliances and utensils to suit.

This may seem like a recipe for a narrowly specialized result, but there's no need to worry. There nothing narrow about New American Cuisine. If anything, it is all-encompassing. In the words of Herbert Wise, "New American Cuisine is not really new. It does not represent a complete break with classical French cooking. Rather, it is an evolution, an adaptation, a refinement, an updating to make it

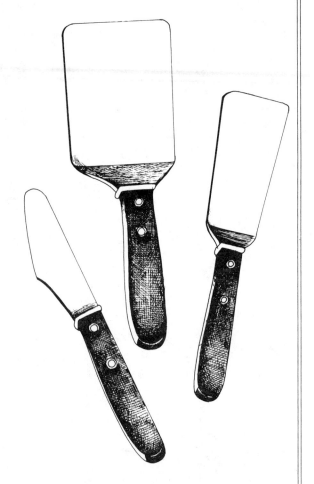

compatible with modern American kitchens, resources and tastes." [p. 9] Thus, alongside The Ranch Breakfast and The American Cookout, one finds The English Breakfast and A Chinese Banquet.

A preliminary section discusses kitchen design at various levels of luxury. The rest of the book is built around a series of menus. With admirable integration, Wise packages all the kitchen details needed to complete a particular menu right in the chapter. The menu, the recipes, the materials, the techniques, the equipment and the completed ensemble are all lovingly explained and displayed in color photographs.

At heart, though, this is an equipment book. Wise views New American Cuisine as bringing together the best aspects of all the others. He reasons that the freshest, finest ingredients and the best equipment should be on hand to produce the right results. Although there are more than 200 recipes in this book, in point of space devoted to them, appliances and utensils win hands down. If each menu were created in turn, the cook would end up with a *batterie de cuisine* unmatched outside an international cooking school. Perhaps this is as it should be, but the bias is most glaringly evident at the back of the book, where the only index provided is limited to pictured implements and manufacturers.

HOME FOOD SYSTEMS

The motto of this book is, "Wrest food production from the factory; return it to its rightful place: the garden, the kitchen, the pantry." Roger Yepsen's *Home Food Systems* (Emmaus, Pa.: Rodale Press, 1981) is both a catalog of systems and a catechism of natural-foods dogma.

Defining a system as "a series of steps that takes food from the garden (or nesting box or barnyard or tree) to the plate," it groups items under the following topics: grains, beans, sprouting, juicing, drying, canning, freezing and cold storage, tongue foods, the home dairy, backyard animals, fish gardening, mushrooms and planning the home.

This book represents one extreme of the shopping spectrum: Don't shop in supermarkets; rather grow, nuture, make, freeze and can your own food. It is a rejection of the current food-marketing system and harks back to 100 years ago—if not in technology, at least in spirit—when "these were processes known to every homemaker."

A chapter typically begins with an essay on the history, nutritional value and social attitudes toward that particular food. In "Beans," for example, we learn that they are not nearly the staple in the United States that they are in countries with fewer sources of protein. Popular varieties of beans are discussed individually—adzuki, black, chick-pea, pinto, etc.—including a nutritional profile, a description, and recipes illustrating how they are most frequently prepared in other cultures. Books relevant to the subject are reviewed in this section. Then sources are discussed, and names and addresses of seed supply companies are listed. A special section in "Beans" concerns soybeans, and the cycle begins anew with a general discussion of its virtues, plus book reviews, photographs and descriptions of special equipment (tofu presses, tempeh incubators), recipes and useful charts, such as the one measuring flatulence from different legumes (peanuts are low, lima beans are medium, kidney beans are high).

The book is well illustrated with hundreds of small black-and-white photographs. It also offers a modicum of humor and nostalgia, as in the section on raising your own chickens, where we learn the answer to the question "Where have all the roosters gone?"

Alas the family farm is being replaced by Agribusiness, large factory farms with single cash crops. Now, the cold ministrations of bottom-line efficiency dominate chicken raising. The fun and games of the family flock are out; the glacial manipulation of Technologial Man are in.

Nowadays, thousands of hens bred for egg production are housed in huge buildings from which they never emerge into daylight (chicken factory no. 1). Walk past one of these plants and you won't hear a single clucking hen. Roosters are put in to mate with the hens, and the fertilized eggs are shipped to an incubator plant.

The rooster in this process is a mere assembly-line gigolo incarcerated within the four walls of the chicken works. His glorious cry is muffled, unheard by his fellow creatures in the free world. For him, gone the sun and the blue sky, the barnyard Eden of chickendom past. [p. 338]

Last, we learn an infallible method of determining a bird's sex: Place some corn or other grain near the bird in question. If he eats it, it is a male; if she eats it, it is a female.

Food
Appreciation

Down through the ages people have found food to be a fit subject for humor, learned inquiry and aesthetic expression. These disparate approaches are lumped together in this chapter because they share a common trait: an unusual way of appreciating food and cooking.

Humorous anecdotes from the past concerning food are pretty rare, but George Lang, restaurateur, author and food consultant, has managed to cram the best of them into one volume, which is reviewed in this section. On the other hand, some of the best humorous writing on food and cooking was produced by the late Ludwig Bemelmans between 1935 and 1970. Currently, satirist Calvin Trillin keeps Americans chuckling on the subject of their own gastronomic foibles.

As for learned inquiry, many foods have a history—like people—with known origins, difficult adolescent years, an adventurous and sometimes glamorous heyday, then a quiet settlement into the mainstream or an inexplicable eclipse. The late Waverley Root had few peers when it came to recounting such histories; few could match his combination of erudition, wit and charm.

Gastronomy, the art of science of good eating, has a strong aesthetic element. Not only do gastronomers love to eat, but they also intellectualize about it, rhapsodize about it, romanticize it, glory in it and, yes, they sometimes get a little arrogant. Justified or not, they feel themselves at a pinnacle (however small) of culture, and they crow from that eminence. As John and Karen Hess demonstrate, gastronomers often feel it to be their duty to point out our gastronomic failings, sometimes with good nature, at other times with bite, but always in hopes of improving us.

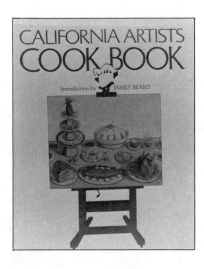

ART

CALIFORNIA ARTISTS COOKBOOK

Chotsie Blank and Ann Seymour's *California Artists Cookbook* (New York: Abbeville Press, 1982) is designed to please both the taste buds and the eye. Produced by the San Francisco Museum of Modern Art, it presents some 200 recipes contributed by well-known artists residing in California (mainly in the San Francisco area), along with handsome samples of their work, reproduced mostly in color. The art selected for inclusion takes food as a subject but does not actually illustrate the recipes. James Beard has contributed an introduction in which he hails this book as an outstanding exponent of the museum cookbook genre, which includes entries from the Metropolitan Museum of Art in New York, the Walters Art Gallery of Baltimore and the Portland (Oregon) Art Museum.

Leading the list of contributors are such notables as Ansel Adams (AA's Sorrel Soup), Judy Chicago (Layered Salad), Richard Diebenkorn (Chicken Renaissance), Claire Falkenstein (Chicken in Orbit), Wayne Thiebaud (Spaghetti with Mizitra Sauce) and "Trader Vic" Bergeron (several recipes, all featuring tofu). Bergeron, in addition to owning a chain of restaurants, is a sculptor and painter.

Various styles and media of art are represented, including painting, photography, prints and sculpture. Likewise the recipes vary enormously, ranging from simple fare to *haute cuisine* and representing many parts of the United States plus Italy, France, the Middle East, Africa and the Orient. There are also black-and-white photo portraits of 40 contributors.

THE FINE ART OF FOOD

Reay Tannahill's *The Fine Art of Food* (South Brunswick, N.J., and New York: A.S. Barnes, 1968) looks as though it might have been a preliminary essay for what later became *Food in History* (q.v.). Apart from a more succinct discussion of historical themes, the book is interesting chiefly for the illustrations, which consist of approximately 100 reproductions of paintings and prints (many in color) that show how artists have looked at food in the context of their own times. The collection is not restricted to Western art but also includes representative pieces from the Indian and Chinese traditions.

These works of art are discussed in the epilogue. Tannahill remarks that until fairly recently artists have preferred to represent food in its natural rather than cooked state. She reasons that raw food has better pictorial values. Before the Renaissance, she points out, "the dishes served consisted mainly of tidbits and of stews, sludgy in texture and either dull brown or saffron in color." As the appearance of cuisine improved, so did its representation.

Since the Impressionists, depiction of cooked food has become more and more a photographer's métier, and for the latter to get their effects they often have recourse to such expedients as substituting shaving cream for whipped cream and Elmer's glue for coffee whitener.

For a well-rounded art selection, this book is hard to beat.

TOULOUSE-LAUTREC CHOCOLATE MAYONNAISE
(contributed by Betty and Clayton Bailey)

8 ounces unsweetened chocolate
½ cup plus 2 tablespoons sugar
1 tablespoon vanilla extract
4 eggs, separated
½ pound butter, softened
Pinch salt
Pinch cream of tartar

Melt the chocolate very slowly with ¼ cup water in the top pan of a double boiler over very hot but not simmering water. Stir occasionally. Remove from the heat, cool slightly, and scrape into a bowl. Using a whisk or a spoon, beat in ½ cup of sugar, then the egg yolks, the vanilla, and last the butter.

Beat the egg whites and salt in a bowl with an electric mixer or a whisk until foamy. Add the cream of tartar and beat 30 seconds more. Add the remaining 2 tablespoons of sugar gradually, continuing to beat until the whites are stiff and glossy but not dry. With a rubber spatula, gently fold ⅓ of the whites at a time into the chocolate mixture until none of the whites show. Pour or spoon into 6 individual serving bowls and chill 6 hours in the refrigerator before serving. *Serves 6.*

Chotsie Blank and Ann Seymour, *California Artists Cookbook* (New York: Abbeville Press, 1982), p. 177.

BIBLIOGRAPHY

BOOKS FOR COOKS

Marguerite Patten's *Books for Cooks* (New York and London: R.R. Bowker, 1975) is a bibliography of modern cookbooks, listed and annotating some 1,500 titles. The selection criteria are broad, including every available type of cuisine and cookery, plus a few books on the history of food, and on science and nutrition. Foreign embassies were asked to submit lists of their most popular domestic cookbooks.

The emphasis is on books that were in print at the time. The task was formidable, and there is no claim that the author tried recipes from all the entries. Annotations are brief, frequently no more than a sentence, stressing contents, special benefits and features, and the nature of the illustrations, if any.

The bibliographic data are more complete than most lists, listing author, title, British and American publisher (and sometimes foreign-language publisher), date, prices for both paperback and hardcover, and number of pages.

The basic arrangement is alphabetical by author's last name, with further access provided by subject and title indexes.

COOKING FOR ENTERTAINING

Nancy and Dean Tudor's *Cooking for Entertaining* (New York and London: R.R. Bowker, 1976) is a cookbook bibliography that provides a basic guide to the literature. As the title imples, cookbooks with a bias toward entertaining are emphasized. The book is intended particularly for librarians who need to build a collection; teachers and students; and, of course, laypersons who seek a well-rounded approach.

The basic arrangement is by subject, with each category carefully broken down into subtopics. The large topics are Reference and Resource Material, General Cookbooks, Menu and Entertaining Cookbooks, Specific Foods, Courses, Special Kinds of Meals, International Cuisine, Wine and Food, Special Appliance Cookery, Party Guides, Periodicals, Societies and Book Clubs. There are also a few listings for such nonprint materials as movies and filmstrips.

The material was selected for contemporary interest, so most of the 800 titles are in print, the exceptions being out-of-print classics.

The authors say they tested a wide selection of recipes from each book. The annotations are unusually complete and often lengthy, showing an in-depth knowledge of each book's contents, giving an exact recipe count and an assessment of the level of expertise required by the book. The usual bibliographic details are given, including price and Library of Congress catalog number.

UNMENTIONABLE CUISINE

Calvin W. Schwabe's *Unmentionable Cuisine* (Charlottesville: University Press of Virginia, 1979) has a neo-Malthusian thesis. A recognized expert on the world food supply, Schwabe suggests that population pressure on the food supply will eventually force Americans to consider eating food that they presently consider to be outside the pale, excluded for irrational motives, although millions of people in other parts of the world find such food delectable. He calls this "unmentionable food."

He is not pleading for a green revolution, or vegetarianism. On the contrary, what he provides here are unexpected sources of *animal* protein that, he points out, are the best sources of protein of high biological value.

This is no doomsday scenario, however. And once he gets through the theory, which takes up only five pages, Schwabe is anything but pompous. He genuinely likes offbeat, not to say bizarre, food. We are talking now of horsemeat; dog and cat meat; the internal organs of beef, pork and sheep; squirrels; groundhogs; guinea pigs; rats; not to mention snakes, lizards, crickets, beetles, termites and grubs.

Ugh? Schwabe makes a convincing nutritional case. For example, under "Locusts and Grasshoppers," he notes, "Most species of locusts and grasshoppers contain 46 to 50 percent protein, as compared to 14.7 percent for T-bone steak." He is also adept at the poetic phrases that add allure to menus and recipes. On cockchafer beetles: "Adults can flavorfully enhance an otherwise insipid or mundane broth. . . . Remove the heads and wings . . . pound in a mortar (or put in an electric blender) and sieve into a hot bouillon." On water beetles in shrimp sauce: "Prepared this way, water beetles are said to taste like Gorgonzola."

He offers hundreds of recipes, all with nutritional pointers, along with country of origin and the title in English and original language.

Schwabe has a nice sense of humor and a good ear for anecdotes, as the following testifies:

POTATOES AND BEANS

I am always on the look-out for temperate substitutes for the sub-tropical rice, because the basic form of the peasant Southeast Asian meal—a bed of rice with a few sprinklings of whatever's going on top—is almost the archetypal simple meal; aesthetically, nutritionally, and economically acceptable. Potatoes mixed with beans are texturally comparable to rice or pasta and nutritionally superior to either. Anything can be used as garnish; but crisp slivers of pork belly or bacon and lots of green or Chinese cabbage, sprinkled with soy sauce and plenty of pepper, is a fine combination.

1 lb (½ kg) potatoes
1⅓ cups navy beans or black eyed peas, boiled
Pepper
A pinch of salt

Boil the potatoes with their skins on. Drain, slice thinly, or leave whole, and mix in with the boiled beans. Season with plenty of pepper and salt.

Colin Tudge, *Future Food* (New York: Crown, 1980).

RATTLESNAKES AND BOURBON

In 1971 I was introduced to a Chinese café owner in a little town in western Montana who also ran a thriving export business in rattlesnakes. Actually his product was a preparation of rattlesnakes drowned in bourbon, marinated (aged?) for 4 to 5 years, filtered through a piece of bread, and then shipped to San Francisco's Chinatown, where it is in great demand as a remedy for rheumatism! I had the chance to inspect his wares, but unfortunately none of the elixir on hand was yet aged sufficiently to uncork and sample.

This gentleman also extolled the culinary value of snake meat and reminisced and waxed eloquent about dishes he had transplanted from China to Montana with interesting modifications. This is one:

MARINATED SNAKE COOKED WITH RICE (TSUH ZO FAN)/CHINA ADAPTED TO AMERICA
The snake is skinned, gutted, and cut into pieces of a size manageable with chopsticks. These are marinated in a mixture of soy sauce, garlic, ginger, and bourbon whiskey. The snake meat is placed over partially cooked rice and the cooking continued until the meat and rice are done.

He also prepared snake by stir-frying the shredded meat or making meat balls with any appropriate vegetables or treating it as red-simmered meat.
[p. 260]

FUTURE FOOD

This is futurology of the burgeoning-population-vs-diminishing-resources type, but with an optimistic slant. Colin Tudge, author of *Future Food* (British title: *Future Cook*) (New York: Crown, 1980, hardcover and paperback; London: Mitchell Beazley, 1980), is a biologist who has also produced a work of solid research on world food supply titled *The Famine Business*. The essential message of his present book is that the 21st century will be a rosy time for the human race if man can learn to do two things: Eat rationally, then organize agriculture on the basis of those rational eating habits.

He takes a broad view of the problem, as the subtitle attests: *Politics, Philosophy and Recipes for the 21st Century*. Politics and philosophy aside, he sets up three categories of food called the First, Second and Third kinds. Food of the First Kind includes potatoes, cereals and pulses, or legumes. They are accorded first place because their yield of protein per acre is highest (after green leaves, which humans are unable to digest efficiently). Food of the First Kind, according to Tudge, should form the bulk of all the world's diets, much as they already do in many Asian diets. Next in importance are foods of the Second Kind, which are flavor-enhancing, and include meat, vegetables and fungi. Foods of the Third Kind include everything else (e.g., spices) and are useful in adding zest and excitement to meals. The remaining 85 percent of the book is devoted to ways of making Tudge's ideas on diet and nutrition palatable.

He maintains that a person can eat very well according to his principles: "We could each of us eat as richly as a medieval prince. It takes a little subtlety, it takes a little knowledge." He gives us more than 200 recipes, divided into food kinds, which tend to be unexciting, as perhaps survival fare should be. They are drawn from a variety of cuisines. One reviewer suggested that if Tudge's recipes had been more interesting, arguments about the big picture would have been unnecessary: Readers would have gravitated toward them without needing to be convinced of their cogency.

ENCYCLOPEDIAS

FOOD

Waverley Root's *Food: An Authoritative and Visual History and Dictionary of the Foods of the World* (New York: Simon & Schuster, 1980) heads the list in point of erudition, wit, literary richness and sheer joy in reading, but not, alas!, in point of completeness. Only about 200 of the world's foods are written about at length, for reasons best known to the publisher. Another 3,000 to 4,000 entries are vouchsafed a few words, a line or two at most, though Root manages to sparkle all the same (e.g., "GRUNT, a worthy food fish so little disposed to leave the water that when removed from it, it makes the protesting noise which accounts for its name.") [pp. 161–62]. The total book amounts to only about one third of the words submitted by Root, according to Craig Claiborne.

Still, the essays that are given here are everything one could wish for, except for recipes. But recipes were not in Root's established style, a style he honed in a weekly column that appeared in newspapers throughout the United States and in some foreign countries for more than 10 years. It originated in his 1958 book *The Food of France* (q.v.), which has achieved the status of a classic, and continued in *The Food of Italy* (1977) (q.v.).

A Root essay is like a biography, a personal history, of a

particular food, mentioning origin if known, personality, good points, bad points, employment, haunts, famous people associated with it and witty things said about it.

Root's essays are to cooking what pure science is to engineering: not much immediate use, but influential in some way yet to be defined. The book wasn't designed for quick reference, either, since the essays are lengthy and each follows its own organizational pattern, so there's no standard place to look for a particular kind of fact.

Nevertheless, the book is impressive, fun to read and a great thing to have perused the night before a trivia quiz. The illustrations are unusual, consisting of reprints that constitute an informal history of food in art, with many representations from the old masters, plus sculptures, drawings, woodcuts and film stills.

It is difficult to quote Root succinctly, since he was not a man of few words, nor an author of one-liners, but the following excerpts from the longer pieces should give the flavor of the whole:

GUINEA FOWL. Ever since our poultry raisers succeeded in taking the taste out of turkey, the most flavorful bird of the barnyard has been the guinea fowl. [p. 163]

HARE. Charles Lamb, in his essay in the series *Popular Fallacies, That the Worst Puns Are Best,* offers this example: "An Oxford scholar, meeting a porter who was carrying a hare through the streets, accosts him with this extraordinary question: 'Prithee, friend, is that thy own hare, or a wig?'" [p. 171]

HORSERADISH. The radish is worth its weight in lead, the beet its weight in silver, the horseradish its weight in gold. We have this assessment from no less an authority than Apollo, who himself received it from the Delphic oracle, which on this occasion seems to have expressed itself with unaccustomed clarity. [p. 185]

PEA. Driven out of Europe by the fall of France in 1940, I boarded an American ship at Lisbon, and at my first meal aboard found myself confronted with peas almost as big as marbles, in color an aggressive chemical green, and in flavor easy to confuse with library paste. I was almost home.

The United States could have peas as good as those of Europe if it were not for two delusions which at least half a century have been playing havoc with American cooking: (1) that bigger is better, and (2) that prettier is tastier. These errors make trouble all along the line, but they are particularly disastrous for peas, for (1) the best peas are the smallest peas, and (2) the sleaziest peas are the best peas. [p. 323]

FOOD OF THE WESTERN WORLD

Theodora Fitzgibbon's *Food of the Western World* (New York: Quadrangle/Times Books, 1976) is that comforting thing, a fine reference book that includes everything and is never boring. "Everything" in this context means all that pertains to food and cookery in North America and Europe. Her entries cover food items as well as dishes, *and* she gives recipes. The book has historical depth, going in many entries to the roots of Western cuisine in ancient Egyptian, Middle Eastern, Greek and Roman cooking, and relating the ancient to the modern.

As you might imagine, the book is a wonderful lexicon of food and cooking terms, in 30 languages. Many foods have multiple entries, and the foreign-language entries are not mere cross-references that send you back to the main article. Under *funghi*, the Italian word for mushroom, for example, she describes half a dozen popular Italian varieties (including taxonomic terms), names and explains typical dishes, then gives a recipe for Italian mushroom sauce *(salsa de funghi)*. There are similar articles under *grzyby* (Polish) and *ciuperci* (Rumanian), among others. The main article, under the English term, is much longer, containing some history, general approaches to cooking, and an extensive list of mushroom varieties, plus a key to subsidiary articles.

Unfortunately, the book is saddled with pedestrian typographical makeup (double columns, small print) and dull graphics (small, black-and-white linecuts and photographs) that seem designed to fatigue the eye.

Many entries are spiced with unusual facts and historical oddities, an in this excerpt:

SNAIL *(Helix pomatia; H. aspera)*, an edible mollusc which lives on dry land. Snails were immensely popular as food with the Romans, who introduced *H. pomatia* into Great Britain. They are still traditional food in the West of England, especially in the area round the Mendip hills, where they are known as "wallfish." They used to be roasted over braziers by workmen, and were also sold in public houses. Until early in this century, the glassmen of Newcastle-on-Tyne had an annual snail feast, collecting the snails on the Sunday beforehand. *H. pomatia* is the snail most commonly eaten, but *H. aspera* is the most succulent, although smaller. In the 17th and 18th centuries snails were thought in England to be good for people suffering from a "decline" and for backward children, and a snail soup was administered to them. Until a few years ago snail soup was drunk by some Somerset miners as a precaution against silicosis. In the London Gazette of March 23, 1739, there was a long account of a £5,000 award being made to a Mrs. Joanna Stephens for her tried and approved pills made from calcined snail-and egg-shells mixed with fat and honey. However, snails are far more popular on the continent of Europe, especially France, than in Britain. . . . [p. 437]

DICTIONARY OF GASTRONOMY

André Simon and Robin Howe's *Dictionary of Gastronomy* (Woodstock, N.Y.: The Overlook Press, 1970) uses a genial approach to the subject. The strengths of this book are its charm and its breadth of coverage. It is arranged A to Z, and one finds entries on food items, cooking styles, dishes (including some recipes), wines, liqueurs, cooking equipment and, occasionally, people.

André L. Simon (1877–1970) was an international authority on gastronomy who made his career in England. He wrote the basic text of this book during World War II. Robin Howe, an English author who has written more than 14 cookbooks, revised and expanded the text for the current edition.

The authors address some 2,000 entries and include 600 line drawings and 64 pages of color illustrations. Nevertheless, the number of entries is too few to support any claim of completeness on the topic; nor can it aspire to become a standard reference work: The entries are often very short, haphazard in their organization, and other reference apparatus, such as an index or even page numbers, are missing. Also, one occasionally runs across an egregious error, such as this one in the article on lettuce: "There are several varieties, but the two main types are the cos and romaine." (Cos and romaine are the *same* variety of lettuce.)

Despite these limitations, the book is valuable and should serve well the audience it was intended for: the "increasing numbers of people who take an intelligent interest in what they eat and drink." This is so because, in addition to satisfying curiosity, the authors have the faculty of increasing interest in the topic under discussion.

MADELEINE

A small French teacake made of flour, butter, eggs and sugar and baked in shallow shell-like moulds.

Some say madeleines were invented by Anice, Talleyrand's great pastrycook, others that they were known long before Anice and were made in the small town of Commercy; they were a favorite at the court of

Versailles about 1730. Stanislaus Leszcynki, father-in-law of Louis XV, introduced them to Paris. It is said that the recipe was long secret but eventually sold to Commercy bakers for a large sum of money. This cake is also celebrated in French literature because it was the taste of a madeleine dipped in tea which sparked off a train of thought in Proust's mind and led him to write his famous novel, *À la recherche de temps perdu*.

Madeleine is also a garnish consisting of artichoke bottoms filled with onion purée and topped with haricot beans.

THE WORLD ENCYCLOPEDIA OF FOOD

My own *The World Encyclopedia of Food* (New York: Facts On File Publications, 1982) is a one-volume reference book about the things people eat and drink all over the world. It is aimed at the general reader and focuses on food rather than cooking.

The coverage is not limited by region or ethnic group. The 4,000 articles are comprehensive but brief, including such elements as alternative names, a description of the food, where it is grown, how it is produced, where it is eaten, what it tastes like, how it is usually prepared, and the literary and social lore associated with it.

The book is written in an uncomplicated, nontechnical style. The text is illustrated with 400 line drawings and photographs (50 in color). There are extensive glossaries of terms relating to cooking and wine and liquor. Charts of nutritional values and sodium content of foods are included. Arranged alphabetically, the text is thoroughly cross-referenced and indexed.

Here's a sampling:

PULQUE
This is a popular, mildly alcoholic, Mexican beverage that was sacred to the Aztecs. It is the result of fermenting the sweet juice of the maguey plant, also known as agave or century plant. Cloudy, thick and slightly foamy, pulque has a heavy taste somewhat like sour milk. Because of continuous fermentation, it must be consumed near the source. Consequently, it is neither bottled nor exported. Usually it is drunk in small bars, called *pulquerías*, with whimsical names like "My Office" and "Memories of the Future." [p. 539]

GASTRONOMY

A FOOD LOVER'S COMPANION

Evan Jones's *A Food Lover's Companion* (New York: Harper & Row, 1979) is a book of excerpts on the delights of cooking and the pleasures of eating. The excerpts are always intelligent and usually stimulating or amusing (sometimes all three).

The pieces are selected from a wide range of historical periods and a variety of literary genres, including poems, epigraphs, essays, stories, journals, diaries and letters. Sources range from gastronomic classics (*The Physiology of Taste* by Brillat-Savarin) through literary classics (*Remembrance of Things Past* by Proust) to contemporary humor ("Living High on the No-Frills Flight" by Calvin Trillin).

These culinary comments are grouped into 12 chapters with such headings as "Country Pleasures," "Moveable Feasts," "Cookery Is Become an Art" and "Gastronomic Extravaganzas."

The following sample is taken from "Cookery Is Become an Art":

> THE MOLNAR "CASE"
> Everyone in New York literary circles knows about the Molnar "case." Ferenc Molnar, author of *Liliom* and a dozen other plays, lives* in the Plaza Hotel in one room. If you are fortunate enough to be invited into his retreat, Molnar will take you at once to see his "kitchenette." It is in the clothes closet, in a steamer trunk. . . .
>
> The top drawer contains various cheeses; the next all sorts of crackers and condiments; fruit preserves are in the next; coffee and tea and eggs fill another drawer; and in the bottom one, where ordinary men carry their shoes, Molnar keeps the silver. There is an electric percolator and an electric stew pan on a small table. [As a cook] the famous playwriter is famous for his *Fondue Bonne Femme*. [p.106] Iles Brody, *On The Tip of My Tongue*.

THE TASTE OF AMERICA

John and Karen Hess's *The Taste of America* (New York: Penguin, 1977, paperback) is a treatise on American gastronomy, or, more to the point, the absence of it. The book is an all-purpose jeremiad on the taste of the public, the food business, restaurants, food critics, cookbooks and markets.

---

* Molnar died in 1952.

It was written in the mid-1970s after John Hess did a stint as a food critic for *The New York Times*, so presumably he knows whereof he speaks. His wife, Karen, is a cook, an expert on culinary history and a food journalist.

The Hesses lived nine years in Paris, where John was a foreign correspondent. They obviously know and love good food and cooking, but they are not hooked on food snobbism. Their basic thesis in *The Taste of America* is that we Americans had it and we blew it, but we can get it back again. Before the Industrial Revolution, they say, American food was as fresh and flavorful as any in the world. Since then, "The real flavors have been bred and processed out of our fruit and vegetables, our fish, our dairy products, our chicken. . . ." [p. 47] The way out of the present commercial food system, the Hesses believe, is tied to the survival of small-scale farming and small-scale food handling. Their final chapter is titled "Hope," and they make it clear that whatever hope there is for the future resides in the consumer. It ends with this peroration:

> The crisis of our society, we repeat, is all of one piece: corruption and pollution, rural decline and urban decay, alienation and cynicism, malnutrition and phony food. We cannot solve any of them without resisting all of them. This requires a new dedication to the quality of life, in all its rich aspects. It should be a happy fight, not a sad one. Let us enjoy our food again. Enjoy, enjoy. [p. 337]

It is impossible here to do justice to all the arguments and evidence with which the Hesses press their case. It should be noted, though, that some of the most interesting parts of the book are those that discuss cooking and gastronomy in the colonial period and give the authors' views on early American cookbooks, such as Eliza Leslie's *Directions for Cookery* (1837) and such classics as Mary Lincoln's *Boston Cook Book* (1883). The Hesses, by the way, find great fault with Fannie Farmer, who "embodied, if that is not too earthy a word, all the major ills of twentieth-century culinary teaching. She was the maiden aunt of home economics." [p. 114]

THE FOOD OF FRANCE AND THE FOOD OF ITALY

For people who enjoy reading about food, these two volumes by Waverley Root make succulent fare indeed. *The Food of France* (New York: Alfred A. Knopf, 1958; New York: Vintage, 1977, paperback) and *The Food of Italy* (New York: Vintage, 1977) are scholarly in thoroughness and detail but chatty and humorous in tone. These are true reference books about their respective cuisines, encyclopedic in all respects except format, but concentrating on regional cooking and provender such as seafood, meat specialties, cheeses, vegetables, pastries and wines. In each case the task proved so vast that he was forced to exclude recipes and, for Italy, specific restaurants.

The Food of France will come as a surprise to the person who has formed a casual impression of French food based on what usually appears on the menus of French restaurants in the United States. A close look turns up the odd fact that there is no "typical" French fare. Instead there is a tapestry of endless variation throughout the provinces. Root divides gastronomic France into three principal regions: the Domain of Butter, the Domain of Fat and the Domain of Oil. The first is the largest, and it has given the world what is usually thought of as French cooking. It includes eight areas, among them The Touraine, Paris, Normandy, Bordeaux and Burgundy. The "fat" centers are Alsace-Lorraine and the Central Plateau, which includes the Périgord. Oil-based cooking—olive oil, that is—predominates in Provence, the Riviera and Corsica. The bulk of the book is a careful discussion of each area within these divisions, with particular attention to French terminology, which so often proves puzzling to the outsider. Root devotes two appendices to a gastronomic tour of France, naming specific provincial restaurants in the first, and in the second naming Parisian restaurants that together can provide such a tour within the confines of the city.

Italy, because of its diversity, presented a bigger problem. Root epitomized it with this anecdote:

What is the basic difference between French and Italian Cooking?" Enrico Galozzi, the noted Italian gastronomic expert, echoed my question. "French cooking is formalized, technical, and scientific. Order Béarnaise sauce in 200 different French restaurants and you will get exactly the same sauce 200 times. Ask for Bolognese sauce in 200 different Italian restaurants and you will get 200 different versions of *ragù*. [p. 7]

Aggravating the problem is the babble of Italian dialects, which Root estimates at 700. Nevertheless, after dividing the country into six gastronomic domains, he makes a particular point of sorting out the terminology no matter how obscure.

Root identifies the three major influences on Italian cooking as Etruscan, Greek and Saracen, each of which left a specific trademark: The Etruscans' is a mush made from

grain called *polenta* today; the Greeks' was fish chowder, called *bouillabaise* in France and *brodetto* (usually) in Italy; the Saracens contributed a flaky pastry called *mille-foglie*. On this historical basis he proceeds to a geographical analysis, noting along the way some 22 other tribal and national influences.

These volumes are excellent starting places for anyone who aspires to a more than superficial knowledge of the cuisines involved. They are as authoritative as any books on the subjects, regardless of language.

FOOD IN HISTORY

Reay Tannahill's *Food in History* (Briarcliff Manor, N.Y.: Stein and Day, 1974, paperback) takes a seemingly limitless topic and capsulizes it into 400 pages of readable, often delightful prose. From the naked ape to the green revolution, it is the story of how food has influenced the course of human evolution, history and culture. Tannahill draws from many disciplines—archaeology, anthropology, biology and economics, among others—but is never pedantic or boring. There is plenty of space in the narrative for memorable anecdotes, such as the role of pepper in the fall of the Roman Empire (it supposedly masked the taste of lead from lead cooking pots that poisoned the Roman aristocracy), how a new type of plow helped stimulate the First Crusade (it improved the food supply, boosted population growth and human energy that was eventually released in aggressive imperialism), why the cow became sacred in India (Aryan dependence on dairy products led to a taboo, which gradually spread throughout India, on the killing of cows), who invented spaghetti (probably the Chinese, but maybe the Indians and Arabs as well) and how the turkey got its name (native to Mexico, the turkey reached England by means of the "Turkey merchants" who came from the eastern Mediterranean and brought goods from Spanish ports; the Aztec name is a real tongue twister, *uexolotl*).

A fascinating chapter in the history of English consumerism is the story of German-born chemist Frederick Accum, who in 1820 published a whistle-blowing book titled *A Treatise on Adulterations of Food and Culinary Poisons*.

THE RISE OF CONSUMERISM
Accum's book . . . revealed to all what was already known in legal and governmental circles. That "crusted old port" was no more than new port crusted with a layer of supertartrate of potash. That pickles owed their appetizing green color to copper. That bitter almonds,

which contain prussic acid, were used to give table wine a "nutty" flavor. That the rainbow hues of London's sweets and candies were produced by the highly poisonous salts of copper and lead. That most commercial bread was loaded with alum. And that the rind of Gloucester cheese frequently acquired its rich orange color from additions of red lead. The storm which broke over Accum's head when his book was published ultimately led to his own retreat from England. But although the enraged manufacturers of adulterated food and drink were for the time being victorious, the public had been alerted and listened with attention when later reformers summoned up enough courage to reopen the question. . . .

Dr. Arthur Hassall, a chemist . . . analyzed 49 loaves of bread from various sources, not one of which proved free from alum, the mineral-salt whitening agent, and recorded that coffee was almost invariably diluted with chicory, acorns, or mangel-wurzel (a type of beet). Other researchers soon discovered that publicans put the froth on their beer by doctoring it with green vitriol or sulphate of iron, and that cocoa powder often contained a large percentage of brick dust.

In 1860 the first British Food and Drugs Act was passed. It was drastically revised and strengthened in 1872. [pp. 345–6]

HOCHEPOT DE POULLAILLE

Take your chicken and cut it in pieces and put it to fry in lard in a casserole; then take a little browned bread and the livers of the chicken and soften them with wine and beef stock, and put them to boil with your chicken; then peel ginger, cinnamon and grain of paradise (cardamom) and dissolve them in verjuice; and it should be clear and dark, but not too much.

GREAT COOKS AND THEIR RECIPES

Anne Willan's *Great Cooks and Their Recipes: From Taillevent to Escoffier* (New York: McGraw-Hill, 1977) is a pleasing mixture of history, gastronomy and artfully reconstructed recipes. Best of all, it is well written and well researched. Moreover, the book's illustrations bring together a fascinating collection of contemporary graphics depicting cooks, kitchens, banquets and dining customs.

Anne Willan is proprietor of the École de Cuisine La Varenne in Paris and former food editor of such publications as *Gourmet* magazine and the *Washington Star*. She has written several books, including *Entertaining Menus* and *French Regional Cooking* (q.v.).

In *Great Cooks and Their Recipes*, she discusses thirteen cooks: Taillevent, Martino, Bartolomeo Scappi, La Varenne, Robert May, Menon, Hannah Glasse, Francesco Leonardi, Amelia Simmons, Antonin Carême, Isabella Beeton, Fannie Farmer and Auguste Escoffier. They were selected not only for their historical roles as innovators but also for the influential books they left behind.

The recipes are unique. Ancient recipes are puzzlingly vague, but here Willan juxtaposes the ancient texts with her modern reconstructions, which should enable any experienced cook to re-create medieval delicacies.

HUMOR

LA BONNE TABLE

A mixture of gastronomy, humor and autobiography, Ludwig Bemelmans's *La Bonne Table* (New York: Simon & Schuster, 1964) is also a grand collection of the author's satirical pen-and-ink sketches. The book is a hodgepodge of short pieces written between 1934 and 1962 for a variety of magazines.

There are three sections: "Behind the Scenes" describes his experiences in New York hotels as busboy, *commis de rang*, waiter and finally assistant banquet manager at the Ritz-Carlton; roles are reversed in the "At Table" section, where Bemelmans, now an affluent guest, comments on menus, food, other diners and servers from the perspective of an ex-waiter. He ends the section with a selection of menus from exceptional restaurants, such as Le Pavillon, Maxim's and La Pyramide; the third section, "Fancies," is a series of fictional sketches offered with the editorial proviso, "Just as it was impossible to categorize Ludwig Bemelmans, so it is impossible to put any neat labels on his work. . . . Fact and fiction are indistinguishable, as they were most of all to the author himself."

Ludwig Bemelmans (1898–1962) was born in Austria and immigrated to the United States in 1914. He served in the U.S. Army in World War I, recounting his experiences in a book titled *My War with the United States* (New York: Viking Press, 1937). In all he wrote 39 books, including 17 children's books and seven novels, plus hundreds of articles and

CHICKEN CASSEROLE

2 slices bread
3½–4 pound (1¼–1¾ kg) roasting chicken, cut in pieces, with the liver
¾ cup (2 dl) red wine
¾ cup (2 dl) beef stock
2 tablespoons lard
salt and pepper
2 tablespoons verjuice*
1 teaspoon ground ginger
1 teaspoon ground cinnamon
seeds of 1 cardamom pod, crushed

Correctly, the chicken should be served on a trencher (a thick slice of bread). . . . This recipe serves 4.

Bake the bread in a low oven (300 degrees F or 150 degrees C) for 30 minutes or until thoroughly browned. Let cool, then work it through a grinder or grind it to fine crumbs a little at a time in a blender. Finely chop the chicken liver and work it through the strainer to remove the membrane. Add the liver to the breadcrumbs, stir in the wine, and let stand 5 minutes until the breadcrumbs are soft. Stir in the beef stock.

In a casserole heat the lard and brown the chicken on all sides. Add the breadcrumb mixture with salt and pepper, cover, and simmer on top of the stove or cook in a moderate oven (350 degrees F or 177 degrees C) for 30 minutes or until the chicken is almost tender. Stir the verjuice into the ginger, cinnamon, and cardamom and stir this mixture into the chicken. Continue cooking 10 minutes or until the chicken is very tender. Take out the chicken and keep warm on a platter. Boil the sauce until it is dark, glossy, and very thick; spoon it over the chicken on the dish. (p. 17)

* TO MAKE VERJUICE: work tart grapes, tart apples, crab apples, or any other tart or unripe fruit through a vegetable mill or strainer, or use a blender to obtain the sour juice; strain if necessary. (p. 11)

Anne Willan, *Great Cooks and Their Recipes: From Taillevent to Escoffier* (New York: McGraw-Hill, 1977).

stories for magazines, and musical scripts for the stage and motion pictures.

Much of his writing was humor of the low-key, satirical sort that tried for a smile rather than a belly laugh and usually struck a wistful note. Following is a fair sample:

TO BE A GOURMET

There is a lot of talk about the gourmet these days and about the rules and the art of eating—in fact, several magazines are devoted to this subject. Any restaurant that would try to satisfy the true gourmet would be bankrupt in a matter of weeks. The popular concept of the gourmet is that of a seallike, happy creature of Gargantuan appetite, who sticks a napkin inside his collar, dunks bread into the sauces and throws on the floor plates that are not properly heated. His nourishment is catalogued as caviar, pâté de foie gras, truffles, pheasant and crêpes Suzette. He drinks only the proper wine, but on closing his eyes and rinsing it in and out through his teeth he is able to tell you not only the age of the wine but also the number on the barrel in which it has been aged. He is thought of as a middle-aged man (never a woman), portly and jolly, given to reciting toasts that are spiked with French terms. His extravagant dinners take on the aspect of an eating contest rather than a good meal.

Actually, the true gourmet, like the true artist, is one of the unhappiest creatures existent. His trouble comes from so seldom finding what he constantly seeks: perfection.

To be a gourmet you must start early, as you must begin riding early to be a good horseman. You must live in France; your father must have been a gourmet. Nothing in life must interest you but your stomach. With hands trembling, you must approach the meal about which you have worried all day and risk dying of a stroke if it isn't perfect. [p. 194]

THE I HATE TO COOK BOOK

This oldie-but-goodie combines wit and practicality. Peg Bracken's *The I Hate to Cook Book* (New York: Harcourt, Brace, 1960; New York: Fawcett, 1978, paperback) offers 180 quick and easy recipes that cover most eventualities.

It was a big best seller when it first appeared. In the ensuing years, no one else has been able to match Peg Bracken's brand of domestic drollery, though Erma Bombeck comes close. The book is aimed at an enduring—and probably growing—segment of the cooking population, "those of us who have learned, through hard experience, that some activities become no less painful through repetition: childbearing, paying taxes, cooking. This book is for those of us who want to fold our big dishwater hands around a dry Martini instead of a wet flounder." [p. ix]

The secret, of course, is to simplify. Bedrock here is a chapter giving 30 day-by-day entrées, enough to get a cook through the month, at which time he or she can begin again.

LANG'S COMPENDIUM OF CULINARY NONSENSE AND TRIVIA

George Lang, restaurateur and expert on culinary affairs, also operates a "think tank" on commercial aspects of food and beverages called the George Lang Corporation. In *Lang's Compendium of Culinary Nonsense and Trivia* (New York: Crown, 1980, paperback) he offers a collection of excerpts and short essays—some informative, all amusing—on such varied topics as breakfasts, origins of dishes, folk remedies, chefs and the language of food and drink. The text is enlivened by a series of diverting satirical sketches drawn by Milton Glaser, the noted illustrator, who also designed the book.

Lang was born in Hungary but made his career in New York, where he has become a well-known figure, first as banquet manager of the Waldorf-Astoria Hotel, then as owner of the famous Four Seasons restaurant. He later became an international consultant in the creation of new restaurants, and at present he runs two restaurants in New York City, Café des Artistes and Hungaria. Lang has written for numerous magazines and is also the author of *The Cuisine of Hungary* (q.v.).

Lang sets the tone for the *Compendium* with the following epigraph: "Culinary history is a collection of questionable happenings, recorded by persons of dubious credibility, about events no one cares about and people of no consequence." [p. 11] After this disclaimer, he proceeds to en-

CLAM WHIFFLE
(3-4 servings)

(A whiffle is a soufflé that any fool can make. This is a dandy recipe for those days when you've just had your teeth pulled. It has a nice delicate flavor, too, and it doesn't call for anything you're not apt to have around, except the clams. You can even skip the green pepper.)

12 soda crackers (the ordinary 2-inch by 2-inch kind)
1 cup milk
¼ cup melted butter
1 can minced clams, drained
2 tablespoons chopped onion
1 tablespoon chopped green pepper
¼ teaspoon Worcestershire sauce
dash of salt, pepper
2 eggs beaten together

Soak the crumbled crackers in the milk for a few minutes. Then add everything else, eggs last, pour it all into a greased casserole, and bake it in a 350-degree oven for 45 minutes, uncovered.

Peg Bracken, *The I Hate to Cook Book* (New York: Harcourt, Brace, 1960), pp. 18-19.

Subsequent chapters deal with accompaniments such as vegetables, salads, salad dressings, potatoes and other starches. Chapters Five through Eleven are devoted to special situations—e.g., potluck suppers, company, luncheons for the girls, canapés, desserts, children's parties and last-minute suppers.

FRENCH BEEF CASSEROLE

(This recipe looks pretty disastrous at first, with all those ingredients and instructions. But actually it's only a glorified stew which tastes rather exotic and looks quite beautiful. You can do it all the day before, too. Just be sure to remember to take it out of the icebox an hour before you reheat it, so the casserole dish won't crack.)

1½ pounds lean beef shoulder, cut in 1½-inch cubes

1 pound can tomatoes

6-ounce can big mushrooms

bacon drippings and butter

1 pound carrots cut in 2-inch chunks

2 green peppers cut in squares

1½ cups sliced celery

salt, pepper, flour, dried basil and tarragon leaves, minced onion

Brown the meat—which you've sprinkled with salt, pepper, and one and a half tablespoons of flour—in two tablespoons of butter and two tablespoons of bacon fat. Put it in a big casserole. Put three tablespoons of flour in the skillet with the remaining fat, and add the juice from the tomatoes and mushrooms. Stir it till it thickens, then pour it over the meat, add the drained tomatoes, and cover it. Bake for an hour at 325 degrees. Then take it out and add all the other vegetables, plus three tablespoons of instant minced onion, and teaspoon each of crumbled tarragon and basil leaves. Re-cover it, bake an hour longer at 325 degrees, cool it, add the mushrooms, and refrigerate.

To serve it, heat the oven at 350 degrees and bake the casserole, covered, for 45 minutes.

Peg Bracken, *The I Hate to Cook Book* (New York: Harcourt, Brace, 1960), pp. 81-82.

lighten us on such things as asparagus ("you can make paper out of asparagus as well as ice cream"), caviar (Italian proverb: "He who eats caviar eats flies, shit and salt"), origin of the martini cocktail (described as having "the kick of a Martini," which was a 19th-century British Army rifle) and insects ("Orthodox Jewish laws specifically permit the eating of grasshoppers and various sorts of locusts").

Witty and erudite, Lang conducted his research in some unusual places. For example, here is an announcement from the bulletin board of the chef's office aboard the *Queen Elizabeth II:*

THE RULES OF THE CHEF
1. The Chef is right.
2. The Chef is always right.
3. The Chef does not sleep, he rests.
4. The Chef doesn't eat, he nourishes himself.
5. The Chef doesn't drink, he tastes.
6. The Chef is never late, he is delayed.
7. The Chef never leaves the service, he is called away.
8. If you enter the Chef's office with your own idea, you leave with his.
9. The Chef doesn't have a relationship with his secretary, he educates her.
10. It is forbidden for Chefs to marry in order that their numbers shouldn't increase.
11. The Chef is always the Chef, even in his swimming costume.
12. If you criticize the Chef, you criticize the Almighty. [p. 102]

AMERICAN FRIED AND ALICE, LET'S EAT

Calvin Trillin is a humorist who often writes about food, poking fun at the half-baked and the overripe. *American Fried: Adventures of a Happy Eater* (New York: Random House, 1979, paperback) and *Alice, Let's Eat: Further Adventures of a Happy Eater* (New York: Random House, 1979) are collections of essays, most of which first appeared in a *New Yorker* column titled "U.S. Journal."

In the middle 1970s Trillin traveled to many parts of the United States in pursuit of "something decent to eat." Although he resided in New York, which is by all accounts the gastronomic center of the country, Trillin is a native of Kansas City. Gastronomically, he makes much of his midwestern origins; e.g., "The best restaurants in the world are, of course, in Kansas City. Not all of them; only the top four or five." *(American Fried,* p. 13*)*

He was referring to barbecue places. In *American Fried* he abominates "Continental Cuisine," and in a bit of wisdom distilled from many sojourns in midwestern cities, he tells the reader: "Through a system of what amounted to ethnic elimination, I had arrived at barbecue as the food most likely to see me through the evening." Many of his opinions on food are drawn out in conversation with such staunch characters as William Edgett Smith, the man with the Naugahyde palate, and Larry "Fats" Goldberg, the New York pizza entrepreneur.

In *Alice, Let's Eat,* Trillin recalls with horror his wife's mentioning his overweight just before he sat down to dinner at his favorite soul-food restaurant, reminisces about a plate of *blaff d'oursins* (sea urchin stew) in Martinique, recounts with glee his $33 picnic on a no-frills flight to Miami and fantasizes about taking Mao Tse-tung on a week-long gourmet tour of New York restaurants.

Occasionally Trillin undertakes restaurant criticism, as in the following excerpt from a piece titled "British Boiled":

PUB FOOD

I resolved to redouble my efforts to find decent pub food in London, or maybe a fish-and-chips café that actually fried the fish when it was ordered instead of in a mass-fry-in with all of the other fish at six in the morning. The closest fish-and-chips café of quality that I knew about was in Brighton. Several people had recommended as the best fish-and-chips restaurant in London, a place that was noted for the length of its wine list—a place I naturally dismissed out of hand, the way I would dismiss a barbecue joint in Arkansas that also served lobster tails and chow mein. The pasties at the pubs I had been eating at in London tasted like meat and veggies cleverly repackaged in a crust hard enough to be of some use if the pub happened to be the sort of place where the patrons tend to start throwing things at each other late in the evening. Whenever hunger overcame me at a pub, I had taken to ordering a Ploughman's Lunch—basically cheese and a roll and chutney—on the theory that its ingredients at least remained immune from attack by the man in the kitchen. I found eating Ploughman's for that reason depressingly reminiscent of a defensive gin-rummy player I once knew whose strategy was based on ridding himself of all high cards as quickly as possible and was expressed in the motto, "Lose less." *(Alice, Let's Eat,* p. 103*).*

LEMON SHRUB

The term 'shrub' comes from the Arabic *shurb*, which means strong drink. It is not, as Smyth's 1667 *Sailor's Word-Book* calls it, a "vile drugged drink prepared for seamen who frequent the filthy purlieus of Calcutta" but a delicious one prepared from orange or lemon (or other acid fruit) juice and rum or brandy. Both Lemon and Rum Shrub taste a bit like dry vermouth and can be drunk with ice and lemon peel or mixed as Pimms with lemonade or sparkling water.

1 bottle Spanish brandy
peel of 1 lemon
juice of 2 lemons
½ bottle dry white wine
2 oz sugar

Put the brandy, peel and lemon juice in a large glass jar. Cover and let it stand for 3 days, then add the wine and sugar. Cap again, tightly. Leave for a day or two in a warm place to dissolve the sugar, then strain through double muslin into clean bottles and seal.

Claire Clifton and Martina Nicolls, *Edible Gifts* (London: The Bodley Head, 1982), p. 82.

PRESENTATION

EDIBLE GIFTS

Claire Clifton and Martina Nicolls's *Edible Gifts* (London: The Bodley Head, 1982) solves the problem of what to get the person who has everything. Edible gifts are unusual, bespeak affection and can be quite inexpensive. This small volume collects some 75 recipes, many of which are delightfully illustrated with color drawings by Glynn Boyd Harte.

The authors are two American women now living in London who between them have lived in such exotic places as Hong Kong, Beirut and Mexico City. While the recipe collection has an international flavor, they have striven to avoid difficult techniques and hard-to-find ingredients.

The recipes are divided into four groups: "Savory," "Sweet," "Spiritous" and "Three Teas." Savories include such things as Orange Chutney, Malt Whisky Mustard and Persian Pickled Garlic. Sweets include Bourbon Balls, Peanut Butter Fudge and Murrumbidgee Cake. Among the spiritous items as Pomander Gin, Cajun Rosemary Digestif and Passion Fruit Brandywine.

Many of the recipes are original, but others are attributed to such well-known cookbook authors as Elizabeth David and Claudia Roden.

FOODSTYLE

The appetite is stimulated by the eye as well as by an empty stomach. Molly Siple and Irene Sax make the most of this fact in *Foodstyle: The Art of Presenting Food Beautifully* (New York: Crown, 1982). Presenting food that beckons to the diner is less a matter of inspired art than acquiring an eye for that sort of thing, learning a few techniques and giving it some forethought. It's not much trouble, the authors say, for "cutting a lemon with elegance takes little more effort than hacking it in half." [p. viii]

The book consists of five parts. The authors devote the first 30 pages to discussing basic principles under such rubrics as arrangement, carving, color, equipment, focal points, garnishes, glazing and sauces. Part Two is the bulk of the book, running some 250 pages. It is a quick-reference section, arranged encyclopedia fashion A to Z, in which specific foods are addressed, from anchovies to zucchini. Part Three concerns table styling, touching on place settings, centerpieces, and such special problems as buffets. Part Four deals with international table settings, dealing specifically with Chinese, French, Greek, Indian, Italian, Japanese, Mexican and Scandinavian. Holiday tables are the subject of Part Five—Christmas, Thanksgiving, etc.

There are no recipes because, as the authors say, this is a food book that begins where cookbooks leave off. Unfortunately, it also lacks an index.

Some 320 line drawings—both useful and decorative— illustrate the text. The writing style is lively and informal, as the following excerpt shows:

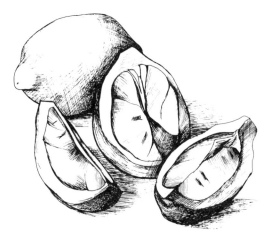

CATSUP
There's no right way to serve catsup. The bottle on the table has no style. But neither do we like the chubby plastic tomato that squirts catsup through its stems. Nor do we want to spoon catsup on our french fries from a cut crystal bowl. Maybe a white ceramic bowl and spoon, a mustard pot, or a small white crockery pitcher would do.

Then again, perhaps certain foods, such as catsup, Rice Krispies, Coke and tins of caviar, are meant to come to the table in their commercial containers. [p. 77]